THE
FIVE
TALENTS
THAT
REALLY
MATTER

THE FIVE TALENTS THAT REALLY MATTER

How Great Leaders
Drive Extraordinary Performance

Barry Conchie & Sarah Dalton

hachette
BOOKS

NEW YORK

Hachette Go, an imprint of Hachette Books
Hachette Book Group
1290 Avenue of the Americas
New York, NY 10104
HachetteGo.com
Facebook.com/HachetteGo
Instagram.com/HachetteGo
First Edition: August 2024

Published by Hachette Go, an imprint of Hachette Book Group, Inc. The Hachette Go name and logo are trademarks of the Hachette Book Group.

The Hachette Speakers Bureau provides a wide range of authors for speaking events. To find out more, visit hachettespeakersbureau.com or email HachetteSpeakers@hbgusa.com.

Hachette Go books may be purchased in bulk for business, educational, or promotional use. For information, please contact your local bookseller or email the Hachette Book Group Special Markets Department at Special.Markets@hbgusa.com.

The publisher is not responsible for websites (or their content) that are not owned by the publisher.

Interior design by Sheryl Kober

Library of Congress Cataloging-in-Publication Data

Names: Conchie, Barry, author. | Dalton, Sarah (Writer on leadership), author.
Title: The five talents that really matter: how great leaders drive extraordinary
    performance / Barry Conchie and Sarah Dalton.
Description: First edition. | New York: Hachette Go, an imprint of Hachette
    Books, 2024. | Includes bibliographical references and index.
Identifiers: LCCN 2024007408 | ISBN 9780306833403 (hardcover) |
    ISBN 9780306833410 (trade paperback) | ISBN 9780306836381
    (trade paperback) | ISBN 9780306833427 (ebook)
Subjects: LCSH: Leadership.
Classification: LCC HD57.7 .C655 2024 | DDC 658.4/092—dc23/eng/20240416
LC record available at https://lccn.loc.gov/2024007408

ISBNs: 978-0-306-83340-3 (hardcover); 978-0-306-83342-7 (ebook);
978-0-306-83638-1 (international edition)

Printed in Canada

MRQ

Printing 1, 2024

This book is dedicated to the oddballs, misfits, disrupters, agitators, challengers, miscreants, antagonists, cajolers, stirrers, provocateurs, mavericks, jesters, trouble causers, protagonists, rabble-rousers, deviants, revolutionaries, contrarians, outsiders, dissenters, eccentrics, debaters, unsettlers, darers, and disputers without whom life would be boring and work tedious. May more of them earn the right to be elevated to leadership positions and break down the barriers erected to protect the elderly, white, male leadership monolith.

Conventional talent management schemes fail because they rarely accommodate mavericks and outsiders who are creative and innovative in their thinking but do not perform well using traditional appraisal measures.

—Marion Devine and Michel Syrett,
Managing Talent: Recruiting, Retaining and
Getting the Most from Talented People

CONTENTS

Contents

PREFACE

Diamonds in the Rough

FIFTEEN YEARS AGO, A MAJOR AMERICAN MULTINATIONAL CONGLOMERATE was attempting a hostile takeover of a British company. With the deal rapidly approaching completion, the conglomerate's CEO was faced with the daunting task of evaluating hundreds of leaders, in almost seventy overlapping global markets, to ensure the success of the union.

The CEO felt that she knew her own leaders but was blind to the capabilities of those joining from the acquired organization. She wisely recognized that the newly combined, culturally divided company would likely succeed only if top positions were filled by the best leaders from both sides. But how could she make these appointments with confidence? Barry Conchie was hired to help answer these questions, and his expertise in assessing candidates was deployed.

The candidates from the CEO's company, whom she and other senior leaders deemed to be their very best, didn't measure strongly when they were assessed. They were team players who were exceptional at driving positive sentiment in the workplace, but this did not translate into metrics that reliably predicted their success in a new environment. Elevating these candidates into more senior roles over others with significantly stronger leadership profiles would put the entire merger at risk.

Companies are not naive about the necessity of making decisions founded on data and evidence; however, they often demonstrate a lack of statistical insight when it comes to their most important business process: selecting new employees.

In this book, we describe in depth the Executive Leadership Assessment that we have researched, built, and refined throughout the last twenty years. You will come to understand the scientific methodology that allows us to predict successful executive leaders with 78 percent accuracy (and to predict unsuccessful leaders with 91 percent accuracy). We hope that this book will convince you of the importance of unbiased, data-driven, and statistically validated methods of candidate selection. As you think about yourself and your current and future leadership potential, the insights gained from our work could be invaluable to you.

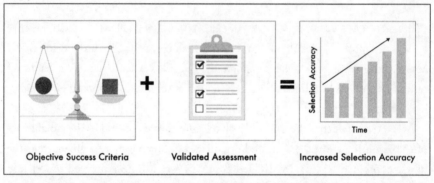

An assessment adds value to a company's selection process only when it is proven to be a consistent, fair, and valid predictor of success in a role.

During our assessment process for this particular acquisition, we identified a leader hidden within the CEO's organization in the Asia-Pacific market. She scored the highest on the Executive Leadership Assessment across every one of the markets we assessed. She was phenomenal, yet completely invisible inside her organization. Because this leader was relatively unknown, and likely because she is an Aborigine and a woman, she was underappreciated and overlooked.

She was obscured below the ranks of a weaker, lower-scoring leader whom we also assessed. It was clear that he felt threatened by her potential, as was evidenced by the poor performance appraisals he had given her in prior years.

She had never featured on any company succession list, yet we recommended that this woman, a "diamond in the rough," be a key player in driving the acquisition. Despite protests from her then manager, she ascended to a top regional leadership position with him reporting to her. As you might imagine, he didn't last long.

She became an extraordinary success, as her assessment predicted, and her promotion served as an inspiration to other marginalized employees battling to advance their careers. In her words, the leadership assessment "liberated" her from a future hamstrung by dysfunctional management. It gave her the confidence to push aside her detractors, step into her rightful role, and share her remarkable talents with the organization.

Unfortunately, this is not a rare occurrence. In nearly every organization that we work with, we find natural leaders whose brilliance goes unrecognized. There are exceptional candidates for leadership roles, many of them women and minorities, who represent one of the largest sources of untapped potential in today's workforce. Nearly all organizations that struggle with challenges in diversity, equity, and inclusion (DEI) and hiring, retention, and succession planning have incredible leaders hidden in their ranks. Discovering this untapped potential has been one of the most personally fulfilling and organizationally valuable outcomes of our assessment practice.

Our key learnings from this experience helped shape our approach in future engagements and ensured that we asked the right questions in every organization:

- Inadequate leaders dislike having talented team members reporting to them. They feel professionally threatened. They fear that they will be overshadowed and overlooked for future opportunities; thus, they are a hindrance to employee development and the organizations they serve.
- The lack of diversity in company leadership is a direct result of poor selection practices—practices that can be improved by using an assessment of the kind we describe in this book. Your organization is as diverse as hiring managers allow.

- Without a credible, objective leadership assessment, senior leaders are blind to the talent and raw potential hiding deeper in their organizations. Although they claim to be immune, they are vulnerable to the judgmental biases we describe in this book that lead to bad hiring decisions.

WHO ARE WE?

Conchie is a company that specializes in executive assessment, selection, succession planning, teamwork, and development. The Executive Leadership Assessment described in these pages forms a basis for building assessments that measure talent and predict success for all key roles in organizations—from entry-level professionals through all intervening roles to executive leadership. We build unique assessments for unique roles and relentlessly pursue excellence and the traits and characteristics that predict it. We try to simplify the complex elements that inform decisions of this type, and our tools—the assessments we build—statistically predict who is likely to perform to a high standard, who might be average, and whom you should likely reject from consideration. The advice provided by these assessments helps our clients make more good hiring decisions and fewer bad ones. Our long-term partnerships attest to our effectiveness.

Barry Conchie set up Conchie in 2013, having previously led Gallup's leadership and development business. He led Gallup's work on some of its most significant client accounts and specialized in advising CEOs and executives in professional effectiveness and team optimization. He contributed as faculty to international MBA programs and frequently presented his Gallup work at conferences around the world. His coauthorship of the hugely successful book *Strengths Based Leadership* positioned him as one of the world's foremost leadership thinkers.

Sarah Dalton joined Conchie in 2016 and became a partner in 2020. Leaders and managers partner with Sarah to better understand the attitudes and behaviors that drive performance and how to select for talent in the hiring process. She is an expert at training teams in interpreting talent assessments and using those insights to facilitate a superior candidate experience, greater confidence in hiring decisions, and world-class performance across all levels of an organization. She is certified in conducting executive-level talent assessments and regularly advises leaders on the ways in which they can achieve success while raising critical questions to help them become more effective.

THE SCIENTIFIC APPROACH

From the outset, we want to make one thing clear—this book isn't the product of smart people pontificating about what they think good leadership looks like. It's a book built on a foundation of evidence and hard science. We want you to feel energized and stimulated by credible ideas that are the result of research and data analysis…a lot of data. We cut through all the noise surrounding what leaders do and how the very best achieve their success. We talk about what really matters.

Few people have a good understanding of science and the scientific method. A 2019 Pew Research Center study[1] showed that in the United States, only 52 percent of the respondents could correctly identify a hypothesis within specific contexts. Only 60 percent of the respondents in the same study recognized the importance of a control group in experimentation. Michael Shermer, in his entertaining yet serious book *Why Smart People Believe Weird Things*, identified the main problem as follows: "70% of Americans still do not understand the scientific process."[2]

Long before the advent of globalized business, perhaps even before the invention of business as we recognize it, ancient cultures were using data to make decisions that would improve people's lives and well-being. In the plains of Mesopotamia, on the shores of the Yangtze River, and throughout the jungles of Mesoamerica, large groups of humans created settlements that persisted beyond the generations that initially inhabited them. These people noticed patterns within the natural world and began to relate potential causes to effects.

In the chapters to come, we explain our own application of scientific methodologies in the context of leadership selection and development in modern business. But first, we need to ensure that everyone shares an understanding of what science *is* and what it *is not*.

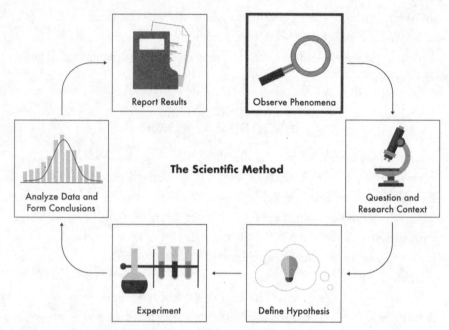

Though rudimentary, early practices of observing, hypothesizing, and experimenting were the foundation of modern science and the scientific method as we know it today.

Meteorology, the study and forecasting of weather, is a good example of using the scientific method in ways that most readers will understand. In ancient times, patterns of weather and seasons were identified, enabling rudimentary predictions to be made. It is this association between observation, data, and prediction that lies at the heart of the modern scientific method and why meteorology is regarded as a science.

Meteorologists gather and analyze voluminous data over long periods of time and across multiple geographies. They capture historical data and compare it to real-time measures and indicators. They run simulations and artificially change variables to assess the impact on their weather models. At the heart of the best science lies the ability to make a prediction and compare inputs with outputs. While the weather forecast might not be 100 percent accurate for every prediction in every location, it is remarkable how accurate it is and how consistently the predictions align with reality and experience.

Contrast this with astrology—star signs. In the same ancient times when observations of the natural world were being made to forecast weather, other people were observing the night skies and attempting to reach conclusions about the relationship between the alignment of stars and planets and their potential impact on the human experience. In these early days, astrology was regarded as a science because, after all, it was based on observation and the study of data in the act of making predictions.

But we now know that astrology is not science; it does not attempt to follow the scientific method, and the reasons are very clear. There is no observable mechanism that explains how particular star and planet configurations interact with the natural world, much less with the life experiences and chances of specific groups of individuals sharing random birthdays.

Astrology fails the ultimate test of science—it has no efficacy. Quite simply, it doesn't work. Its predictions lack specificity and are so general and meaningless as to provide no real insight. While meteorology is very much a science, astrology quite definitely isn't. Keeping this comparison in mind will be important as you work through this book. We demonstrate our approach to leadership assessment through the lens of the scientific method and describe the predictions made by our assessment and how accurate these predictions are.

Calculating probabilities, testing hypotheses, and interpreting data are skills that underlie the most important business decisions. Without applying scientific rigor to selection decisions and empirically measuring the results of those decisions, most companies are practicing astrology when they hire, promote, and terminate their employees. Today, meteorologists can predict (with enviable accuracy) weather in every region of the globe. Their forecasts are supported by huge repositories of atmospheric data, and when they do get it wrong (although rarely), they can explain *why* using that data.

What if companies could forecast the outcomes of personnel selection decisions as reliably as meteorologists forecast the weather?

WHAT YOU WILL LEARN

Every good detective story begins with a collection of seemingly random and imperfect evidence but eventually reaches a very powerful conclusion. When we talk about the scientific method as a means of asking questions and gathering data to test our assumptions, we are attempting to bring you along a path of discovery that leads to conclusions every current and aspiring leader will benefit from knowing.

This book is an account of our endeavor to apply the scientific method to the field of candidate selection, particularly candidates for executive leadership positions. We describe how we devised our research, how we conducted experiments and studies, and the astounding results we discovered. This book is not a scientific article (as you will no doubt be glad to hear), and the topics covered are written in a way that will resonate with people at every level of an organization. There are some concepts that we necessarily define and describe, such as adverse impact or Cronbach's alpha. There are many more that we can reference only in passing, such as conformity bias or complexity bias. We hope that you will research these on your own and gain greater mastery of the subject matter.

Beyond our methodologies and data, we share our holistic framework for comprehending the complexities of leadership. We define the talents and behaviors exhibited by the very best leaders from around the world. Our opinions are not the result of singular anecdotes or case studies; during the course of our research, we assessed and collected data on over fifty-eight thousand executive leaders representing small companies and global enterprises in a variety of industries. Our terminology has been painstakingly reviewed, debated, and refined in an attempt to simplify a profoundly intricate subject.

There is no single quality that makes a leader exceptional, nor is leadership an acquired skill. Ten thousand hours of practice will not transform an intrinsically weak leader into one who is world-class. Rather, leadership is a compendium of talents that different people express in their own unique way. Among the highest-performing leaders, no two are alike—there are no rigidly defined rules that they all adhere to. But there are definitely traits and characteristics that can help us discriminate those individuals who have the potential to perform at the highest levels of executive leadership. We have used our research to refine a model that benchmarks an individual against the most talented leaders across the globe and reliably predicts their potential to convert their unique talents into meaningful performance.

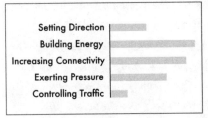 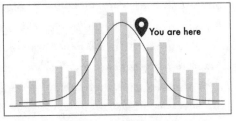

Our assessment model highlights an individual's dominant leadership strengths and benchmarks them against the most talented leaders across the globe.

As you apply these research findings to yourself, we hope you discover a key that helps you identify and unlock your true leadership potential. In the final chapter of this book, we invite you to take an online version of the Executive Leadership Assessment that you will come to be familiar with through these pages. Every person reading this book would benefit from an objective measure of their unique talents and an understanding of how to maximize them in a leadership role. We provide the tools and resources for you to interpret your results and offer a mechanism for receiving feedback to those who are eager to learn more.

HOW IT ALL STARTED

This book is the culmination of my life's work and how Conchie came to be the company it is today. Throughout the following chapters, I share the significant experiences that influenced me to apply the scientific method to selection decisions. When I do so, the text is italicized to emphasize that these are my personal experiences.

—*Barry Conchie*

PREDICTING FUTURE CAREER CHOICES

At fifteen years old, I had no clue about what career to pursue. When my small, rural high school in the United Kingdom introduced the latest career planning technology— a paper survey of questions about individual preferences that, once submitted and processed, would return a list of potential career paths—I felt a mixture of curiosity and prejudice. After all, this must be mumbo jumbo. How could a simple personality test lead to insights that would affect the trajectory of my career—and my life?

As a working-class kid from Northern England, I had never been encouraged to engage in self-reflection. I didn't think deeply; I just did things to survive and earn a bit of money to help the family. "Work hard and show respect" were the values my parents instilled in my brother and me. I never really thought beyond that with respect to my character or self-development.

When the results finally arrived, there was an atmosphere of laughter and surprise in the classroom. Some kids were destined to be lawyers or architects. Others were bound to be doctors. One of the more imaginative suggestions was "fashion designer," which I had never even heard of as a career.

I looked at my results and immediately hoped no one would ask about them. Apparently, the best this high-tech program could suggest for me was radio officer in the Merchant Navy or funeral director. At no point in my life had those possibilities crossed my mind. My earlier prejudices were instantly validated: "Who came up with this nonsense?" I recall feeling troubled and disconcerted about it for quite a while. How could I take these recommendations seriously? Ultimately, I vowed to prove the test and its creator wrong. I decided to forge my own destiny.

Suffice it to say, I never became a radio officer (military or merchant), and I certainly never became a funeral director. Looking back on the career test, I thought, "How meaningless. What a complete waste of my time."

It was only much later in life that I came to recognize a hidden intuition in that guidance and how much more it revealed about me than I had ever thought possible.

Twenty years into my career, I encountered an actual radio officer and was startled to recognize how characteristically similar we were to each other. Radio officers spend most of their time cooped up in a small room beneath the ship's deck handling ship communications, which appealed to my solitary tendencies. In speaking to this experienced officer, I realized that I would likely have rebelled against the military authority this officer described and respected. I had always been puzzled by the specific category of merchant rather than military navy in my career results. But in listening, I realized that I disliked blindly obeying authority. This career program had picked that up.

As my life progressed, I met a few funeral directors under predictably sad circumstances. I knew I would not have enjoyed that career path, but I admired their detached, unemotional professionalism and their sheer sincerity—words others have used about me.

As I reflected on this experience, I realized that all those years ago in high school, I made the mistake of looking negatively at the specific job titles. I failed to consider what these recommendations were really saying about me as a person and how accurate that assessment truly was.

PART ONE

MISCONCEPTIONS ABOUT LEADERSHIP AND SELECTION

CHAPTER 1

What People and Companies Get Wrong About Leadership

WHAT IS LEADERSHIP? WHAT DIFFERENTIATES AN EXCEPTIONAL LEADER from one who is just average?

Let's assume we are sitting in a room together talking about leadership, and we are trying to come up with a list of leaders we most admire and respect—people we could study. Who would be on that list? Would we even agree? Could we find even ten common names? Would our list be confidently compiled, based on a deep knowledge of the individuals and the success they achieved, or would it be more subjective, hesitant, and impressionistic?

You might put Steve Jobs on your list, but he wouldn't be on ours. We might argue for Herb Kelleher and you for Jack Welch. Rather than Welch, we would want his colleague Jim McNerney. And so the discussion would progress.

What would be striking about this discussion is how hard it would be to get to ten at all, let alone ten which we would agree on. But if we got to that number and then tried to draw conclusions about what was important in leadership based on these individuals, we'd be hard pressed to come up with a consistent and holistic answer because the individuals would be different from each other in significant ways—some observable and some not.

Each of our chosen leaders is undoubtedly successful, but they achieved their success in unique ways. Their paths to success were the consequence not of varied strategic choices but rather of each leader's innate characteristics. They thought and behaved differently—not only from the general populace but also from each other. Their natural tendencies influenced how they viewed their businesses and the choices they made regarding the team members who surrounded them. Each leader harnessed these various elements to achieve phenomenal outcomes. They led highly successful organizations that directly reflected their personal characteristics and values. They didn't just lead an organization—they led *their* organization.

It's hard to look at Southwest Airlines today and not see Kelleher's fingerprints. Apple and Jobs. Boeing and McNerney. General Electric and Welch. The answer to what made these titans such successful leaders is difficult to ascertain from such a small group. Fortunately, truly inspiring leaders exist all around us—although they may not be household names. They are legends hiding inside their organizations and communities. They are the individuals to whom others look for advice, guidance, purpose, and growth.

Over the course of our work, we have identified thousands of exceptional leaders, many of whom would likely measure more strongly than the household names previously highlighted. Identifying these individuals has allowed us to create a holistic framework for leadership and to answer the question "What makes the very best leaders unique?" Before we can answer, it's important that we help you unlearn ideas that aren't helpful in developing an understanding of how the very best leaders achieve their success.

LEADERSHIP: THREE TRAPS AND THE TRUTH

The path to high-performing leadership is obstructed by too many books and thinkers who fall into one of three traps, making their writings and opinions confusing and contradictory. Many of these authors are extremely smart, but books that lack credible research to inform their findings often miss the target, as is true of many leadership books. The three traps are evidenced by a swift glance at the leadership section of most business bookshelves.

Students of leadership should be skeptical of writers and thinkers whose work falls into one of these three common traps.

The First Trap: Successful Leaders Do This *One* Thing

Leadership is a highly complex endeavor, but you wouldn't think so from browsing the business or self-help sections of the local bookshop. There are dozens of authors who claim that the secret to great leadership is one specific trait or simple characteristic. These arguments are appealing to a general audience because nearly everyone would like to believe that they can become one of the very best leaders. As fantastic as that would be, the evidence all around us shows that this is simply not true. However, books that make such claims have been wildly successful bestsellers.

Good to Great: Why Some Companies Make the Leap and Others Don't by Jim Collins identified humility as a driving force for success in attaining his "level 5 leadership."[1] His argument was founded on limited investigation and interpretation of a handful of companies. The small sample of leaders he studied were mostly white, older men, which raises concerns about the validity of his claims and their applicability to a wider population. Critics such as Steven D. Levitt were quick to apply measures to these claims.[2] Levitt tracked the stock performance of the companies that Collins had identified in the eight years since the book's release and found that "overall, a [stock] portfolio of the 'good to great' companies looks like it would have underperformed the S&P 500." If these companies were operating under the very best leaders, humble or not, we should expect to see this reflected in their stock performance.

A year after Collins's book, Robert Greenleaf released *Servant Leadership: A Journey into the Nature of Legitimate Power and Greatness* to mainstream success.[3] Like Collins, Greenleaf proposed an understanding of leadership that contradicted the procession of late-twentieth-century books extolling the importance of "leading from the front." The compelling leadership narrative was based on his reading of Herman Hesse's *The Journey to the East*, which described a humble servant whose value to his colleagues was appreciated only when he left the group and they realized he was really their leader.[4] It's an excellent concept of nonhierarchical, distributed leadership that led to the development of ideas about CEOs existing in service of their organizations rather than the other way around. Much research has been undertaken to apply empirical measures to Greenleaf's claim, but "problems have arisen from poor construct clarity, poor measurement, and poor design."[5]

Collins's and Greenleaf's books are important. They gave a voice to characteristically less assertive, but equally effective, leaders who achieved success with more subtle forms of leadership. These books defined leadership in terms that were more naturally encouraging for female and minority leaders, who had historically been discriminated against for not exhibiting the aggression once considered necessary for strong leadership. For this reason alone, these books have been necessary in shifting leadership into a more inclusive space for everyone—although it would have been nice if Collins and Greenleaf had highlighted this fact themselves.

These books fall into the same trap that has plagued leadership studies for decades. They attach disproportionate emphasis to one leadership characteristic over others. For Collins, it was humility, and for Greenleaf, it was service. Philip Rosenzweig, in his thoughtful book, *The Halo Effect... and the Eight Other Business Delusions That Deceive Managers*, highlighted this exact problem: stories of business success and failure constantly exaggerate the impact of leadership style and management practices on a firm's outcomes.[6]

Effective leadership is the product of more traits and characteristics than those highlighted by Collins and Greenleaf, and although neither author was attempting to codify everything that goes into great leadership, their emphasis on these two characteristics wasn't strongly supported by research evidence. Other students of leadership have realized this too, and approaches are gradually changing. Various other publications have unfortunately veered in the opposite direction entirely—rather than focusing on one all-important leadership characteristic, authors have attempted complex descriptions of everything leaders could do. This leads us to the next trap.

The Second Trap: Successful Leaders Do *All* These Things

The trend of trying to define every aspect of leadership has been around for a while. Dozens of business authors and journalists have published lists of skills, habits, or practices that, once learned, will give an organization what it needs to succeed. Stephen Covey claimed that to be effective, you need to acquire his seven habits;[7] Glenn Llopis said there are fifteen things every successful leader does;[8] and Michael Page said there are actually just eight qualities that define an effective leader.[9] Which is it? Seven...eight...fifteen...thirty?

The abundance of these lists is likely overwhelming for the motivated student of leadership, and adhering to one or more might leave the reader confused. A discerning review should help them to realize that most of these claims are simply the opinions of the authors, substantiated by little more than cherry-picked examples of already successful companies or leaders. Without data and rigorous study backing these qualities or habits, they should be considered little more than musings. Few authors have attempted to empirically study these topics, and those who have done so have made claims that we should be equally skeptical about.

"We believe every CEO, manager, and entrepreneur in the world should read this book...you can build a visionary company." This was a claim from Collins (again) along with his coauthor Jerry Porras in their 1994 book *Built to Last: Successful Habits of Visionary Companies*.[10] Since its introduction, this book has become one of the "most influential business books of our era."[11] The authors surveyed one thousand CEOs, of whom roughly one-fifth responded, to provide a list of companies that were considered visionary. From there, they worked backward to see which patterns could be influencing this sentiment. They identified nine "habits" demonstrated by these companies.

The central claim of the book was that if you inculcated these habits in your own organization, success would follow. The late Nobel laureate Daniel Kahneman, in his seminal book *Thinking, Fast and Slow*, dissected this conclusion: "The basic message of 'Built to Last' and other similar books is that good managerial practices can be identified and that good practices will be rewarded by good results. Both messages are overstated. The comparison of firms that have been more or less successful is to a significant extent a comparison between firms that have been more or less lucky."[12] Kahneman continued, "On average, the gap in corporate profitability and stock returns between the outstanding firms and the less successful firms studied in 'Built to Last' shrank to almost nothing in the period following the study."

A better title for the book might have been *Built to Regress to the Mean*. This lens of critique should be consistently applied to any claims about business success and leadership. First, determine whether the claims are supported by any data or research whatsoever; this threshold should knock out the majority. Second, determine whether the quality of data and research has any validity. The claims should be true across long stretches of time to remove the influence of market events. They should be testable in other companies and provide predictable, measurable results. Very few books can pass these two checks.

The Third Trap: Follow Jack Welch's Path to Successful Leadership

Books describing similar leaders proliferate on the business bookshelves. The premise seems to be that these leaders were successful, and so, if you emulate what they did and how they operated, you too will be successful. Some leader biographies and autobiographies stray into this trap.

While useful information can be gleaned from reading a leader's life story, what they write and how they describe themselves is unique, just as the challenges and opportunities facing you will be unique. We were once contacted by an individual who thought he would benefit from our executive coaching work. We asked him whom he admired just to get a sense of his leadership thinking. He was very clear in his answer—he idolized Jack Welch. "I want to be a leader just like Jack Welch and feel that I can get there. I just need your help." It was a short conversation—"How about we help you become the very best version of yourself? Jack does Jack better than anyone. How about we get you to do the very best version of *you*?"

The best leaders are the very best versions of themselves, but not everyone knows what this looks like or can describe it in rich and vibrant tones. The language they use to describe themselves tends to be general and lack specificity. They paint themselves with extremely broad brushstrokes when finer details would provide a richer and more compelling narrative. Leaders who don't think they can describe the best version of themselves should at least try to provide a better narrative of the characteristics they can describe. This is where a credible assessment can provide the best start. It will likely describe you in terms that you might not even consider strengths. The assessment that we describe here does exactly that—it shines a bright light on a person's talents and potential to perform at the highest levels of executive leadership.

For a definition of leadership to be trusted, it must be measurable and predictable—it should be scientific. This is a difficult problem to solve because, as we mentioned earlier, successful leaders are vastly different from one another, each achieving success through unique means. But what if there were underlying similarities that all successful leaders possessed...a collection of traits or characteristics that reliably predict the best performers? This is the foundational question that our research sought to answer.

The Truth: Great Leaders Possess a Constellation of Talents

The conclusion of our scientific research is that exceptional leadership is the result of high capability across a range of specific leadership Talents. We capitalize the "T" in Talent for a reason. In the modern business world, "talent" is used in multiple contexts to mean entirely different things. Someone describing the "talent" on their team might just mean "employees." Someone who is proficient with a certain tool or procedure might be described as "incredibly talented." Neither of these usages meets our definition of Talent. For us,

> Talent is a measurable, innate characteristic that a person demonstrates consistently in order to achieve high performance. Talents are strictly defined. A person who has a strong measure in a specific Talent will perform predictably better in tasks related to that Talent.

Talents cannot be learned or taught; they are not habits. They are the natural characteristics that we are all born with. Contrast this with skills and knowledge, both of which can be attained through effort and practice. A person's unique constellation of Talents is enduring and pervasive. The influence of an individual's strongest Talents is visible in nearly everything they do. They leave their idiosyncratic signature on all their accomplishments. It is extremely rare for two individuals to have the same measures of Talent, which helps explain how dramatically disparate leadership styles can achieve the same exceptional results. Through the Talent lens, the past achievements of the consistently best leaders can be understood and their future success predicted.

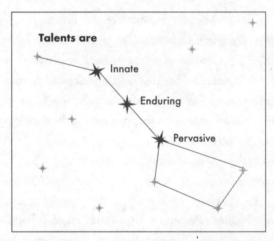

Talents are part of who we are and how we think (innate), consistent over time and resistant to change (enduring), and present in our daily work and personal lives (pervasive).

The measure of natural Talent—and the predictions we make from these measures—underpins the core work of our business practice. Our clients trust us with this work. Not only do they base their selection decisions on assessment results—using them to guide their decisions about whom to hire and in what roles—but they also use this data to build comprehensive succession plans, assessing internal leaders to help guide their professional development.

The assessment and measurement of Talents have allowed us to help reduce the uncertainty associated with historically risky business decisions:

- In selection decisions, we measure the Talents of candidates to provide insight into who is most likely to perform best in a role.
- We determine the Talent composition of different teams and advise our clients on the ways a promotion or termination will affect the team's capabilities.
- We identify the Talents of executive leadership teams to guide high-risk successions and leadership of significant projects.

In Part Three of this book, we organize our framework for assessing leadership Talent into five chapters that describe what high-performing leaders do:

- **Chapter 5: Setting Direction**—The very best leaders we've studied are driven by a vision of a positive future state when plotting a long-term course for their organization. They apply focus to goals, rather than activities, and look ahead to anticipate problems, issues, and opportunities rather than waiting to be overwhelmed by them. Talented leaders, when setting direction, help their organizations navigate through complex situations and articulate the value that many employees find motivational and engaging.
- **Chapter 6: Harnessing Energy**—While the short-term focus of Talented leaders is inward on how to drive organizational improvement, their long-term focus is outward and considers competitive positioning, market trends, and external influences. Driven by a burning work ethic, Talented leaders set an exacting example. They measure their progress and effectiveness and recognize that the most Talented employees beneath them demand their greatest attention and support.
- **Chapter 7: Exerting Pressure**—Talented leaders are comfortable speaking to, inspiring, and motivating large audiences, groups, and teams. They relentlessly focus on driving progress and improvement, and they agitate for change, provoke thinking, and never settle for average outcomes. They make employees in the organization feel uncomfortable in a positive sense that drives commitment and engagement. They assert a clear point of view and are persuasive in their approach.

- **Chapter 8: Increasing Connectivity**—Talented leaders establish effective and powerful followership through purposeful and ethical behavior and through care and concern for those they lead. They build relationships that differ from those of average leaders, contradicting the belief that better management involves maintaining distance from direct reports. Instead, our research clearly establishes that it is desirable to "get close" to direct reports, but in a way that doesn't compromise the leader's objectivity when evaluating performance.

- **Chapter 9: Controlling Traffic**—High-performing leaders understand how organizations work, what makes them tick, and how they drive superior performance. They manage pace and complexity with seamless assurance and use data and evidence to inform their progress and stay on track. Talented leaders tend to be exceptional planners, which is based on two juxtapositional characteristics— first, the need to establish protocols and guardrails to guide work and second, the need for agility and flexibility when circumstances change. This juxtaposition isn't always easy to achieve and is one of the reasons why exceptional leaders achieve exceptional results.

We developed our framework through multiple years of discussion, study, and validation. For every individual we assess, we ensure that we can appropriately describe their Talents within this framework. In our leadership database, no two leaders are alike, and our research has identified the varying paths these leaders have taken to achieve their success. For each of the Five Talents, we describe how leaders who think very differently from each other can meet these demands and achieve phenomenal results. You will likely recognize your own natural strengths in some of these chapters, but other qualities will be less familiar.

INDICATORS OF NATURAL TALENT

Why are some people just so good at something? Why do you gravitate toward some tasks over others? Talent tends to be the arbiter of these situations. Lurking in our subconscious, our predispositions guide us to make decisions that allow our Talents to shine. Hardly anyone wakes up on a particular morning and decides that they are going to be a genius in an area that is challenging for them. People tend to be averse to activities in which they struggle, and no amount of effort or training seems to make a difference. Public speaking is an excellent example. The mere thought of standing in front of a large group causes panic in many people. It is often stated that the three greatest stresses in life are the death of a loved one, divorce or separation, and giving presentations. By way of contrast, outstanding public speakers can't wait to get on stage.

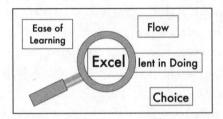

If you look closely, there are clues that will indicate the natural Talents that make each person unique. These talents represent their greatest development opportunities.

Flow

Anxiety and other negative emotions concerning an activity are a great indicator that someone likely does not have Talent in that area. Conversely, strong positive emotions when thinking about or performing an activity are a rudimentary measure of underlying Talent. In *Flow: The Psychology of Optimal Experience*, Mike Csikszentmihalyi posited that people are happiest when they are in a state of Flow, a state of concentration or complete absorption in the activity at hand. This state is felt by the individual and observed by others as "being in the zone."

Csikszentmihalyi described Flow as "being completely involved in an activity for its own sake. The ego falls away. Time flies. Every action, moment, and thought follows inevitably from the previous one, like playing jazz. Your whole being is involved, and you are using your skills to the utmost."[13] One of his key observations is that there must be an effective balance between a person's Talents and the specific demands of the situation. If these are out of balance, Flow cannot occur. Talent and expectation must match at a high level. If the task expectation matches, but at too low a level, the result is apathy, and otherwise

Talented people end up going through the motions even if the activity suits their predispositions.

Tasks that seem to be beyond the capabilities of others are achieved by some with minimal effort. These individuals exhibit phenomenal levels of concentration and application. Our conversations and interviews with high-performing leaders reveal that all have experienced this state of Flow, some more regularly than others. On occasion, these leaders can predict when a state of Flow is likely to happen by reviewing the nature of the tasks ahead of them. They describe such a sense of connection to an activity that they might fail to hear a phone ring or notice that someone is at their office door. When such signs are observable in others, it could well be an indicator of underlying Talent. Try to find out exactly what the person was doing when they experienced this feeling of Flow—this might be where one of their natural talents and capabilities lie.

Choice

Similarly, observing what a person chooses to do when they are not constrained by other requirements can indicate Talent. Given free choice, people tend not to do things they dislike or to perform activities in areas where they consistently struggle. Something surprising, as many people take too long to discover, is that some people love doing the things that you dislike. They can't get enough of them. We've met leaders who hated completing expense reports, only to discover an admin support person who loved this and who derived a significant sense of achievement from submitting these reports accurately and on time. The very best outcomes are achieved in situations where an assigned activity is completely aligned with a person's unconstrained choices. This leads to the very best application of a person's Talents in practice.

Ease of Learning

Some people seem to be able to learn difficult things with extraordinary ease. We tend to notice this more in areas where we personally struggle. Their achievements seem to stand out in contrast. Areas of rapid learning can be quite diverse. We've worked alongside leaders who pick up foreign languages for fun and who can credibly hold significant business discussions in those new languages. The speed and ease with which they learn is beyond the reach of many. Regardless of the activity, being able to quickly adapt to new knowledge and skills can indicate an underlying Talent in that area.

Excellence in Doing

Think of occasions when you have felt frustrated because someone told you how to do something that you had already figured out. Maybe you could already perform this task to a higher degree than the person interjecting. This may be a clue to discovering your natural Talents. Talk to female leaders who feel this frustration at having to listen to explanations from their male colleagues, and you'll begin to understand where the term "mansplaining" originated.

A person with natural Talent in a specific area will tend to perform in the top echelon compared to the general population. Excellence, by definition, is attainable by only a few. If an individual consistently measures as a top performer in an activity, they are likely demonstrating their natural Talent. Consistency is important because top performance can be influenced by limitless external factors. Over multiple iterations, the likelihood of results being driven by chance decreases, and Talent emerges as the key contributor to success.

Excellence shouldn't be reserved only for those with extensive track records. Additionally, excellence is not always measurable. Sometimes the sign of excellence is a glimpse of a very specific thing that is special, extraordinary, but usually fleeting. It can manifest as the potential a person might be indicating, something that captures our attention and makes us wonder "Is something there?" A younger emerging leader who shows promise could give us one of these glimpses. They might be showing Talent in its nascent stages of development. Being alert to different means through which excellence manifests enables us to be clear about the type of Talent we are identifying.

If such a glimpse is a true indicator of Talent, that reality will emerge. A person will seek out and repeat the activities that provide the satisfaction they receive from achieving something through their innate Talents. Individuals who consistently engage in and enjoy a specific activity are likely continuing to do so because their Talents allow them to succeed with ease.

What kind of work do you gravitate toward? What are you the quickest at learning? What are you consistently the best at? What can you do such that hours pass in minutes? Using these basic tests, you can start understanding what your Talents might be. The next question you might ask is "What do I do with my Talents?"

FOCUSING ON TALENT ELEVATES OUR BROADER ACHIEVEMENTS

Another mistake that leadership "gurus" make is that they assume that a leader must be well-rounded to be successful. We see examples in books claiming that X number of habits or qualities drive top performance and that if an individual does not have them, they need to learn them. This is as far as possible from the truth. The very best leaders don't continuously assess their deficiencies and try to correct them. They dive headfirst into the activities that allow their Talents to shine. Rather than focusing most of their attention on their deficiencies, they seek to build complementary partnerships with Talented people in contrasting areas. In other words, they manage their deficiencies rather than focusing on them.

Consider again the lack of innate Talent and the anxiety and nervousness this produces for some people in public speaking. This negativity obstructs effectiveness, and not just during the activity. Barbara Fredrickson, in her 2004 paper "The Broaden-and-Build Theory of Positive Emotions," found that negative feelings measurably limit performance in a range of unrelated areas where an individual was previously strong.[14] In contrast, positive reinforcement leads to elevated achievement across a broad area of functioning. Spending our time in areas that provoke negative sentiment limits our capabilities and hinders overall performance. Spending time in areas where we feel good, that are aligned with our Talents, elevates performance beyond the scope of those areas.

THERE'S NO SUCH THING AS BEING "TOO TALENTED"

Are there any downsides to being Talented? A common myth we need to dispel is that "your best strengths can become your worst weaknesses."[15] The pervasiveness of this belief is staggering, and any applicability is only superficial. The idea originated in a published article that reads more like a philosophical analysis than empirical research. It was repeated unconvincingly by Adam Grant and

Barry Schwartz in their 2011 paper, "Too Much of a Good Thing: The Challenge and Opportunity of the Inverted U."[16] The claim fails a basic tenet of good research because it assumes its own conclusion, i.e., "We see people behaving in less-than-optimal ways and this must be due to a tipping point where a strength becomes a weakness." This supposition is a poor derivation of the 1908 Yerkes-Dobson law, which states that optimal performance arises in situations where just the right level of pressure is applied.[17] Too much pressure, and performance deteriorates; too little pressure, and performance fails to improve at all.

The belief that strengths are in fact weaknesses is widespread, including in Tomas Chamorro-Premuzic's recent book *The Talent Delusion: Why Data, Not Intuition, Is the Key to Unlocking Human Potential*.[18] We have yet to find an example where it holds up under even mild scrutiny. To illustrate this, let's examine the story of Dan Rockwell, author of the *Leadership Freak* blog, in his own words:

> I'm a talker who married a quiet person.... Over the years I've learned that my strength is my weakness. I talk too much. I've learned that I don't have to fill silence with the melodic sound of my own voice. I've also learned that a few moments of silence is an invitation for my wife to begin talking, and when she starts talking I listen. She's quiet, not dumb. When she starts talking, she says so much smart stuff my head spins.[19]

Dan claims that "talking" is both his strength and his weakness. His interpretation is that because he talks a lot, he is a Talented speaker. Is a high quantity of speech a strength? We would say no. A better measure is whether he is an effective communicator. Under this lens, Dan is mediocre. We deduce that he has the capability of speaking but that he is prone to dominate conversations. His Talent for communication is not exceptional if he runs into the issues he described.

Let's return to the original proposition, that too much of a strength turns it into a weakness. Can we ever be too effective at communicating? So Talented a communicator that no one can stand listening to us? What about someone who plays the violin too well? The clear issues in the "strength is weakness" argument are semantics and poor definitions of what constitutes a strength. Dan did not effectively define his strength; he combined multiple distinct characteristics—speech quantity and communication quality—and treated them as if they were the same.

In our framework, a Talent is a measure that counts only upward, from bad to good. Strong and weak are measures that are both on the same continuum. There are no U-turns. There is no danger in using your strongest Talents to achieve your best performance. We encourage it.

WHAT ROLE DOES EXPERIENCE PLAY IN LEADERSHIP?

Another common belief that we encounter is that leaders are forged through challenging experiences that cause them to rise to the occasion and lead. If this were the case, we could take any individual and ensure that they become an effective leader by designing the appropriate series of challenges. This is false even though the training and development industry would love you to believe it is true. Instead, what we see is that individuals with Talents that predict strong leadership are able to meet the challenges they face, whereas individuals without those Talents are not. Experience is additive to a Talented leader and is largely irrelevant to a weaker or average leader.

Nearly every top-performing leader has persevered under difficult circumstances in their career, but attributing the source of their leadership effectiveness to those experiences would be to fall victim to Survivorship Bias.[20] Plenty of other individuals faced similar challenges and failed and therefore are not top-performing leaders. For experience to be a reliable means of creating top-performing leaders, it would have to be reliable and reproducible for a measurable proportion of the leadership population. It isn't.

This isn't to say that experiences aren't important; it's just that they aren't a means of producing top-performing leaders. Experiences can help already Talented leaders to develop beyond their current capabilities, but they will not help mediocre or less Talented leaders become exceptional. Our conversations with the very best leaders during in-depth reviews across a wide range of companies have helped us to identify experiences that show up consistently in many of their careers. We provide details of these experiences in Chapter 10, where we outline the career experiences that are most essential to a leader's development.

When you think and reflect on the role of high-level experience in the business world, it is usually beneficial, but not always. The key question is whether a leader is sufficiently aware of areas of potential downfall. Too few are, in our experience. These leaders tend to think they know best, and they are happy to communicate this belief freely to others. Too many people credulously listen. The following account shows that experience isn't always what it's cracked up to be.

Experience Provides a Veneer of Competence

On Monday, January 18, 1977, I emerged from a college lecture to find that Dougal Haston, a Scottish mountaineer, had just died in an avalanche while solo skiing in the Swiss Alps. He was a prodigious talent in rock climbing, mountaineering, and alpinism. One of the very best. He had scaled some of the most ferocious mountains around the world. For a young climber like me, he was a cult figure—an idol. I had seen him in Scotland the previous winter while on a skiing trip to the Cairngorms near Aviemore. He was an imposing figure, a commanding presence, and was possibly the most experienced British mountaineer of his day. He had survived some of the wildest and most extreme environments on Earth. Yet he died in an avalanche.

He had been skiing solo near his home in Leysin, Switzerland. Avalanche warnings had been posted there that very morning. Indeed, Haston, who was head of the International School of Mountaineering in Leysin at the time, had posted the exact same notice at his school so that people would be informed of the potential danger and hopefully heed the warning by staying away from the mountain that day. A warning he ignored.

Why did one of the most experienced mountaineers on the planet end up dying in a predicted and prewarned avalanche?

Haston was no stranger to avalanches and their destructive, often deadly force. He had spent the best part of his life navigating harsh and extreme mountain conditions. When he climbed the North Face of the Eiger by a direct route with the American climber John Harlin (who sadly died after falling several thousand feet when a rope—which Haston told him not to use—snapped), it was regarded as possibly the greatest feat in mountaineering history. I made thirteen attempts on that mountain and failed every time.

Haston needed to be able to exercise good judgment in order to minimize objective dangers such as ice and rock falls as well as avalanches. Why did someone of such

supreme experience make decisions that made little sense and ended in his death?
I have three observations that typically apply to the most experienced practitioners
across many areas of human endeavor.

Experience Breeds Overconfidence

What does a little solo skiing mean to a mountain expert who has spent his life facing
challenges of the kind that others view as impossible? The posted warnings of ava-
lanche risk in precisely the area where he chose to go skiing suggest either a complete
disregard for his own safety or the belief that the notice didn't apply to him because he
was special. He had more experience in exactly these conditions than almost anyone
else. He was the head of a mountain school, for goodness' sake, teaching programs on
topics such as avalanche safety. Haston wasn't some irrational risk junkie—he was
calm and calculating. Yet his incredible experience might have contributed to his
death. Hundreds of people were on vacation that day in Leysin, everyday skiers with
barely a fraction of his experience—and none of them died. Haston did.

Experience in One Area Doesn't Always Transfer to Other Areas, Even When You Might Think It Does

There's something very different about looking at a mountain through a climber's
eyes compared to a skier's. For one thing, the climber must evaluate the easiest and
safest uphill route toward their goal, whereas the skier is concerned about coming
down. When Haston climbed the famous Point Five Gully on Ben Nevis, the hardest
part wasn't the one-thousand-foot-high frozen vertical waterfall in the gully; it was
navigating the treacherous snow slopes below—slopes where the wrong step could
lead to a fall into a crevasse or trigger an avalanche. Haston knew this and read these
situations extremely well. But skiing is downward directed, and usually at speed,
and little time is spent looking up at a slope from below. All of Haston's experiences
were the exact opposite and counted less in this environment. His experience failed to
transfer effectively.

Experience (and the High-Level Achievement That Usually Comes with It) Can Push the Risk Boundary Too Far

There is a close relationship between experience and self-confidence. This is under-
standable because as your experience contributes to your success, it can lead to even

more risk-taking. And at the very top of the experiential ladder, the line between danger and safety is imperceptibly thin—the margin of safety narrows and, as in Haston's case, inverts. When that risk is an extension of your experience, it can lead to breakthrough achievements, as was certainly the case with Haston's climbing career. But it can also lead people to think that they "should be good" in related areas. I can climb on snow and ice; therefore, I can ski on them. If I'm good on a road bike competing in the Tour de France, I "ought to be good" at mountain biking—after all, they both involve bikes. But there is a reason why people don't frequently switch between these sports. I thought it was the height of hubris when US Hall of Fame basketball player Michael Jordan announced that he was going to switch to Major League Baseball. Although Haston's case is a little different, high levels of experience can lead people to feel that they can do pretty much anything. They can't.

Three key findings behind this story should live at the heart of every organization:

1. *Experience breeds overconfidence.*
2. *Experience in one situation doesn't transfer to other situations.*
3. *Experience can lead to pushing the "risk" bar too far.*

It would be desirable for experience to be more of an effective predictor of future leadership success than it is because, after all, experiences are tangible and easy to identify and manage. But they contribute little to the overall prediction of a future leader's success. The best we can say about experiences, however significant or impactful, is that they are no more than "table stakes"—nice to have but lacking independent, predictive value.

DISCOVERING YOUR TALENTS

At the beginning of this chapter, we outlined what most books get wrong about leadership. Some of these books sold many copies and have been extremely influential in leadership thinking. It's no surprise that leaders attempting to follow their advice have ended up in a confused mess and have followed selection approaches and organizational designs that have failed to deliver real value and fallen short of the high-level achievements they so obviously desired. We talk more about these failings in the chapters to come. We intend this book to help tidy up such sloppy thinking and reasoning as we outline The Five Talents That Really Matter.

We shared some behavioral clues that can help an individual identify areas where they may have natural Talent. These can be helpful for personal awareness and development, but they fall short without the robust description of the Five Talents.

We have also laid waste to the rather silly idea that your strengths can become your greatest weaknesses. This very damaging claim seeks to unnecessarily detract from individuals' greatest capabilities. Psychologists, it seems, are so focused on human dysfunction, psychosis, and varied disorders that they can't wait to get their hands on the few things that humans do well and twist them to match their prejudiced thinking. This book won't let them get away with it.

Finally, we encourage caution to those organizations chasing high leadership performance through an experiential focus. While it is tempting to believe that key experiences matter, in research terms, they do not. Experiences must be viewed as table stakes, not differentiators. This realization comes with less reliance on résumés in the initial selection of candidates.

Having outlined how most leadership books get their focus wrong, our next chapter traces these mistakes into companies and organizations. It shouldn't be a great surprise that companies seeking to emulate key writings in leadership end up making the same errors—errors that have huge implications for selection practices, particularly with respect to executive leadership. Our aim is to begin the significant task of correcting these errors.

CHAPTER 2

What Companies Get
Wrong About Selection

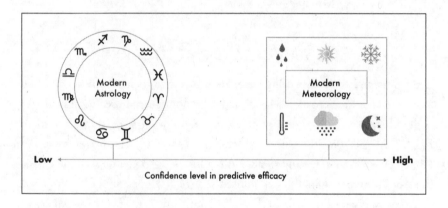

Modern
Astrology

Modern
Meteorology

Low ⟵————————————————————⟶ High

Confidence level in predictive efficacy

IMAGINE A SCALE THAT MEASURES AND RATES PREDICTION ACCURACY. ON
one end, you have a field with high predictive value, such as meteorology, where
the forecasts are nearly always correct. On the other end is astrology, which has no
demonstrable predictive value. Now think of your own organization's candidate
selection methods. Where do those methods fall on this scale? Is there a consistent
process that reliably predicts the future success of the candidates you hire? Do your
decisions have any data-driven component?

If you answered yes to these questions, your organization is among the few that fall closer to meteorology on the scale. Based on our experience, it is much more likely that your organization is among the majority where the predictive value of the methods used to select employees is akin to practicing astrology.

From a research perspective, the current era of candidate selection focuses heavily on the development of employment testing that is fair, valid, and reliable. Statistical methodologies continue to improve, and a large library of scholarly articles that better describe behavioral psychology has been amassed. The number of organizations that deploy some kind of candidate assessment when hiring employees has increased significantly. We would like to say that this has resulted in a plethora of organizations operating with the precision of meteorologists in identifying the very best people for their most suitable roles. If you've been employed in the past fifty years, you're probably aware that this isn't the case.

So what went wrong?

THE STATE OF CANDIDATE SELECTION

Truly outstanding leaders bring tremendous value to their organizations by creating the conditions that allow individuals to flourish and the business to grow. Sadly, there seem to be too few of them. Research on leadership performance has shown that only 18 percent of global business leaders deliver more than 88 percent of their company's value.[1] A landmark 2013 Gallup study of engagement at all organizational levels showed that only 30 percent of US employees are actively engaged in their work.[2] In 2023, this percentage grew—but only to 33 percent.[3] This should alarm you.

These numbers are symptomatic of a deeper, more systemic issue, the results of which likely deprive companies of hundreds of billions of dollars annually. From our perspective, this issue is the product of organizations making serially poor selection decisions and refusing to acknowledge, and learn from, their mistakes. Despite advances in the fairness, validity, and reliability of assessments, they haven't proven to be very effective in predicting superior job performance.

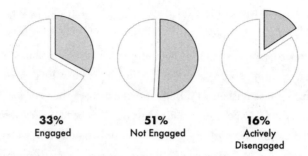

33%
Engaged

51%
Not Engaged

16%
Actively
Disengaged

Poor leadership selection practices have a predictable impact on company performance and employee engagement.[4]

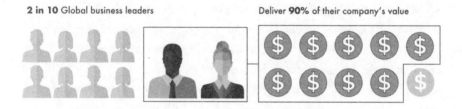

2 in 10 Global business leaders   Deliver **90%** of their company's value

FLAWED APPROACHES TO LEADERSHIP SELECTION

Companies often proclaim what should be obvious—that hiring the most Talented employees is essential to their future. We agree and assert that decisions about whom to appoint to leadership roles are particularly important, as these people's influence reaches every corner of the organization and impacts the experience of every stakeholder who interacts with them. Every selection decision that companies make is a prediction, and rather than focusing on making that prediction accurate, companies make a series of easily correctable errors when selecting leaders. There are seven key errors.

1. Selection Decisions Are Left to Chance

We met a CEO who, forty-five years earlier, had founded his company and was now nearing retirement. His company had enjoyed much success due to an effective product mix and sparse competition. Recently, new players had captured a worrisome chunk of the market, and this organization now had to learn to play offense and defense. The change in function necessitated a change in form, most importantly at the leadership level.

Agile leaders were (and are) in short supply, which we explained to the CEO as we introduced him to our assessment methodology. He wasn't enamored. "I just need a strong, firm handshake. I'll know when I can see the whites of their eyes!" he exclaimed. The CFO position remained unfilled, as he had burned through two of his favored candidates within a year. "Why did they leave?" we asked. "They weren't up to the job," he explained, failing to address the fact that they had both had strong handshakes and the right hue of white in their eyes. This is a pattern of behavior we see all too often—selection decisions made on instinct and gut feeling.

Although this is an extreme example, consider the implications for your own organization's selection methods. How many people are hired because they effectively wooed the interviewers? Does exceptional interview performance transfer to exceptional role performance? What biases are inherent in interviews that hinder an organization's ability to be objective? Despite very well-intentioned and capable leaders trying to do the right thing, our observation and evaluation of many selection processes suggest that companies really have little clue as to what they are doing. Their results are rarely better than what could be achieved by chance.

2. Face-to-Face Interviews Reward Likability

We are often asked for examples of companies that are regarded as using best practices for executive selection. Truthfully, each company's circumstances are unique, and there isn't a template that works universally. Some companies perform well in certain parts of the selection process, particularly candidate sourcing, but we have yet to find a company that has it completely figured out. The biggest impediment we see to effective selection is an overreliance on face-to-face interviews, and almost every company uses them.

Without a clear focus, assessment criteria, and effective questioning, face-to-face interviews are a waste of time. Likability factors have a huge and disproportionate impact on how a candidate is perceived and weighed against others. Generally, a candidate's affability will have no correlation to how well they can perform within a specific role—we've checked.

If these types of interviews are a key component of your organization's selection process, you shouldn't be surprised if your company's composition most resembles the kind of people your hiring managers could be friends with. A company that struggles with diversity will see progress toward equitable representation only when its leaders realize that their organization is a result of whom the hiring managers are prepared to allow in. What happens when the most talented, capable candidate doesn't get along well with the interviewers? This happens all too often and hinders companies that want to appoint the best leaders to drive exceptional performance.

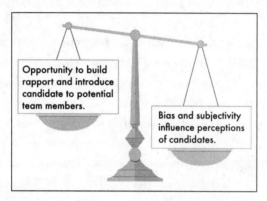

Companies should weigh the pros and cons of face-to-face interviews very carefully and recognize that the bias that influences perceptions of candidates needs to be balanced by more objective evidence of a candidate's qualifications.

3. Unstructured Interviews Show Poor Validity

This issue is compounded when interviews are entirely unstructured, meaning there is no formalized process by which the interviewer conducts their questioning or evaluates candidate responses. Every candidate for a role will have a different interview experience as the hiring manager racks their brain for difficult and esoteric questions they believe will provide some ultimate insight into whether the candidate will fit the role. If you have ever been asked (as an adult) what you'd like to be when you grow up or what items you'd bring to a desert island, you were a victim of this crime. Companies that should know better, like Google, have an appalling reputation for asking bizarre questions during face-to-face interviews. "How many golf balls can you fit in a school bus?" is just one of countless silly questions. Whatever Google thinks it learns from candidate responses, we can guarantee that the outcome is nonpredictive in terms of performance.

Unstructured interviews cannot meaningfully predict future performance because they rely on the subjective opinions and interpretations of both parties. By their very definition, unstructured questions introduce variability into the selection process. You cannot produce a reliable prediction of employee effectiveness with such variability.

Some organizations do attempt to apply structure to their interview process, and they create templates of questions that are a better match for the requirements of the role. However well-intentioned, these often fail on two fronts:

First, typically no credible research has been conducted to explore the range of responses an interviewer might encounter and which of them is more predictive of job performance. Any response that sounds good in the moment may prevent interviewers from asking more critical questions about a candidate's characteristics.

Second, training in how to interview candidates is inconsistent and poorly conducted, and many executives don't think they need it. They are wrong. Interviewers introduce their own preconceptions and biases when interpreting a candidate's responses. As a result, no two interviewers will interpret an interaction in quite the same way, and the recommendations that follow are clouded by misjudgment.

Free-form, unstructured interviews produce very little evidence that might help companies improve their selection decisions. The problem worsens when companies opt to include more interviewers in the process, conducting "round-robin" interviews over a span of several days or even weeks. Candidates are introduced to executives and board members, and their opinions and evaluations are magically assimilated in a cursory and subjective way. The process is rarely done collectively, and the lack of preparation and agreed-upon selection criteria is staggering.

4. Misleading Candidates Damages a Company's Brand

Face-to-face interviews often have the unintended effect of misleading candidates who are not likely to be selected for the role. In part, our natural desire to have positive social interactions means that interviews are usually friendly, affirming conversations. Companies want applicants to feel valued and important during the process, and this can result in communications that inadvertently mislead candidates to develop a stronger view of their chances than is potentially warranted.

Beyond the lack of predictive value offered by face-to-face interviews, mismanagement of the process in this way is damaging to the candidate as well as the company's recruitment brand. Too few organizations apply serious care to handling the outcome of selection decisions, particularly the experience of unsuccessful candidates. Companies that get this part wrong, effectively "ghosting" those they have rejected, are undermining their future recruitment efforts one jilted candidate at a time.

Chapter 10 contains, along with other tools to improve your company's selection process, a Selection Charter—a disclaimer sent to candidates that clearly outlines expectations for the process they'll participate in. A tool like this can greatly reduce the confusion and uncertainty that candidates face. Companies that have adopted a similar charter have gone a long way toward ensuring that their brand is viewed as fair and transparent by both successful and rejected candidates.

5. 360 Assessments Are Subjective at Best, Biased at Worst

A 360 assessment requires individuals who are peers, direct reports, work partners, or supervisors to score a leader on a series of defined characteristics. As established research has clearly shown individuals' flaws and biases in evaluating others, aggregating these flawed judgments doesn't correct these errors.[5] Zenger-Folkman, a company whose business model relies on conducting 360 assessments, stated that these assessments primarily measure the current engagement level of a leader and their direct reports.[6] Furthermore, they have a significant history of reinforcing the biases that cause diversity challenges. A growing body of research has indicated that 360 assessments lead to unfair judgments of women and minority individuals.[7]

These assessments lack the objective capacity to reliably predict a candidate's future performance, which should disqualify them from inclusion in any selection process. Beyond this, they introduce issues for candidates, especially executives, where confidentiality precludes disclosing their pursuit of other career opportunities to their current employer where these 360 assessments would be required to be conducted. Violating this confidentiality can diminish a hiring company's brand and will lead to the early withdrawal of otherwise excellent candidates.

Given these detractors, it is surprising that 360 assessments are currently a key component of some organizations' hiring process. The driving factor we have identified is their adoption by search firms seeking to gain quick and relatable insight into a candidate's experience and personality.

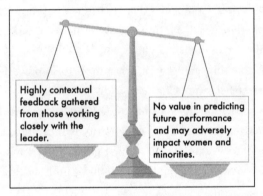

Highly contextual feedback gathered from those working closely with the leader.

No value in predicting future performance and may adversely impact women and minorities.

360 assessments can be a useful tool to aid a leader's growth and development, but they cannot provide an effective measure or prediction of performance.

6. Misaligned Incentives with Traditional Search Firms

Traditional candidate search firms are a juggernaut in the realm of employee selection, especially at the leadership level. They exercise phenomenal influence and control over who is deemed worthy of their advocacy and support. Over the past twenty years, their role in selection decisions has expanded beyond simply identifying eligible candidates and passing them on to a hiring company. Many search firms, especially at the executive level, have acquired assessment tools so that they can market themselves as "full-service" selection, succession, and guidance providers. These companies search for candidates, vet them internally, and then make recommendations to their clients.

There is a troubling flaw in this model. Search firms that identify candidates and then determine their capabilities through their own assessment services are guilty of a serious conflict of interest that we have yet to see effectively addressed. These firms are most profitable when they are able to quickly recommend candidates for a role, secure their commission, and then move on to the next role. They are implicitly incentivized to advocate for candidates who are already on their rosters rather than identifying entirely new applicants who might be better suited for a role.

The assessments they use therefore need to be broad enough that whoever they source will fit a role somewhere and quickly. Unlike the assessment industry, which has to meet stringent legal requirements for reliability, validity, and fairness, the search industry is largely unregulated, subject only to voluntary codes of conduct. The assessments that search firms use lack predictive value because they rarely measure the long-term performance outcomes of their recommendations. We are unaware of any that freely publish such data.

Occasionally, we have the good fortune to work with highly professional and talented individuals who happen to be employed by a search firm. They distinguish themselves from their peers by focusing entirely on the needs of their client rather than the candidates on their roster. When a search firm professional becomes a candidate's advocate, it loses all objectivity in a way that is damaging to its credibility and is not helpful to the candidates or the companies that pay their fees. It is our expert opinion that hiring companies should set the expectation that searching and assessing will be performed independently from the beginning of their relationship with a search firm.

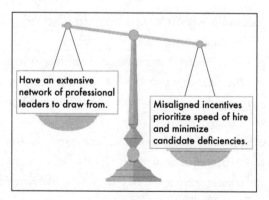

Search firms rarely measure the long-term outcomes of their recommended candidates. Leaders should be diligent with their questioning to evaluate the professionalism of any search and selection partner.

Ending the Search Firm Stronghold of Identifying and Assessing Candidates

We argue strongly that traditional search firms exert too great an influence over all aspects of executive selection and that few companies will succeed in transforming their organizations by consuming the menu these firms provide. In its otherwise excellent report on the use of psychometric assessments in the search process, the Association of Executive Search and Leadership Consultants (AESC) failed to outline the need for this clear separation.[8] The tension that exists between search firms and independent assessment providers is very real and predictable. Each is evaluating the candidate through a different lens, and this tension is essential to obtaining the best outcome for the candidates and hiring companies.

The expertise of search firms lies in identifying candidates who seem to have the requisite skills and experience for the role in question. The assessors are then able to objectively measure who will most likely succeed. By splitting sourcing and assessing between independent parties, the conflict of interest is resolved and the company can trust that the best, rather than the first, candidate will be hired.

When building a relationship with search firms, we suggest companies seek the following information:

- What legal standards do you adhere to in the fulfillment of your duties?
- What data can you provide regarding your effectiveness for similar roles in this industry over time?
- What percentage of your recommended candidates were hired?
- What was their average tenure? What was the tenure range?
- What percentage of hired candidates achieved top-quartile performance?
- What percentage of hired candidates chose to leave after they were appointed to pursue other opportunities?
- What percentage of hired candidates were terminated? Within what time frame?
- What informal studies, reports, or formal validations of your work efficacy can you provide?

- Do you disclose competitor companies with whom you work whose candidates are "off-limits"?
- What performance dashboard will you use to establish your effectiveness in this engagement?

Detailed and validated answers to these questions should help companies differentiate between the search firms that can add value to their selection process and those that can't.

7. Confidential Reference Checks Are Unreliable

Every failed executive, either those fired because of poor performance or those who committed ethical violations, came at the top of a search firm's list of recommended candidates and received glowing references from someone claiming to know them well and able to vouch for them. So why did they fail?

The previous section described the limitations of search firms, and their failings are relatively easy to explain once their business model has been outlined and understood. But how can reference checks be so wide of the mark? How can it be that a referee—someone who is prepared to put their reputation on the line to vouch for a candidate—can get it so terribly wrong? The reason is simple, and we've already explained it. People aren't that good at picking people—even people they know well. Why should it be any different with a professional referee? Why should we assign to them powers that no one else possesses?

A close working relationship with someone doesn't confer special powers of evaluation. You might work shoulder to shoulder with someone for ten years and come to know this person better than anyone bar their spouse, but your experience and evaluation will be in a unique set of circumstances in one role. And that person might have excelled alongside you or under your guidance. But the characteristics observed by a referee might be unique to that role and those circumstances and may not translate to an elevated role in a new company with a new boss, different expectations, and unique systems and processes, however much you may think they will.

Just think for a moment about the loss of your expertise and contribution alongside them—that's not easy for you to describe and is difficult for you to take into account. How much of their success was due to your influence...to you just being there, nudging them at the right time and making small suggestions they might not have noticed? On balance, professional referees are no more capable of evaluating a person than anyone else, and you should stop assigning weight to their perspective.

The evidence is all around us. We don't need a bunch of technical research papers to point out that the people we think we know the most about—internal candidates—still flame out in elevated roles with failure levels that are shocking. If professional proximity is as good and reliable as some people think it is, then we should see no failures at all. Yet we've all experienced numerous examples in recent memory—every current leader in every organization has seen this several times in their own lifetime.

In their landmark 1998 research paper, "The Validity and Utility of Selection Methods in Personnel Psychology: Practical and Theoretical Implications of 85 Years of Research Findings," Frank Schmidt and John Hunter found that reference checks had half the validity of structured interview assessments in predicting future job performance.[9] In the same paper, they found that job experience, which is heavily favored by most search firms, had half again as much validity. The ignorance of these findings shown by most organizations is staggering. Search firms thrive, reference checks persist, yet both offer a poor return on investment and add little of value to selection decisions.

So what use are reference checks? Do they have any utility? At this point, we are going to sound contradictory, so follow along carefully. We believe that reference checks should always be carried out and diligently considered, but with this important caveat: if all you hear is a glowing reference with limited insight and no serious reservations, you should discount the information entirely. It simply isn't credible. The referee lacks objectivity (as most do). This also extends to those references that mention, in "criticism" of a candidate, that he or she "works too hard and doesn't know when to stop" or where the worst that can be said about a person is that they "don't like to take credit for the many significant achievements they have accomplished." You get the picture. Ignore them all when considering your decision; this applies to nearly all reference checks. However, if you do hear significant negativity that is supported by evidence, then you should always take it seriously and give it additional weight in your considerations. Unfortunately, in our experience, this happens all too rarely. Just accept that most of the work that goes into reference checks will be a waste of time.

One final quirk regarding references and the role of search firms. Many search firms offer to check references on your behalf—to do the work that companies might prefer to avoid. Never outsource this work; always do it yourself. Do we need to explain why? In our view, there is no substitute for hearing evidence firsthand rather than having it relayed back to you in filtered form via a third party strongly sponsoring a candidate under consideration.

EVALUATING YOUR OWN SELECTION PROCESS

Addressing these significant errors requires every organization to audit and then evaluate its own selection process. For each of our clients, our aim is to measurably increase the rate at which selection decisions predict future successful performance. Sometimes this involves incorporating our assessment tools into an existing suite; other times it means a complete transformation of a company's selection practice. Each situation is unique, but our strategy is consistent: we introduce tools and processes to steer hiring, succession, and promotion decisions toward a structure that is defined and has measurable outcomes.

The first step in any engagement is to realistically appraise the company's current process and results. We recommend keeping these questions in mind as you investigate your own company's hiring methods:

- Do face-to-face interviews dominate selection decisions?
- Are interviews structured or free-form?
- Do we consistently score important role characteristics in interviews?
- How well do search-firm-recommended versus otherwise-sourced candidates perform?
- Do we objectively measure the efficacy of our selection decisions at all?

Honestly examining the current state of your hiring is difficult. In a large company, there may be many disparate approaches to selection. A smaller organization may have only a skeletal definition and improvise its approach with each opportunity. If your company is like most others, your current selection process is comprised of mostly subjective measures and doesn't track its own validity, reliability, or effectiveness. This leads to hiring decision efficacy that is no more predictable than chance. Any company can make improvements to its selection process and shift its predictive capability further toward that of meteorologists. In the final section of this book, we outline tools that could help transform your organization's selection practices.

At the heart of an effective, predictive selection process is a validated assessment that helps identify the individuals who are best suited to the role they're being considered for. Whether it's for development, succession, or selection, the first step in being able to identify individuals with the Talent to become world-class leaders is to study the leaders who are already the best. This is the endeavor that we started over twenty years ago. In the next chapters, we describe our methodology: how we designed our Executive Leadership Assessment, the rigorous testing and validation we undertook, and how we interpret the results. It is our hope that a greater number of companies can benefit from the profound insights we have gained through this work.

PART TWO

BUILDING A PREDICTIVE ASSESSMENT

CHAPTER 3

Researching the Very Best Leaders

CORRECTING THE MANY MISTAKES THAT COMPANIES MAKE WHEN SELECT-ing leaders required us to build an assessment of the Talents that really matter. Rather than focusing on just one thing or trying to measure everything, we needed to define and assess the specific Talents exhibited by the very best leaders. We wanted a reliable means of predicting which individuals were capable of being top-performing leaders. We wanted to forecast the weather. The difficulty arose when determining how we could accomplish this. What data could we use that would be consistently available for every candidate we wanted to measure? How would we know which aspects of that data were meaningful and relevant?

Leaders are unique, achieving their success through their own idiosyncratic methods. What data could we possibly use to compare them with one another? How could we define exceptionalism in leaders across entirely different organizational functions? Do exceptional leaders even exist? These questions were the foundation of our research and needed to be answered before we could consider any kind of experimentation.

Our aim to build an assessment that could predict the highest leadership performance would progress through a series of research and testing phases:

- We needed to define clear performance criteria: a means of determining who the best leaders were.
- We needed to find enough leaders who met these criteria to study—we determined that we needed to study and research at least one hundred.
- We needed to put these leaders under the microscope and find out as much as we could about their leadership characteristics and Talents—we needed to define what was common and what was unique.
- We needed to build a model of their Talents and define questions that would enable us to test this model. This testing would need to be conducted on leaders we knew nothing about—blind testing—to determine whether our synthetic assessment (essentially our prototype assessment) had any predictive potential.
- We needed to ask far more questions during synthetic testing than would be needed in our final assessment because we knew some questions wouldn't work—the responses of leaders to some questions would not provide evidence for top performance.
- Following synthetic testing, we would be able to finalize a model that captured the varied Talents exhibited by the highest-performing leaders we studied along with the questions that would help us predict the likelihood that future leaders we assessed might surpass their achievements—or fail trying.

Since first starting our research twenty years ago, we have built a huge leadership database of over fifty-eight thousand of the top business leaders around the world from predominantly larger companies. We had to be patient and persistent as we built our database and had to persuade many individuals to help us reach this large number. After a massive initial effort, we continue to systematically add leaders at a rate of about two thousand individuals per year.

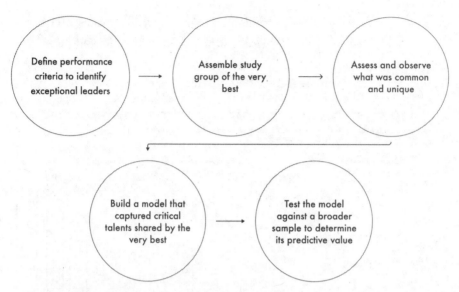

Our assessment model captures the natural variation that exists among even the highest-performing leaders and accurately predicts an individual's chances of success eight times out of ten.

This database contains many CEOs from companies small and large. It includes an overwhelming number of top executives who report to CEOs, enabling us to describe interesting Talent profiles of commercial leaders, general managers, marketing executives, heads of HR, general counsels, operational leaders, and many other functional and commercial roles. It also includes leaders who report to those top-level executives, the ones typically considered for promotion and who often populate succession planning lists. As our database grows, so does the strength of its functional and positional representation, enabling much deeper analyses and more accurate predictions.

As demographic, country, and functional representation grows, so has the number of records that include at least six years of complete performance data—currently more than nineteen thousand of these leaders. This enables us to constantly monitor the effect size, fairness, reliability, and validity of our assessment. We can determine how effectively the assessment works in real time, ensuring that our claims about Talents being enduring and consistent are verifiable. The quality of the data increases our confidence in the predictions made by the Executive Leadership Assessment regarding external job applicants and provides a robust measurement against which to benchmark existing leadership teams and individuals whom companies describe as having "high potential."

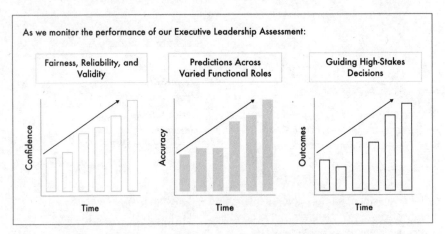

Not all of the fifty-eight thousand leaders in our database are exceptional, and to understand what that means, we need to define exceptional leadership.

DEFINING EXCEPTIONAL LEADERSHIP PERFORMANCE

We began asking questions about the indicators to look for in exceptional leadership. What metrics really mattered? We discussed this with the leaders we were studying but didn't get a consistent answer. The responses we received, however, helpfully narrowed our focus. Rather than capturing every metric that might matter, we wanted to capture the most important. This work wasn't as easy as we had hoped because every leader and every company expressed their performance measures and expectations a little differently.

We eventually identified three criteria that we felt defined exceptional leadership and have debated these criteria ad nauseam within our company and with our external partners. These conversations rarely produced agreement, but they helped us understand why we believe what we do. This shaped our research approach and provided the parameters to identify a sufficient group of leaders to study who exhibited the following criteria.

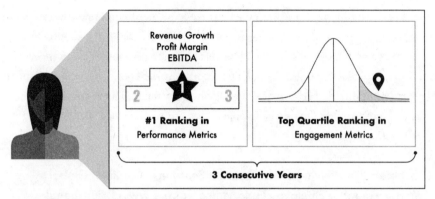

Truly exceptional leaders deliver outstanding performance through changing business cycles. Only those leaders who could consistently grow their business while treating people well qualified for our research study.

Criterion 1: Achieving Number-One-Ranked Performance (Against Their Peer Group) in Three Independent Finance and/or Process/Functional Metrics Within a Company

Finding individuals who achieved number-one status in three measures was extremely difficult, but we stuck to our guns. We rejected those who might have come first in two measures but second in the third. They had to be first in all three metrics. What kind of financial/process/functional measures qualified? We considered execution to budget, operating margins, overall revenue growth, earnings per share (EPS), EBITDA, and so on. These financial measures were helpful in comparisons between companies since their formulas are standardized.

Process/functional metrics were more varied because these are determined largely by the business of each company. However, quality metrics were common and often expressed as the cost of poor quality. Supply chain and distribution elements were especially data rich. We took a company-by-company approach, carefully considering what was most important to each particular company as it described excellent performance. We learned that these metrics were similarly designed but reflected the uniqueness of each company's priorities.

We were studying top-level leaders and felt that these broader measures were an indication of their effectiveness. One problem we encountered was that companies quite often didn't rank their leaders against these metrics, and we ended up doing a lot of this work ourselves. We learned a lot about the performance orientation (or lack of it) of these myriad companies throughout our efforts. Much of our research work and findings turned out to be helpful to them in redefining their performance management systems. Where previously their assessments of individuals lacked objectivity, our work helped them correct this problem.

Criterion 2: Achieving a Top-Quartile Score in a Credible, Global Measurement of Employee Engagement (at the Overall Functional Level—Not Just a Direct Report Team)

Plenty of stories were recounted to us of leaders who were basically bullies and who exhorted their teams to deliver results in conditions akin to captivity. Their team members could rarely exercise free expression and were certainly not engaged. With this in mind, we decided that another important measure of effective leadership was the measure of the engagement of employees within a leader's functional organization.

By measuring the engagement of their functional organizations, we aimed to eliminate leaders whose toxicity is fundamentally incongruent with an acceptable definition of leadership. We chose the top quartile in this criterion because an average score does not signify excellence. We typically used engagement data measured and provided by credible organizations such as Gallup and factored in how engagement measurement improved over time.

Criterion 3: Achievement of Criteria 1 and 2 for Three Consecutive Years

Studying leaders who had achieved the first two criteria for three consecutive years caused our research to take far longer than we would have liked. There were many individuals who would qualify one year and then fail in subsequent years. The worst cases were those where participants succeeded for two years but missed just one financial measure in year three. It was sometimes distressing, but we stuck to our standards. Our plan was to find one hundred qualifiers.

To improve cohort selection, we considered leaders who met these criteria in the year we met them and then worked backward to analyze the previous two years of performance. This allowed us to identify candidates immediately rather than waiting the three years.

But why impose such a strict measure? Did it really add any value? Our reasoning was simple. Broader market conditions, along with internal company dynamics, can create a favorable environment for some leaders to "outperform" in one year, but when those conditions become more challenging in subsequent years, some leaders fail to adapt and deliver the same high-level performance as in their previous achievement. Additionally, we wanted to reduce the possibility that their performance was the result of simple luck. We have been diligent in measuring the consistency of our claims to ensure that our findings aren't simply a random occurrence, an effect of regression to the mean.

We wanted higher confidence that the leaders we identified as exceptional could push through the performance curve and deliver superior performance through changing business cycles. As exacting as this criterion was, and as much as it gave us a collective headache, we persisted because we felt that it would separate outstanding leaders who could turn in amazing levels of performance year over year rather than just studying those who could do this only once.

DEMOGRAPHIC REPRESENTATION

These criteria were not our only considerations. We wanted our research group to include reasonable demographic representation. Due to the still present underrepresentation of marginalized groups in leadership roles, true statistical representation of society at large would be nearly impossible, but we at least wanted our group to be representative of the organizations from which these leaders were drawn.

We were committed to validating our assessment thoroughly during the synthetic testing phase, where we could better reflect more representative proportions. Considering the overrepresentation of white males in the study group, we paid particularly close attention to validity measures of adverse impact. It was good fortune that the initial one hundred qualifying leaders provided evidence of more varied demographic representation than we had expected, although it was still far from ideal. We divided companies into four size classifications based on revenue, assets under management (AUM), and number of employees:

Large (>$12 bn revenues or ≥$50 tn AUM and ≥50 k FTE employees): 12

Medium-Large (>$6 bn revenues or >$25 tn AUM and ≥20 k FTE employees): 66

Medium-Small (>$800 m revenues or >$10 tn AUM and ≥5 k FTE employees): 11

Small (>$200 m or >$5 tn AUM and ≥500 FTE employees): 11

In a study of 100 leaders:

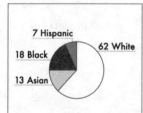 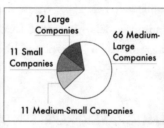 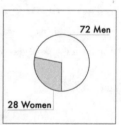

Our group of 100 leaders was composed of 72 men and 28 women, compared to the proportion of women CEOs in Fortune 500 companies as of 2023—only 10.4 percent.[1] The group had 62 white, 18 Black, 13 Asian, and 7 Hispanic leaders.

These aren't perfect groupings by any means, and we certainly don't claim that there is much significance in how we created these delineations, but we needed consistent categorizations for later analysis. Our study group was skewed toward larger companies. Given the number of different industries, our study group was a poor representation, but this was something we knew we would recalibrate and validate in the synthetic testing phase:

- Manufacturing: 2
- Retail (excluding Luxury Goods): 9
- Financial Services & Insurance: 11
- Automotive: 6
- Luxury Goods (excluding Retail): 10
- Hospitality: 18
- Media/TV: 9
- Health Care: 15
- IT: 18
- Construction: 1
- Transportation: 1

Given our exacting qualifying criteria, we expected some gaps in our representation. In some industries, such as wholesale distribution and logistics, we had no representation at all in our initial one hundred leaders. As with the demographic representation, it was our aim to address these issues through careful selection during the synthetic testing phase. Awareness of biases in our cohort allowed us to effectively plan for the rigorous validation we would need and to be confident in any of our findings.

Now that we had our one hundred leaders, the very best among tens of thousands, it was time to learn everything we could about their superlative leadership.

STUDYING THE VERY BEST LEADERS
UNDER A MICROSCOPE

We already had multiple years of performance data for our leaders; now we needed to gather a far richer image of who these individuals were. We interviewed them and examined their résumés and career highlights. We captured their academic qualifications and GPAs. We observed them in typical work situations. We interviewed people who worked with them. We carried out 360 assessments and administered a series of standardized and validated assessments of personality, critical thinking, verbal reasoning, comprehension, and numerical and spatial awareness. They all took exactly the same assessments, enabling us to compare their results.

We ended up knowing a lot about these individuals, in incredible detail. We needed to reduce the complexity in front of us so that we might identify patterns through a slightly wider lens. We used the heaps of data collected for each individual—interview recordings, observation notes, performance metrics, and employee reviews—and did our best to synthesize broader thematic definitions that were still descriptive of the individual in question. This process was somewhat abstract, and we were careful to reduce the influence of our own preconceptions about leadership as much as possible.

To accomplish this, one team member would create the synthesis of a random leader, ensuring that the result was anonymized to hide any revealing details. Next, a group of colleagues would attempt to match the synopsis to the leader that we felt it best thematically described. The team correctly named the leader from the synopsis eighty-six times out of one hundred. This gave us confidence that although we had simplified some of the complexity of these leaders, they were still being described in a way that reasonably captured their traits and characteristics.

Having reduced the initial complexity of the cohort, we sought to answer the question "What patterns are we seeing that make a difference?" Our first discovery, which we referenced in our exploration of Talent, was that even the very best leaders were dramatically different from one another. In some cases, they were radically different. In hindsight, this makes complete sense given the various ways leadership is presented in the world, but it was still an important discovery.

Our overriding concern was that perhaps there is no way to categorize leadership characteristics in a way that would enable us to predict leadership effectiveness, and instead, we would discover that these characteristics are always unique and essentially random. We persisted in trying to identify patterns, and eventually, we began to see expressions of similar qualities between disparate leaders. Over time, we began to define overarching categories that these qualities matched and clearer definitions for the subcategories within.

BUILDING OUR LEADERSHIP TALENT MODEL

The framework that eventually emerged was a holistic definition of leadership. This definition took years to hone, but even in its initial permutations, it could be used to describe every leader in our cohort. We discovered the Five Talents That Really Matter in exceptional leadership. We explore the framework fully in Part Three of this book; however, this is the thesis:

> From our study of a cohort of one hundred exceptional individuals, we learned that the very best leaders possess a variety of Talents that enable their success at the highest levels. We organized these Talents in a framework we devised that could fully explain our observations. At the root of this framework are the Five Talents That Really Matter.

These broad Talents define domains of behaviors and characteristics. They help us describe *what* leaders do. Each contains a number of narrower descriptors—these are smaller categorizations of behavioral tendencies that help us describe *how* leaders achieve their success within each of the Five Talents.

The detailed descriptions of leadership behaviors that we captured are a unique product of our research.

Setting Direction

Setting Direction: How leaders evaluate goals and opportunities, decide what to do, and plot the path ahead.

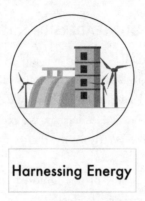

Harnessing Energy

Harnessing Energy: What motivates leaders to set high standards for themselves and others.

Exerting Pressure

Exerting Pressure: How leaders get people to act and commit to the right path.

Increasing Connectivity

Increasing Connectivity: The meaningful network of connections leaders cultivate to ensure that essential work gets done.

Controlling Traffic

Controlling Traffic: How leaders build the systems and processes to ensure that work is effectively organized, transacted, and managed.

But First, Let's Talk About Schoolteachers

In the early 1990s, I met with a group of high school head teachers in the United Kingdom. They represented various tenures but tended to have higher experience levels and many years on the job. Some were inspirational; others were decidedly less so.

They all complained about the poor quality of young entrants into the profession.

When I asked them to explain why, these head teachers simply weren't confident that the applicants they were dealing with actually liked children. It wasn't that they actively disliked children; rather, they lacked an affinity for dealing with them. They seemed to be missing the joy of interacting with the variety of children in any given classroom.

I asked about the typical questions that the head teachers were using in their applicant interviews, and the most common question they asked was "Do you like children?" Although it appears to get straight to the heart of the problem, this is a poor question and undoubtedly contributed to the instances of hired candidates who later underperformed. Who would answer no to this question? Even the least capable applicant for a teaching position would see the poorly concealed trap. I felt sure there must be a better question.

After countless interviews with teachers and direct observations of their practices, that question became clear. The very best interview question to ask to determine whether a teaching job applicant actually likes children isn't "Do you like children?" It is "Are there some children you don't like to teach?" The response to this excellent question tends to polarize candidates on the very issue the head teachers were seeking to uncover. Patient and effective teachers, who view the classroom as a place for collaborative learning, unconditionally like children—all children, even the challenging ones. After all, a challenging child is often an indicator of a curious mind. Their answer to the question is a resounding no.

Impatient teachers, who are often angered by disruptive behavior, see this question as a reflection of the reality of life. Humans are imperfect, they might think. In broader society, there are bad people—full prisons are an indicator of this. They opt to present themselves as realists and respond consistently with what everyone knows—there are bad people; ergo, there are bad children. "Yes," they might say, "there are some children I don't like to teach." An affirmative response to this question is a predictor that, if hired, they may not deal effectively with classroom conflict and may ultimately underperform and fail.

"Are there some children you don't like to teach?" is a powerful question, but there is no single question you could ask in an interview that would be the ultimate discriminator of who will be a world-class, rather than an average, teacher. I realized that it is only through a line of structured questioning, each one making a statistical contribution to the definition of effective teaching, that you can predict differences in teacher behavior and performance. It was the application of this thinking that influenced my approach to predictive questioning in the field of human selection.

BUILDING OUR ASSESSMENT PROTOTYPE

Building the questions that we could test in our assessment prototype was demanding work. Through our study of the top one hundred leaders, we had identified and categorized the underlying Talents that these leaders clearly possessed. Now we needed questions that would effectively test whether an individual outside this group had one or more of these Talents, and whether they had enough Talent for us to predict their subsequent success. A good question was one that top-performing leaders answered consistently in one way and weaker performing leaders consistently answered another way. If we could find over one hundred questions that achieved that separation, we knew we had the potential to build an assessment that worked.

Here's a question that we eventually developed that successfully predicts an individual's Talent in strategic thinking, which we define as a process of generating and evaluating multiple plausible ideas:

"What type of meeting do you prefer the most?"

a. One where you consider ideas and plans?
b. One where you take action?
c. One where everyone's voice is heard?

Each of these responses is highly plausible and desirable. Who doesn't enjoy a meeting that leads to action? Who thinks that hearing everyone contribute isn't a good thing? Imagine how good a meeting it would be if you just achieved "b" and "c." During the synthetic testing of our assessment, we learned that top-performing leaders chose option "a" over the other attractive and credible options. Ideas are so important to them and they enjoy thinking and talking about ideas so much that they elevate this option above any others. Weaker leaders rarely select this option because they focus more on getting things done or ensuring that people feel good about the process.

Eventually, we accumulated over one hundred questions that separated respondents based on their intrinsic characteristics. These questions addressed the detailed characteristics we discovered in the Five Talents of our Talent Model—Setting Direction, Harnessing Energy, Exerting Pressure, Increasing Connectivity, and Controlling Traffic. We knew that the assessment we built wouldn't capture everything a leader does, just the most important things that predict exceptional leadership. No individual leader measured strongly across all Five Talents. Rather, they provided evidence of enough of them to achieve their success.

TESTING OUR ASSESSMENT PROTOTYPE

For an assessment to work—to deliver the results it predicts—it first must be tested against "blind" candidates. This is called synthetic testing. It required us to find a large sample of leadership candidates who were "blind" to us. We would not know anything about their capabilities or performance profiles. We knew some would be highly regarded by their organizations, and others would be seen as more problematic owing to either behavior or performance.

For synthetic testing to be effective, and for the assessment to be judged as valid, we needed the assessment results to at least correlate to the performance descriptors provided by these candidates' organizations. Were the synthetic testing candidates who achieved the highest test scores also the top performers as defined by their companies, and were the synthetic test candidates who achieved the lowest assessment scores evaluated lowest in performance by their companies?

We designed our Executive Leadership Assessment to paint a picture of an individual's innate capabilities—their Talent constellation. This cumulative measure has two purposes:

First, to determine whether they are likely to be a strongly performing leader at all. Is there sufficient evidence across the elements we measured that they meet the high standards for success in statistical terms?

Second, given the unique ways that different leaders achieve their success, to determine what particular combination of capabilities this particular leader exhibits. How does their Talent constellation help them meet the expectations of their role? And in what ways might they be hindered?

We worked with a number of companies and identified 4,074 participants to test our assessment prototype. Of these, 2,412 were considered outstanding performers and 1,662 weaker by their companies' standards. We were extremely careful to advise these companies on how to balance the previously mentioned demographic and functional variables to better represent the population at large. When the time came for synthetic testing, each company simply provided a list of participant names, and we scheduled their assessments.

ANALYZING THE RESULTS

At the end of the testing phase, our partner companies shared their participant performance designations and we learned who were the stronger and weaker performers. We compared this information to each participant's assessment score. Our first step in the analysis of the results was to eliminate questions that didn't work—where there was no statistical difference across respondents. We originally asked 164 questions, and we eliminated 61. This left the results for 103 of the strongest questions that showed the greatest variance between top and weaker performers.

The results of our synthetic testing supported our hypothesis. By the end of our experimentation and data collection, we could confidently claim that leadership performance can be predicted and our assessment was capable of doing exactly that. Over the years since our synthetic testing, we have continued adding records to our database, which has further solidified our initial findings and strengthened the statistical confidence of our claims. Our analysis showed the following:

- The assessment score correlated to top performance eight times out of ten (r = 0.78).
- The assessment score correlated to weaker performance nine times out of ten (r = 0.91).
- The higher a candidate scored, the more likely they were to be a top performer.
- The lower a candidate scored, the more likely they were to be a weaker performer.
- Our assessment was valid in terms of the criteria (performance) predicted.

In the years since these discoveries were made—the Five Talents That Really Matter—we have used the Executive Leadership Assessment to dramatically improve our clients' hiring processes to increase the likelihood of successful appointments and reduce the chance of unsuccessful appointments. Our assessment isn't the only measure our clients use—and we would never advocate for it to be the lone arbiter of selection—but it introduces a reliable measure into the decision-making process. This reliability has been one of the most consistent positive feedback items that our clients have shared with us. For them, being able to raise the probability of one of their most critical responsibilities—hiring the best leaders—is a compounding benefit.

Fairness

It isn't enough for an assessment to be valid—it also needs to be fair. Fairness is about determining whether an assessment is biased toward one group of people over another. This is a crucial measure in determining whether you can trust a system or tool.

Determining fairness in selection is more than just calculating the impact of assessment results for different demographic groups. For example, candidates needed to be treated equitably throughout the entire process, to be given the same opportunities as other candidates to present themselves and answer questions, and to experience each part of the selection process in the same order and in the same way. Judging the fairness of the overall process requires that each part of the process be intrinsically fair, and this applies especially to assessments. Too many companies fail even this simple test.

Considering whether an assessment creates adverse impact is extremely important. For example, let's assume that one of the questions in an assessment asks you to determine which is the outlier from the following list:

- The Lincoln Memorial
- The Washington Monument
- The Korean War Memorial
- The Statue of Liberty

Asking this question outside the United States could lead to unfairness, for while everyone might recognize each of these as an important monument in the United States, it is less likely that they will know that three are in Washington, DC, and one is in New York City. Even asking this question within the United States would likely be problematic because not everyone will have received the same standard of education or been in the country long enough to determine the correct response.

The past decade has been unprecedented in terms of worldwide migration, and many countries have seen an increase in individuals from diverse backgrounds. For assessments to be considered fair, they must take this level of diversity into account. Anthony J. Kunnan, in his 2001 paper "Test Fairness," proposed a five-point framework for determining whether assessment tests are fair:[2]

- Validity
- Absence of bias
- Access
- Administration
- Social consequences

Each of these points is worth exploring, as they are all rich topics that can expose unfairness in any circumstance. It's a helpful framework because it forces a holistic approach to fairness that incorporates all parts of a selection process (even though it wasn't written precisely for selection purposes). His basic approach was to highlight that bias can creep into the most innocuous parts of any process and that being especially vigilant to this risk ensures that the right protections can be put in place.

Adverse Impact

The concern to avoid any form of adverse impact was high during the development of our assessment. We followed the guidelines of the Equal Employment Opportunity Commission (EEOC) with respect to the four-fifths rule. This requires that, minimally, assessment scores for the lowest-scoring group (typically defined by demographics) should fall no lower than four-fifths of the score of the highest-scoring group. If the average score on an assessment for women is 50, then the score for men should be no lower than 40 to meet this standard. In our view, this is a rather lax standard, and our aim was for there to be no discernible difference at all.

For our synthetic testing candidates, the mean score for men was 37.7 and the mean score for women was 37.6. In statistical terms, these scores are regarded as identical—as good as they can possibly be. When considering race, all assessments tend to report greater variation, although some of this is driven by low numbers (where we statistically would expect wider variation). For racial designations, we did discover slightly wider variance, but still far surpassing the EEOC guidelines.

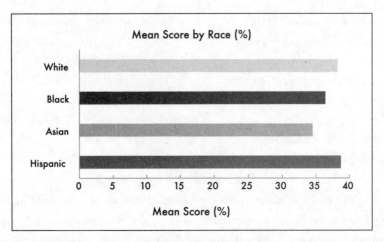

White (not Hispanic or Latino): 38.2 percent (98.7 percent of highest-scoring group)

Black or African American: 36.4 percent (94.1 percent of highest-scoring group)

Asian: 34.5 percent (89.2 percent of highest-scoring group)

Hispanic or Latino: 38.7 percent (highest-scoring group)

In the years since first determining these values for the synthetic testing group, these differences have remained extremely stable.

Our assessment is measurably fair across demographic groups, and it can therefore cut through the biases inherent in the selection process that perpetuate organizational homogeneity. We see these differences firsthand in our work with our clients. When objective measures are a core component of selection, the danger of face-to-face interview subjectivity is kept in check, and more diverse and talented candidates are deemed "qualified" and subsequently appointed.

Reliability

Our assessment is valid and fair, but it is also important for it to be reliable.

Reliability is a measure of confidence. In assessments, it describes whether the instrument provides the same results each time it is used, in the same setting, with the same type of subjects. Do the same inputs return the same outputs? Reliability, for our purposes, isn't the number of recorded failures but the consistency or dependability of the results over time. Reliability contributes to an assessment's overall validity.

Our greatest reliability measure was the test-retest value of our assessment.[3] Essentially, did the assessment show similar results for the same individual after a period of time had elapsed? This measure was key to ensuring that what we were testing represented innate, permanent characteristics rather than an individual's shifting disposition. This was measured on a scale from 0 to 1, where values closer to 1 represented a nearly identical result over time. Acquiring this measure required that specified individuals take the assessment at varying time intervals under conditions that replicated those of the initial assessment. This was extremely hard to do. The calculation, however, was simple—the correlation between the two assessment results. Our data showed the following test-retest correlations for the individuals we selected:

After Two Years: 0.91

After Three Years: 0.89

After Four Years: 0.88

After Five Years: 0.86

A second reliability measure that we used is a measure of internal consistency—Cronbach's alpha.[4] This statistic helps determine whether a collection of survey or test items consistently measures the same characteristic. It quantifies the level of agreement on a standardized scale from 0 to 1. Where groups of test items/questions are intended to measure the same construct (such as a theme or dimension), a high level of responses across these items suggests consistency and indicates that the measurements are reliable and that the items are therefore measuring the same characteristic. Conversely, low values suggest a lack of response consistency, meaning items/questions are not measuring the same construct.

What is an acceptable Cronbach's alpha score? For psychometric assessments, the typical acceptable score range is 0.7 to 0.9. An assessment that falls within this range is regarded as having excellent internal reliability. The Cronbach's alpha score for our Executive Leadership Assessment is 0.84.

The Five Talents That Really Matter

These results suggest an assessment that is remarkably reliable at measuring the Five Talents That Really Matter.

Through building a predictive assessment, testing and validating the initial prototype, and deploying it in real companies selecting real leaders, we have built up a candidate database of over fifty-eight thousand global leaders. The questions we have been asked the most are "What have you learned? What has this rich source of information revealed about leadership Talent and the organizations seeking to exploit it?" These are questions that we have asked ourselves, and before we engage in the detailed description of leadership Talent that lies at the heart of our assessment, we want to highlight some of our key learnings.

Some of the findings that follow are shocking, especially with respect to interview and selection bias. As we enter the middle years of the twenty-first century, we should all be asking why so little progress has been made toward advancing the Talents of everyone. By shining a bright light on these findings, we aren't seeking to embarrass organizations and leaders. Instead, we hope to galvanize them to take the right actions, many of which are outlined in the final pages of this book.

CHAPTER 4

What Have We Learned?

HAVING AMASSED OVER FIFTY-EIGHT THOUSAND LEADERSHIP ASSESSMENTS from around the world, our analysis hasn't been limited to individuals and our predictions of their future performance. We have asked many questions of our database and have sometimes been presented with interesting and worrisome findings.

EIGHTEEN INSIGHTS FROM FIFTY-EIGHT THOUSAND ASSESSMENTS

The Assessment Scores of Women in Executive Leadership Positions Are Considerably Higher Than Those of Their Male Peers

In our entire leadership assessment database of over fifty-eight thousand global executives, the mean assessment score is 37.7 for men and 37.6 for women—statistically identical. However, the mean leadership score for those who are appointed to executive-level positions in a competitive selection process is 42.2 for men and 45.1 for women. Why the difference? On the face of it, it seems that women are being held to a higher standard than men. In order to be appointed, women must demonstrate greater capability than their male counterparts. This won't surprise those women who occupy executive leadership positions—but it might surprise many men, and it will likely be denied by most of them.

We also see that the score range for men being appointed to leadership positions is far wider than the range for women, suggesting that it is easier for less talented men to be appointed than women based on consideration of other factors such as experience or perceived intelligence. The practical effect of this wider score range is that more men with much lower leadership assessment scores are being appointed to executive roles for which we would predict that they lack critical Talent and have increased potential for underperformance. Female candidates do not seem to be afforded the same leniency.

The Assessment Scores of Minority Ethnic Leaders in Executive Leadership Positions Trend Higher Than Those of Their White Peers

This seemingly contradicts many people's assumptions about race and leadership. As highlighted earlier, Hispanics or Latinos are the highest-scoring racial group in our entire database, followed by white and then Black and African American and then Asian leaders. This gives the lie to the widely held, but seldom expressed, opinion that minority race candidates lack the requisite leadership capabilities. Our data suggests that there are no good reasons for this opinion. The challenge that most organizations face is the paucity, even more than of women, of credible minority race candidates from whom to select. We have found, though, that even when these candidates are found and assessed strongly, they aren't being appointed for reasons not related to their leadership capabilities. Some would argue that it is due to the persistence of subliminal racism and prejudice. It is findings of this kind that fuel the term "institutional racism." This issue demands an answer.

Current Executives with Lower Leadership Assessment Scores Not Only Perform Worse Than Their Peers with Higher Assessment Scores but Also Tend to Select Weaker Team Members

Ask a leader whether they always aim to appoint strong candidates to their team, and everyone says yes. Push them further about whether they seek stronger candidates than themselves, and most still say yes. But neither response is supported by data. We have analyzed the results of our leadership assessment across the top levels of many organizations. In some larger organizations, where this number can total several hundred individuals, the pattern is clear, consistent, and pervasive— weaker leaders definitely perceive a threat from stronger leaders and are reluctant to appoint them, finding many creative excuses not to do so. There might be many reasons for this, such as concern about their own career chances or having strong controlling tendencies that might be questioned by a stronger team member reporting to them. It's a major problem that we see few organizations exploring or addressing.

We wish we could see evidence that stronger leaders are more likely to select stronger team members, and although we do see stronger individuals appointed by them, there are far fewer than we expect or desire. Even strong leaders with higher assessment scores, it seems, aren't averse to relational sophistication and likability when it comes to selecting candidates.

In our entire leadership database, where we were able to assess a leader and their entire direct report team, only 37 percent of team leaders had a person on their team with a higher assessment score than the team leader. Only 17 percent of leaders had at least two team members with stronger assessment scores than the team leader. This is a recipe for perpetual mediocrity and is just one reason why so many companies struggle to put performance daylight between themselves and their market competitors. This leaves attempts to build effective succession plans dead on arrival. One bright spot is that when we educate high-scoring leaders on effective selection, their hiring and selection practices change overnight; they become strongly focused on finding higher-scoring team members and place a much stronger emphasis on this aspect in their selection practices. For the very best leaders, it becomes a focus on which they will not compromise.

Leaders Across All Assessment Score Ranges, from Strongest to Weakest, Prefer to Select Candidates Who Demonstrate Characteristics Similar to Their Own While Claiming to Do the Reverse

Ask any leader if they intentionally select leaders like them, and they will say they do the opposite—they pick people different from them. There is clearly a "right" answer to this question, and everyone seems to know what it is. The problem is that this answer is nowhere near the truth. Most teams that we have studied at the leadership level have as much Talent diversity as the genetic diversity you might find in a remote village in western Nebraska (with apologies to the inhabitants of western Nebraska).

One of the great achievements to which most leaders can lay claim is that they have succeeded in self-replication—rather than seeking and achieving Talent diversity, they have all but stamped it out. Yet Talent diversity predicts stronger collective performance advantages. For over fifty years, psychologists have consistently found and reported that leaders pick team members in their own image (sometimes even physically). A rather cruel indicator of the lack of effectiveness of our investment in HR is that almost nothing has changed, with just a tiny number of incredible standout outliers.

Again, this situation changes with higher-scoring leaders who receive education in selection training and development. After this education, understanding the lack of variation in key Talents becomes a main selection focus for high-scoring leaders. Raising awareness, and deploying our leadership assessment, it seems, drives the right actions in populations of high-scoring leaders. They are given clear data and are willing to act on the results. Conversely, we see no change in the selection practices of lower-scoring leaders, even when they are given the right selection tools.

Most Organizations Have a Significant Leadership Deficit in Strategic Thinking and Growth Orientation That Is Typically a Product of Poor Initial Selection Decisions for First- and Second-Level Managers

"Where are all the strategists?" one of our client CEOs lamented. And he was right. An analysis of the top three levels of his organization uncovered a dearth of creative strategists. But our assessment wasn't needed to confirm what was in plain sight: poor commercial thinking, a multitude of failed projects, uncoordinated execution, and an iterative rather than groundbreaking product and service pipeline. The answer to his question wasn't what he expected.

We had already deployed one of our other selection tools at lower levels in his organization and discovered that the organization had some very good thinkers who showed strategic promise. But they didn't survive long or make it to leadership levels. Either they left because they didn't feel appreciated or activity-focused managers terminated them...quickly. These thinkers didn't play well at lower levels, where the focus was on speed and getting done what you were told to do. Too many middle managers saw the tough questions these thinkers asked as a sign of insubordination or general awkwardness. So a scant few made it close enough to the leadership team to be afforded protection and air cover, and most were let go.

The answer to the strategic deficiency in most companies is internal; it's deeper in the organization. Even knowing this, too many executives don't have the patience to solve a problem that might take five to ten years of focused attention, so it becomes an executive-level selection problem. Any hope that the face-to-face interviews typically deployed by these companies are geared up to detect the strategic thinking they are looking for is no more than wishful thinking.

An Overwhelming Number of Women Appointed to Leadership Positions Exhibit Characteristics, Traits, and Behaviors More Stereotypically Associated with Men

The stereotypical male leader is not difficult to describe, and there is much to appreciate and admire in some of their qualities. But elevating these qualities into desired values and behaviors for everyone can be problematic. We are tired of educating leaders that there isn't one firm template (a stereotypical male template) that predicts leadership success—there is no cookie cutter. Effective leadership is based on the compendium of Talents described in this book. Yet aggressive and assertive behaviors are valued, sought after, and demanded. Even when these behaviors cross the line, they are often excused and tolerated, particularly if carried out by a "high-performing" man.

There are many smart people seeking to develop their careers in companies, and these lessons are easily observed and learned. The characteristics of those who exhibit these behaviors are rewarded through promotion, and when individuals lower in the hierarchy exemplify the same behaviors, they too are rewarded. They are noticed with positive feedback and affirmation. When we assess female leaders at the executive level, we find that over 80 percent of them possess the same more aggressive characteristics. It isn't that these women aren't successful, because quite often they are; it's that it becomes extremely difficult for women with different capabilities, such as creative strategizing—softer characteristics, traits, and dispositions, if you will—to be positively noticed, and they are more readily overlooked.

When beginning our work with new clients, we start by asking HR leaders what data they have collected on this issue—whether they even see the problem. For too many, it is the first time they have heard the question.

Female Leaders Are Little Different to Their Male Counterparts in Keeping the Glass Ceiling Closed and Impenetrable

The justifiable complaint from many women—that the glass ceiling exists and remains impenetrable—is a very real problem. However, despite seeing a very small improvement in the numbers of female executives over the last decade, many of these promoted women pull the ladder up behind them, and are as reluctant as their male counterparts to appoint women to executive-level positions. Rather than champion the cause of the women they represent, the data shows they appoint women to promoted roles with similar ratios to men, often while proclaiming to do the opposite.

There Is an Overwhelming Preference and Desire to Appoint Leaders with a Strong Action Orientation Across All Roles and Functions, Including When the Board Selects the CEO

As Marshall Goldsmith famously said, "What got you here won't get you there."[1] He was writing about how the characteristics that cause people to be promoted and rise through the corporate ranks get a person to a certain level but no further, as other qualities become more essential. It's surprising how many leaders haven't figured this out. We have already highlighted the concern about the lack of strategic thinking at the top of many companies; this is a product of leaders placing too high a value on reactivity and action orientation.

It is no surprise that these qualities remain so valued at the expense of more comprehensive thought processes. There are individuals who attend leadership team meetings and become bored by the discussion of ideas—their dominant thought is "When are we going to get something done?"

Our analysis of top teams across many companies shows a strong predisposition toward action as their most evident characteristic, typically at the expense of conceptual, strategic, and commercial thinking.[2] We are not stating that action orientation lacks value; rather, we are saying that too many teams are overloaded with players who primarily value action orientation. The imbalance is evident, and too few teams operate with awareness of this bias or show interest in revisiting any of their many mistakes.

Higher-Scoring Leaders Are More Likely to Take Longer to Fill Vacancies Than Lower-Scoring Leaders

Some HR departments place high value on "time to hire" as one of their key performance metrics. This is almost as bad as call centers thinking that the speed with which operators answer customer calls is a more important metric than actually solving customer problems. Quickly hiring a poor performer carries no upside. But of course, no one believes they are hiring a poor performer because their selection process fails to measure this effectively.

We discovered two common virtues of leaders who score high on our assessment:

> *First,* they are always recruiting. They constantly cast their net, build connections and new relationships, and keep an eye on their competitors. When they find individuals who show potential, they put them through our assessment to see what else they can learn and whether their initial interest was justified. If it was, they go about creating a vacancy. An existing weaker team member is moved along, and a better player is brought in. If this sounds callous and uncaring, then maybe you aren't cut out for top leadership.

> *Second,* they know that it is better to wait for the right person than to compromise on Talent. This lesson seems impossible for weaker leaders to learn because their bar is already lower, and they will always find more qualifying candidates. We are fortunate to work with a small number of HR professionals who understand this. Most don't. Time to hire is a terrible metric for HR to use, and "quality of hire" is a better metric that most HR functions struggle to measure.

Lower-Scoring Leaders Take Significantly Longer to Terminate Poorly Performing Team Members (and Often Never Get to the Point of Terminating Them) Than Higher-Scoring Leaders

This isn't meant to imply that leaders who score higher on our assessment are impetuous and lack patience. It's that they set stricter timescales for performance improvement plans (PIPs) and don't allow individuals who are struggling to be coached to death over a protracted period. These decisions don't need to play out over years, yet for lower-scoring leaders, they typically do. Quite often these protracted support plans are thought to be helpful for struggling individuals, but they rarely are.

If a job doesn't fit, then it is in everyone's best interests for the termination decision to be made quickly and respectfully. We have yet to meet a leader who, on reflection, felt they acted too quickly in these situations. They nearly always criticize themselves for taking too long. Furthermore, the terminated employee is more likely to thank the high-scoring leader for making this decision, as it releases them from the misery they were experiencing in their role.

This is one of the hidden costs organizations pay for tolerating weaker (but likely technically capable and likable) leaders.

In Every Organization, We Find Outstanding Leaders (Often Women and Minorities) Deeper in Their Structures Who Are Being Held Back, Undermined, Suppressed, and Generally Mismanaged by Weaker, Typically Male Leaders and Executives

We find this issue occurring in nearly every company that we study, yet nearly every company denies it is happening. "Not here," they say. The reason is clear: most executives' perspectives on Talent are shaped by the people beneath them, and these are sometimes the blockers who think that denying the leadership abilities of high-potential people beneath them is in their best interest. We also see too many succession planning processes that fail to go deep enough into the organization along with a general reluctance to promote younger leaders who might skip levels. The risk aversion is overwhelming.

Even when we do see succession planning activities being carried out by the top leadership team, we see a lack of rigor in setting this expectation at deeper levels of the organization. Consequently, weaker managers are able to survive, and the stronger players who are hidden on their teams never receive the oxygen they deserve. Leadership succession is a much bigger problem than CEOs and top executives realize. Our assessment work carried out at depth in organizations is some of the most exciting and rewarding work we do. On too many occasions, we surprise leaders who should really know their people better than they do.

Too Many Leaders (Usually but Not Always Lower-Scoring Leaders) Say They Encourage Debate in Team Settings yet Have a Hard Time Handling Dissent

In three separate studies, we found that leaders who possessed challenging characteristics, traits, and dispositions—who spoke their mind and stood up to other leaders they believed to be making bad decisions—invariably received lower performance evaluations than more compliant and less challenging individuals, even though objective performance measures contradicted this. Lower-scoring but more relationally compliant leaders, who tended to be easier for their supervisors to manage, were invariably rated higher in their performance.[3]

Of course, there is a fine line between making an argument and being argumentative, and asserting a point and being overbearing. Highly Talented leaders understand these distinctions and manage them to good effect. Weaker leaders see these characteristics as a threat to their authority and have a hard time managing people who possess them. We should also point out that female leaders who exhibit these characteristics seemingly have a much harder time being effectively and accurately evaluated by weaker, typically male leaders who manage them.

With Some Notable Exceptions, Most Executives in Most Companies Appoint Candidates to Positions Based on Their Relational Sophistication and General Likability, Even if These Candidates Have Low Assessment Scores

Too many leaders find it hard not to "fall in love" with certain candidates based purely on their likability and strength of relationship building. Once this initial relationship has been established (call it "chemistry" if you will), it is hard to balance this perspective against more objective evidence such as an assessment score. Research evidence has already shown that we rate a person more highly if we think they agree with us, and we believe they are Talented and capable across a broad range of areas if we find that they are competent in one.[4] All of these are danger signs in selection, but those most susceptible to these kinds of biases are the ones who most vociferously deny it. These leaders can quickly explain away a low assessment score as an aberration or within the margin for error that is part of every assessment. But what is the chance that these leaders possess special gifts of divination that are beyond the reach of everyone else?

Talented, High-Scoring Leaders Are 5.6 Times More Likely Than Less Talented, Low-Scoring Leaders to Promote a Talented Younger Employee Across Multiple Skip Levels

Younger employees who possess high natural Talent but may lack experience are much more likely to be sponsored and promoted by high-scoring leaders. In all our years of research across over fifty-eight thousand executives, we have found only a tiny number of lower-scoring leaders prepared to take this risk. Longitudinal performance analysis suggests that these risks were largely justified and these skip-level promotions delivered high performance outcomes and also went on to subsequent promotions.

Black and African American CEOs and Executives Are Much More Likely to Appoint Black and African American Candidates Than White, Asian, and Hispanic or Latino Candidates

Black and African American CEOs and executives seem to have little difficulty finding and appointing Black and African American candidates across the score range to top leadership positions—candidates whom their white peers claim don't exist or can't be found. However, Black and African American CEOs and executives seem to have difficulty appointing Hispanics and Latinos and Asians despite their relatively high assessment scores.

Lower-Scoring Asian Leaders Are Eight Times More Likely Than Higher-Scoring Asian Leaders to Select Asian Candidates over Candidates of Other Races

Furthermore, the Asian leaders who were selected tended to be selected for perceived experiential capabilities rather than measured Talent and tended to exhibit below-average scores on the leadership assessment. Lower-scoring Asian leaders are far less likely to select African Americans than they are any other racial group.

Candidates for Whom English Is a Second Language Score Higher When Taking the Assessment in English Than When Taking It in Their First Language

The average assessment scores for non-English speakers who take the online version of our leadership assessment in English, rather than their first language, are higher than non-English speakers who elect to take the online assessment in their first language.

This defies logic but may lack any causal value. One explanation is that leaders who don't speak English as their first language, who choose to take the assessment in English, may naturally have to concentrate harder on the questions or think more carefully about their responses.

In Every Organization Where We Have Assessed High Potential Populations, the Results Have Conformed to a Normal Curve of Distribution...and They Shouldn't

Whether they admit it or not, or publish the details or not, nearly every organization has a list of high potential leaders—people viewed as having exceptional talent who can occupy roles above them. Indeed, getting onto this list is seen as a considerable achievement in many companies. Yet when we assess these leaders their results conform to a normal curve of distribution—the opposite of what we would expect.

Accepting that the overlap between the ranking on this list and assessment score will never be perfect, our assessment places nearly 20 percent of these "high potentials" in the bottom quartile of our database. Why? What might explain this complete disconnect?

The first explanation is simple. These lists show internal, not external, comparisons. They might well track to real potential defined in the company, and that will indicate how low the bar has been set. It shows the product of mediocre selection practices playing out over many years. Companies are limited in their definition of excellence.

The second explanation is a point we have already covered in this book. These lists comprise "nice" people, not necessarily the most effective leaders.

When we ask to see the objective evidence that put candidates on the list, we have to wade through a tidal wave of wishy-washy, subjective likeability comments. They are undoubtedly good people. Their managers love them. But they aren't destined to top leadership when predicted by our assessment data.

The great thing for us is that companies don't always follow our advice, and when they promote some of the individuals on their list, the lower-scoring leaders—who are thought to demonstrate high potential leadership capability—fail nine times out of ten. In this definition, "fail" is an inability to achieve top quartile performance in comparison to their peers. Many do achieve average outcomes and too many organizations find this acceptable. Their bar for talent is nowhere near high enough.

THE LEARNING LEADER

We continue to learn from our data, and the examples here are just a sample of the issues we have uncovered. Some of them are hard for organizations and leaders to swallow. It's not easy to own up to our failings, and in the case of bias, isn't it something that other people suffer from?

The exciting part of this book comes next because the most important discovery we made was the characteristics that predict effective leadership—the Five Talents That Really Matter. At the end of the book, you'll learn how you can take our assessment and find out more about yourself than you currently know. Until then, you will learn the most by keeping an open mind, reading through the Talents, and being ruthless in your self-awareness.

Reading about the Five Talents That Really Matter will open your eyes to the traits and characteristics that define high-performing leadership—the aim of every credible and aspiring leader. For each of the Five Talents, we break down the description into more tightly defined attitudes, values, and behaviors that capture the variability we see in the very best leaders. No two leaders are the same, and it will be important for you to think about how this variability captures aspects of your leadership and helps describe your qualities and capabilities.

Just as we have yet to find the perfect leader (despite meeting some who think they are), neither will you be perfect. Considering the descriptions we highlight might help you to identify the highs and lows of your own capabilities. We have broken down each of the Five Talents to help you in this task. Each of the narrower descriptions you encounter starts with a Research Definition followed by more expansive details drawn directly from our initial and ongoing research. It is against these detailed descriptions that you should consider your own leadership Talents. For those wanting more accurate help, the opportunity to take our Executive Leadership Assessment is described at the end of the book.

In my case, I've always known from an early age (although I didn't have the vocabulary to describe it then) that I struggled with relationships. Part of it was due to being too judgmental of others. Part of it was due to being too competitive. But most of it was because of insensitivity. It wasn't that I didn't care about people but that I was indifferent to showing that I cared. As much as I might have wanted to have been regarded as a great manager of people, I probably never was.

As I admit this to you in the pages of this book, can you read these pages with the same self-awareness? If you can, your leadership journey will be long and productive. And if you can't, you really don't need to read the remaining pages because you are already perfect, and we should all be learning from you.

PART THREE

THE FIVE TALENTS THAT
REALLY MATTER

CHAPTER 5

Setting Direction

I BECAME MESMERIZED WITH MAPS AS A CHILD ON THE RARE OCCASIONS *when I would ride in a car (we never had one of our own). It was a thrilling adventure, tracing my finger along the lines and symbols of these colorful mosaics, decoding roads and landmarks and eagerly anticipating the next turn. Throughout my adult life, I've collected maps for nearly everywhere I've been fortunate to visit, sometimes for road directions but mainly for mountain running and climbing locations to help me find my way around. I became extremely proficient in navigating with a map and compass, and the mistakes I made were usually when I failed to account for magnetic variation in the compass needle, especially in wild, foggy weather when I was under stress to get back on course in a high-mountain race. Mapping a journey and reading the directions made the trip extremely efficient, but make a mistake and it often took miles to realize*

and correct. GPS technology has taken the skill of navigation away from us, but it has evolved to such an extent that it helps actively manage the journey versus simply arriving at a destination. The GPS in my car suggests restaurants and cafés according to the time of day and highlights nearby gas stations when fuel levels fall below a certain threshold. It checks for congestion along the roads ahead and provides alternative routes when time and distance advantages are calculated. The system becomes smarter each day as historical data from other users enables it to more accurately predict traffic patterns and driver behavior. And each morning, as I load my Irish wolfhounds into the car, GPS has already teed up directions to our favorite coffee shop, although I'm not sure why.

It should be clear from this analogy that leadership is about much more than defining a destination. The magic is in managing the journey and keeping everyone onboard. The best leaders look ahead and anticipate in much the same way that GPS does. They collect data to anticipate traffic delays and adjust action in real time. They try to avoid costly backtracking to important places of interest. They sometimes switch to a slower back road because speed is relative and a road closure along their planned route would leave passengers feeling frustrated by the lack of progress. Thus, the best leadership navigators continuously manage engine load and passenger engagement. They keep people, and the vehicle, appropriately fueled.

There are two critical issues for leaders when mapping their journey:

First, the destination must be a place worth going to—a place that excites passengers and fellow travelers. There will certainly be a sense of accomplishment in completing the journey, particularly if it went well, but the destination itself must feel as though it was worth the effort.

Second, the route choice needs to be interesting—the journey needs to be fulfilling, with engaging layovers and visits to interesting and important landmarks. We tolerate driving by sprawling oil refineries and ugly industrial areas because of the upcoming river gorge, mountain pass, or fields of flowers. Maybe we share the driver's seat to keep people involved.

Paying attention to where and how is a critical function of leadership. How great leaders find answers to these questions is illustrated ahead. They achieve this mainly through how they define meaning and purpose and through communicating what matters—answering the questions *where* and *why*. Balancing thought and action ensures that the answers to these questions remain relevant. By becoming better thinkers and avoiding the cognitive traps that ensnare too many leaders, high-performing leaders ensure that strategy and execution are aligned. Establishing clear goals and targets and making essential trade-offs ensure that decision-making is effective.

Setting Direction involves

  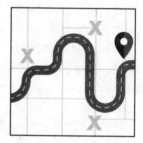

| Communicating What Matters | Balancing Thought and Action | Setting Targets and Making Trade-offs |

DEFINING MEANING AND PURPOSE

Research Definition: High-performing leaders see the future with vivid clarity and articulate a compelling picture of how value is created and how each individual role and leader contributes to the effectiveness of the organization.

Establishing a sense of direction, even a specific destination, has the potential to align people with a leader and develop a shared commitment that is equally important to everyone. It is the articulation of a vision that has the potential to differentiate one leader and one organization from the next. With so many companies competing in overlapping markets, with similar products and services, this direction and specific destiny might be the only things that make you distinct.

Strong direction at the leadership level of an organization builds cohesion toward a future state. This attracts people who don't work in organizations just because of compensation or to fulfill some technical or experiential need. They do it because they believe in what the organization stands for and is trying to achieve. Their work has real meaning. It is the role of leaders to encourage and develop this.

Putting a Man on the Moon

When President Kennedy visited NASA at Cape Canaveral in 1962, he noticed a worker clearing leaves with a broom. Never one to miss an opportunity, he went to the employee and introduced himself with a question: "Hey, I'm Jack Kennedy. What are you doing?" Anyone who works in aviation will tell you that the presence of debris in the vicinity of accelerating aircraft can be destructive. The backdraft from engine thrust can suck the debris into the engines and cause catastrophic failure. This was the most obvious and logical answer to the president's question, but the employee looked back at Kennedy and said, "I'm part of the team that's going to put a man on the moon."

When Gallup completed their research into employee engagement, they captured what came easily to JFK: "Does the mission and purpose of your company make you feel your job is important?" In asking the question, Gallup realized that it wasn't knowledge of the organization's mission and purpose that is important (although that's a good starting point), it's that employees can express this knowledge through the value they create in their own job.[1] Sure, the employee at NASA is sweeping up leaves, but his value is much greater. He sees his job as critical to the mission of NASA, and he just happens to contribute through sweeping up leaves.

What had to happen for this employee to respond this way? It required leaders, starting at the top, articulating the organization's values and mission in a way that helped each person realize why their job had real meaning and value. It's a difficult challenge. Too often leaders focus on overly tactical communication—the what, how, and when. They lead and manage through tasks, projects, and activities. They value people who are busy in the belief that this makes them productive.

Fundamentally, they get the psychology of human motivation wrong. This focus on projects and tasks leaves the bigger questions unanswered: Why am I here rather than somewhere else? Is my contribution noticed and valued? Am I making a difference? Is our work meaningful to others? Exceptional leaders ensure that these questions are answered in a way that drives higher levels of engagement and commitment. People want to follow leaders like this.

Questions about meaning at work are not new. When writing about workplace alienation in his critique of capitalism, Karl Marx defined three contributing ingredients—the lack of a voice or influence, poor person-job fit, and perceived lack of meaningfulness at work.[2] This doesn't differ much from research analysis of the benefits of employee engagement (the flip side of alienation). Many of the most common measures of employee engagement reference the need for employees to derive meaning from their work by providing real value to themselves, their company, or the broader society.[3] It seems that business leaders advocating the benefits of employee engagement are really closet Marxists. Who would have thought?

Communicating What Matters

We want to highlight five important principles derived from our research on meaning and purpose from a leadership perspective. These principles establish a framework for communicating with employees that motivates and excites them and aligns their work contributions with a greater good—something larger than themselves that they believe has significance, importance, and meaning to them. Top-performing leaders follow and advocate these five principles:

1. Being totally dedicated to work or activities in the service of others predicts a leader who can articulate a clear value proposition for what they do at work. Central to this principle is the belief that doing things for the benefit of others makes people feel that their lives are more enriched and have more value.[4] At a time when so much has been written about the demands of newer entrants into the workforce for work with purpose and greater meaning, this leadership principle is gaining in importance.

2. Having clear, consistent, and unchanging values about ethics, integrity, and the right way to treat people makes meaning evident through

everyday interactions. This principle has seemed timeless since the early beginnings of modern management practice. It continues to differentiate companies today.

3. Be conscious of the reasons others come to you for advice and guidance—do they just bring work issues, or do they pour their hearts out? As you think about what the right answer is to this question, be careful not to define your role and position with a firm underline that separates you relationally from those you lead. We've lost count, in our research, of leaders who erase artificial dividing lines and instead get as close to their employees as they can in support of them.

4. Engage others in effective and compelling storytelling that paints pictures in their minds. Leaders often forget that "vision" is less about goals and objectives than about what you can see and feel. In fact, when you reach the final days of your leadership career, one thing will become much clearer than it might seem now—of all the things you will achieve with others, you will be remembered less for the aggressive goals you set and for the businesses you led than for the advice you gave and the sponsorship you provided. Above all, you will be remembered for how positive and good you made people feel.

5. Work hard to ensure that, following every meeting and every interaction, people leave your presence feeling more positive, more engaged, more motivated, and more committed than when they came.[5] Exactly what is the focus of your influence when you discuss issues with team members or other leaders? Do people leave your presence with a spring in their step or carrying the burden of the world on their shoulders? There's only one good answer to this question.

You might believe that leaders have enough to do or that people are paid to work and we shouldn't need to apply extra effort to helping them find meaning. You'd be wrong, and if you can't articulate purpose and value from the work that employees do, they will eventually leave and go to a workplace where they do get this.[6] High-performing leaders understand this all too well because it explains how they remained committed and energized throughout their own careers.

Five Principles for Inspiring Meaning and Purpose
1. Total dedication to work that benefits others
2. Unwavering beliefs about ethics and integrity
3. Investment in close proximal relationships
4. Helping others see and feel what is possible
5. Making every interaction count

BALANCING THOUGHT AND ACTION

Research Definition: Reining in the common tendency to drive quickly ahead to action and implementation, with all the inefficiencies and frustrations that predictably occur, highly talented leaders think contingently and configuratively about the opportunity or problem that confronts them. They weigh the risks and look for hidden opportunities before making up their mind.

The most effective leaders operate much like the smartest GPS devices when mapping their journey, balancing speed with efficacy given the available information and options. Of course, there are leaders who, knowing their destination, feel confident in relying on wit and intuition and either don't think they need GPS or spend the entire journey arguing with it and contradicting its recommendations. These tend to be the same overconfident individuals who feel that they can dispense with instructions when assembling flat-pack furniture—and we all know what that looks like, if not immediately, then in a few months when everything starts to fall apart.

"What Kind of Meeting Do You Enjoy the Most: One Where You Discuss Ideas, Possibilities, and Plans or One Where You Get Things Done?"

We often ask this question of leaders, and very few express a preference for discussing ideas...the allure of action is all-encompassing. Humans tend to enjoy a sense of accomplishment in seeing things being done and progress being made. The perceived pain of deliberation and overanalysis is relatively rare. The bigger problem comes from making rapid assessments and lazy assumptions and then finding that the ideal path is anything but.

Balancing, and effectively managing, depth of thinking with speed of action is the capability that best typifies those destined to be enterprise-level leaders from those who will remain lifelong senior managers. When Marshall Goldsmith and Mark Reiter wrote their book *What Got You Here Won't Get You There*, they were making a similar observation.[7] There comes a point as you climb the leadership hierarchy when all the characteristics of hard work and perseverance that got you there count much less at the next level. At the most senior levels, the quality of your thinking matters more than how busy and active you are in the moment.

Too Much Faulty Thinking

The idea of rational thought, once the dominant belief in human reasoning, is quite amusing. Humans aren't rational at all, and this has been known since the seventeenth century, when the Italian philosopher Baruch Spinoza became the first to suggest the primacy of emotions controlling the human brain.[8] Not only is the brain emotionally driven, but it is also the laziest organ in our body. This isn't a great combination if your preference is for rational reasoning. Thinking is hard, which is why many individuals default to more instinctive reasoning.

Much of this is a by-product of our evolutionary past, when it was far more important for our thinking to contribute to our survival than to be "right" in any pure sense of the term.[9] Hearing footsteps behind us while walking down a poorly lit street on a dark night in Baltimore isn't something about which we should overdeliberate...probably best to just get out of that situation as quickly as possible. In doing so, we survive, we live to procreate, and the genes associated with that behavior stand a greater chance of becoming "fixed" in the population.

Another cognitive shortcut to deeper thinking and analysis comes through pattern recognition, which humans are remarkably good at.[10] For example, we are far better at recognizing familiar faces in crowds, or where images are blurred or incomplete, than at recognizing unfamiliar faces.[11] We put labels on nearly everything, providing us with a visual and experiential shorthand that helps us navigate complex situations reasonably well.

One of the more damaging findings for business leaders is that people are less likely to think through a situation if it looks familiar and they have encountered something similar before.[12] We categorize problems as being of a certain type, and where we have prior experience, we already have an imprinted memory of what actions we might take to address them. But problems of a particular type rarely exhibit the same characteristics, meaning preferred "solutions" are often wide of the mark, and our lazy brains don't see this. One of the most often stated frustrations within companies is with unanticipated consequences—things that should have been thought about in advance but weren't—leading to imperfect execution, backtracking, and inefficiencies.[13]

The cognitive resources that could address these failings are hard to muster, and our intuitive judgment about what's possible and feasible just isn't that reliable.[14] Our brains are trivially easy to fool and extremely resistant to becoming fully engaged. This creates situations in which business leaders are more likely to implement ideas that easily come to mind.[15] Mark Twain famously wrote, "It is easier to fool people than to convince them that they've been fooled." Scientist Richard P. Feynman stated, "The first principle is that you must not fool yourself—and you are the easiest person to fool." Nassim Nicholas Taleb, in his book *The Black Swan: The Impact of the Highly Improbable*, stated that we humans constantly fool ourselves by constructing flimsy accounts of the past and believing they are true.[16]

Over the past forty years, a whole slew of cognitive impairments and biases that afflict human reasoning have been identified.[17] It seems that even when we think hard, we aren't very good at it. Indeed, the brain isn't very flexible, and if we concentrate hard on a particular task, we are less likely to see something specific and potentially important. The brain finds it hard to switch between cognitively demanding tasks, in much the same way that a person concentrating hard on their work can sometimes be difficult to distract. This becomes worse if the task is physically demanding, as problems in our reasoning occur when different parts of our brain compete for resources.[18]

When we do reach a particular judgment, we are more likely to believe arguments that support it, even when those arguments are demonstrably unsound.[19] One of the more bizarre research findings has been termed the "anchoring effect"—where sometimes erroneous data shows a statistically significant relationship to the choices people make.[20] People are prone to establish logical coherence between unrelated events/issues. If we are in a good mood, we are less likely to engage in deep thinking and more likely to make decisions based on cognitive ease. Conversely, when under stress, we tend to be more vigilant and are better able to identify errors, but then concentrating on those issues leads us to miss other important factors.

We have even seen compelling research that suggests that repetition of false statements is all it takes for many people to believe them.[21] As we write this book, the demonstrably false statements of former president Trump about a "stolen election" in 2020 are supported and believed by 71 percent of Republicans despite many Republican state officials and Trump's attorney general stating that there was no evidence of this.

This delusion might also be the product of another credible finding—that things that are often repeated are viewed more positively.[22] A CEO colleague I knew for many years would repeat praise of his executive team to the point that he became convinced that they were the best team he had ever worked with, even though most people (including the team members themselves) viewed them as dysfunctional individuals who lacked trust in each other.

Another condition that makes us more likely to believe blatant lies and untruths is when we are distracted by other cognitively demanding work.[23] Psychologist Solomon Asch discovered the "primacy effect," which showed how much the first word or image in a series predicted how a person would think or feel.[24] He produced a series of descriptive words to describe an arbitrary person: "intelligent; industrious; impulsive; critical; stubborn; envious." He then produced these descriptive words to describe another arbitrary person: "envious; stubborn; critical; impulsive; industrious; intelligent."

He found that people perceived the first person as "an able person who possesses certain shortcomings which, do not, however, overshadow his merits." People perceived the second person as "a problem, whose abilities are hampered by his serious difficulties."[25] Asch also demonstrated how susceptible individuals are to group opinions when they are in the minority—something most leaders would deny, although it happens frequently.[26]

With respect to hiring people, if a person creates a good first impression, we are more likely to like them, and even though we know very little about them, we are much more likely to attribute many positive qualities that we haven't observed to them.[27] For employees who are our colleagues, we are much more likely to think they will be good at a wide range of tasks if we have seen them perform well in one. There is also the problem of dealing with people who claim to know things that they don't, which is called the Dunning-Kruger effect.[28] It seems that people would rather pretend to be smart than lose face in front of others, so they lie or misrepresent their capabilities. This is similar to the tendency of some people to believe that bias is something that afflicts others but not themselves.[29]

The human brain is irrational and lazy

Six Cognitive Traps to Avoid
1. **Caution:** Watch for overreliance on past problem-solving and pattern recognition.
2. **Intuition:** This may shape perceptions of what's possible and feasible.
3. **Overconcentration:** This can lead to overlooking critical details and errors.
4. **Alert:** Good moods may decrease vigilance.
5. **Repetition:** There may be increased susceptibility to believing repeated untruths.
6. **Beware:** There may be a false sense of immunity to biases.

The lazy brain is a very real problem.[30] Many of these examples have been taken from the late Daniel Kahneman's book *Thinking, Fast and Slow*, and his research findings have been replicated by many other psychologists studying heuristics and decision-making.[31] Considering the totality of Kahneman's work, the percentage of people showing susceptibility to these biases is within the 75–88 percent range, which is a remarkable number. This means many leaders and teams will be equally limited by these cognitive biases, and based on the work that we do, we can certainly confirm that. However, the statistics suggest that 12–25 percent have some natural resistance to these biases, and this group is particularly interesting to leadership researchers like us.

As gullible and influenceable as the overwhelming majority seem to be, what are the characteristics of the resistant few? What are they doing that potentially insulates them from some of these effects? Unfortunately, we don't know whether this group is a consistent population of individuals uniquely protected from all bias—it might be the case that everyone is susceptible to some, but not all, biases. Nevertheless, what some individuals do to shield them from the worst effects of biases is eye-catching, and we offer some perspectives below that other leaders might emulate. As mentioned before, thinking is hard.

So what to do?

Becoming Better Thinkers

Let's explore three different elements that can productively contribute to a more effective thought process—breadth of perspective, configurative and contingent thinking, and upside or opportunity analysis.

Breadth of Perspective

How much of their world does a leader consider? How broad is their perspective?[32] We see this as similar to a photographer selecting a lens prior to taking a photograph. A telephoto lens is excellent for capturing detail at long range, but it effectively eliminates everything outside its focal range. It is selective and exclusionary. A macro lens takes a reverse step and illuminates in considerable detail, where the naked eye lacks the capacity to process all the information available, a close object like the tiny follicles on the underside of a green leaf so critical to photosynthesis—but the green leaf is the only thing in view. A wide-angle lens is the preferred choice for landscapes and broad vistas where specific details are less important than the overall picture. It is less selective and more inclusionary but lacks detail. For breadth of perspective, leaders must first select the wide-angle lens—they need to capture the whole picture to its fullest extent.

In business, we use the term "big-picture thinking" to describe this attribute. We need to keep the big picture in view to prevent our close focus from driving decisions without evaluating their consequences elsewhere. This isn't easy. In many organizations, the value of thinking is that it guides us toward what to do. Many people quickly leave the big picture behind and become consumed with activities and implementation. Quickly latching on to the practicalities that drive action rapidly draws them away from the big picture and to ground level.

At some point, the photographer's lens analogy falls apart because the "big picture" isn't sufficiently well-defined or clearly visible at all. It might not even be big enough. We might see only 60 percent of it and hope the brain can fill in the gaps. And the brain does fill in the gaps; it just isn't concerned with getting the overall image right.[33] Leaders need to stretch themselves to look even more broadly or consider more information—in some cases information they don't even know exists. This requires them to actively shift their thinking from what they see and what they know to what they don't know and can't see.

Leaders can benefit from constantly reminding themselves about the importance of breadth of thinking and perspective. To help leaders in this challenge, we typically ask them to describe what they read and where they go for new information—information that might enlarge their big picture. Most leaders don't read enough, and they tend to get what information they do read from a pitifully narrow range of sources, typically dominated by their role or industry focus.[34] Leaders would benefit from being exposed to ideas and ways of thinking that might legitimately make their brains hurt. Reading like this not only helps to fill out the big picture but also has the potential to change its composition. Our professional recommendation is that every leader read at least one reputable science journal, like *Nature* (*National Geographic* doesn't count).

Configurative and Contingent Thinking

If there were as many strategists in organizations as individuals who claim to be, why have so few companies figured out how to break away from their competitors and drive a huge growth-based wedge between them? Most companies are systemically challenged strategically.[35] It's a problem that can't be wished away. So what is strategy, and how does it relate to configurative and contingent thinking?[36]

The first mistake people make is to assume that strategy is a thing. You frequently hear questions that embolden this view—"What is your strategy?" Far more than a thing, strategy is a process, a way of thinking, and it's extremely rare. To simplify, it's helpful to see strategic thought on a continuum.

At one end is creative thought and opportunity analysis. This is configurative strategy. Here, we typically see individuals who can reassemble a myriad of parts into something much better. Without changing the components too much, they develop and add functionality and capabilities or simplify and reduce operational complexity. They seek to amend, improve, and create. Sometimes these improvements are incremental, but more often they are significant. The other end of the strategy continuum is occupied by contingent thinking.[37] The important part of contingent strategy is the ability to look ahead and plan for the changes that others can only react to. Doing so provides the advantage of time and the ability to prepare. When you hear people talk about

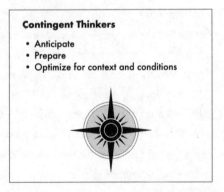

Configurative Thinkers

- Innovate
- Harmonize
- Optimize for efficiency and effectiveness

Contingent Thinkers

- Anticipate
- Prepare
- Optimize for context and conditions

The best strategists are never short of ideas. Strategy refers to a process and a way of thinking rather than a thing or a plan.

"looking around corners," they are really talking about the ability to think contingently.

We've never met a serious strategist whose first thought when developing ideas was to narrow their options. But far more than developing alternative scenarios, contingent strategists

- create backup plans that can be swung into motion when circumstances change—this requires identifying potential roadblocks in advance;
- tend to be excellent at mitigating risk, as they try to imagine what might go wrong and plan for the worst; and
- are excellent with numerical dashboards that help them look to the future and plan for the changes they see coming.

The value in this way of thinking should be obvious, but there is one variable that often prevents a good strategist from contributing effectively—time. A contingent strategist isn't always quick to evaluate the situations that confront them, and their methodical, analytical approach often increases the time it takes to get to a plan or response. From our experience, it's unclear whether the urgency that so many organizations imply and expect is justified. Given the choice between an immediate response that might be a toss-up in terms of likelihood of success, most organizations would gamble and fail to see the benefit in sacrificing two extra days to reach a 70–80 percent probability. Urgency rules. When leaders are asked whether they would like to be "slow and right" or "fast and wrong," they reply, "I like to be fast and right." Good luck with that.

Upside and Opportunity Analysis
There is a third aspect of strategic thinking that is even rarer than what we've just described. It seems that as desirable as growth is, too few individuals possess the ability to understand how to create and build the platform necessary for growth to occur. Put more succinctly, they are fearful of failure to the extent that they don't think the risk is worth it.

We should state at this point that the description of upside and opportunity analysis we provide here is sometimes mistaken as being similar to the work of Carol Dweck in her book *Mindset: The New Psychology of Success* and related research.[38] We have not found compelling evidence to support this work, and other recent research has reached similar conclusions.[39] We highlight this for anyone who might assert that a growth mindset is a choice leaders can make, that it is teachable—it's not. Dweck misleads her readers.

In our definition, an upside or opportunity analysis is a way of thinking that is best defined as the productive balance between risk acceptance and opportunity value, and it occurs naturally; it isn't a choice. When Kahneman and Tversky found that humans were defective at calculating probability, it was their work on risk aversion that opened the door.[40] Using gambling games and simulations, they established that people would place extremely risky bets from losing positions (where they stood to lose even more) and extremely conservative bets from positive or advantageous positions (where they stood to gain the most). It made no mathematical sense.

They went on to describe a business case study in which people were asked to choose between two options regarding an intention for a company to open an office in another country. The cost of the investment in both options was $60 million:

- **Option A** guarantees you will make $20 million—one-third of your first-year investment.
- **Option B** yields a 30 percent chance to make $60 million—which would be a break-even on the full year-one investment.

Which would you choose? An overwhelmingly large number of people are so risk averse that they would rather be certain of $20 million than face a two-thirds risk of losing everything. It is this risk aversion—generalized across our leadership research database—that contributes to the rarity of upside and opportunity thinking. This isn't to imply that upside and opportunity thinking is simply an acceptance of risk that others deem unacceptable. Rather, risk is part of a calculated judgment that builds from the breadth of perspective highlighted previously. Identifying and illuminating as many variables as you can that could impact the situation you are seeking to exploit enables you to balance the risk inherent in moving forward with whichever option is favored.

Narrower, more tactical thinkers focus too much on the specifics and practicalities of the situation. For all the ideas in front of them, they see all the reasons why not, and their preference drifts toward ease of implementation based on their intuition. They find it harder to see the big picture, which makes it harder for them to balance or mitigate risk. This description captures the overwhelming number of leaders, and it's the reason so many companies struggle with growth.

Upside and opportunity thinking that leads to growth isn't just about entrepreneurial opportunism and good commercial judgment. Leaders exhibiting these characteristics also have a very good sense and awareness of the conditions that need to exist for growth to be realized.[41] Critical among these is consideration of important Talent characteristics—the innate and enduring dispositions and traits that enable a person to be world-class in their role.[42] It is worth pointing out two measurable elements we see in growth-oriented leaders:

> *First*, they are acutely aware of their own strengths and limitations, and they are obsessed with finding individuals to partner with who best complement their own capabilities.

> *Second*, they appoint some people to their team who are stronger in both technical and leadership capabilities than they are. They aren't threatened by Talented individuals; they thrive in the presence of these team members.

Upside and opportunity–oriented leaders spend significant time and energy on selection, recruitment, and development. They understand all too well that Talented team members find ways to achieve outcomes despite challenges and limitations that might be too much for others. For all those who believe that hard work and determination are what is needed to succeed, these leaders know the answer is much more nuanced and lies in people's innate, natural Talents and capabilities.

Correcting Faulty Intuition

We've just described three attributes that broaden our perspective and expand our thinking about what is possible to achieve, attributes that improve a leader's sense of direction. The challenge is in managing our action orientation to question our assumptions and generate more ideas about where we could go and what we could do. Assuming or believing you are right is an insufficient reason to commit to a course of action.

The term "superficial plausibility" describes the state we reach where our confidence exceeds our perceptions of risk and we believe, confidently, that we are right. It has been well established in research that if we are able to build a compelling narrative about a situation we encounter, we will be more likely to think the story is true, and we will repeat it as though it is.[43] But in too many cases, the decisions we make based on that confidence come back to bite us hard when obstacles and errors abound. It turns out we didn't think things through, we didn't challenge our assumptions, we didn't put our ideas under sufficient stress, and we ended up being wrong, or only partly right. Our thinking seemed plausible but was superficial.

There are effective ways to insulate ourselves from the dangers of superficial plausibility, but none of them is easy, and for some leaders, they could well be impossible. Here are some ways for leaders to build confidence that is justified:

- Be open to the idea that you are wrong and share this assumption with others as a way of encouraging them to challenge you.[44] Make it clear to your team and those who work with you that they can contribute no more important value than coming up with data, evidence, or argument that disproves your thinking.
- One of the less surprising research findings in feasibility studies is that almost none return a null verdict and recommendation not to proceed.[45] There's a simple explanation—smart people can come up with justifications for almost anything.[46] Clearly define the evidence that would prove you are wrong and go look for that evidence with zeal.[47]

- Encourage disagreement, argument, and outright dissent.[48] Disagreement is an important first step because it encourages people to lay out their reasoning against one proposition or in favor of another. Dissent states, "I'm not going to do this." "I'm not going to comply." "This does not have my support." Without dissent, we end up with compromise and compliance covering the cracks with a paper-thin facade.

- Quite often we find that the best idea isn't the first one, a fact clearly established by neuroscientist David Eagleman.[49] Instead of asking, "What should we do?" you can drive more plural thinking by asking, "What *could* we do?" Try this approach and you will see two effects. Each member will produce more ideas and possibilities and will be less wedded to a single preferred approach.

- Never default to the ideas and recommendations of credible professionals, but always consult them and highly weight their ideas and perspectives, particularly if they contradict your own.[50] Be equally careful about seeking advice from people who claim to be experts but aren't. It wouldn't be a great idea, for example, to address questions about quantum physics to Deepak Chopra.[51]

- Do a better job of pressure testing and challenging the assumptions, ideas, and suggestions that do emerge.[52] When a team member comes to you with a suggestion and their rationale, ask, "What two ideas did you seriously consider and reject before you brought me this one?" It's a powerful question because most people don't think this way...yet they should.

- Prior to decisions being made, ask, "Have we done an effective job of identifying potential hazards and obstacles we could meet in the future, and what are our contingencies for dealing with them?" Contingency planning is hard, and too many leaders aren't prepared to expend the cognitive effort that would make these risks and challenges easier to manage. Relying on your wit and intuition when problems become more immediately visible partially works in lower-level positions, but it is not acceptable for executive-level leadership.

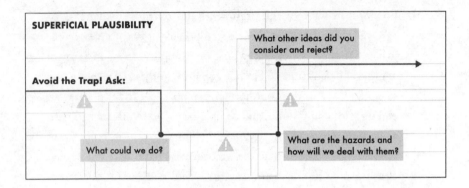

TARGETS AND TRADE-OFFS

Research Definition: Leaders who establish clear and consistent team processes for making decisions prevent unnecessary confusion and overload and increase alignment and accountability regarding where time is best spent.

The lack of a destination, a goal, or even a clear sense of direction is debilitating. It causes confusion. *It reminds me of a school friend who once went to our local bus station and asked for a "round-trip" ticket. "Where would you like to go?" asked the ticket agent. "Back here, please."*

Let's explore two different elements that can help eliminate confusion and task overload—a clear and consistent process for making decisions and prioritizing the tasks and activities that get you closer to your destination.

Decision-Making

Our research on decision-making highlights one key finding—leaders talk to too few people. It isn't the "decision" in decision-making that leaders get wrong (although they often do); it's the poor consultative process that precedes it. Too many leaders focus on decision-making as a technical issue—getting the decision right. For this reason, they tend to talk to people they believe can best help them in that task—people with domain expertise and a track record of successfully navigating similar challenges in the past. We make no argument against this; in fact, we encourage it. Our point is that it is insufficient; too few ideas will emerge and too few people will be involved.

Leaders should be encouraged to think of decision-making in three distinct phases: (1) the need for the decision, (2) the discussion and debate about options, and (3) the specific decision itself.

Let's take each of these in turn.

Addressing a Need or Opportunity

There is a pretext and broader context for every decision. Typically, an issue is identified from data dashboards or some other information source, and the need for a decision is realized. At this stage, the leader needs to identify a decision owner. The decision owner will be charged with several small but important tasks at the outset and will play a critical role in bringing the overall process to a conclusion:

- Write a "problem statement" that clearly defines the issue to be resolved.
- Collect relevant information and data that are readily available so that the context for the decision is understood.
- Identify key stakeholders who can assist in the identification of, and the discussion and debate about, options and possibilities. This net needs to be wider than leaders initially think.
- Set a date and time by which the decision will be made.
- Share this outline with a broader set of peers who need visibility of the decision but may not play a part in the process.

Discussion and Debate

Effective consultation opens the door to discussion and debate, which need to be far-reaching and rigorous. The decision owner needs to create a climate in which argument and disagreement are encouraged and expected. This isn't always easy, but it is essential. Assertiveness is not a learned trait, and this should influence the selection of participants whose job it is to develop options and possibilities and then subject them to testing and stress in search of the very best outcome.

There are two important constituent groups to include in your consultative plan—those responsible for implementing the decision and those who will be affected by it. These two groups extend far beyond the inner circle that surrounds a leader, and their involvement could well make the difference between an idea that will work and one that won't. Not everyone needs to be consulted, but certainly a representative sample does.

Consult with executionally minded employees who will be implementing the decision to

- consider whether the idea or approach is capable of being integrated into other systems and processes related to the issue,
- identify challenges and barriers that could otherwise detract from the overall plan, and
- provide insight into how to make the process better and more efficient.

Consult with the often overlooked majority who will be affected by the decision to

- influence their level of engagement and perceptions of value,
- give them a stake in the idea and get everyone on board,
- help people prepare for changes to come and give them a head start on implementation, and
- make them feel that they, and their job, are important.

When people are legitimately and seriously involved in examining an issue and are enabled to offer their opinions, they are more likely to support the outcome, even if they don't fully agree with the final decision. We don't want to be too distracted by discussions of consultative methodology; the important thing is to make consultation feel real and genuine to employees. A commitment to consultation of this nature is a difficult but virtuous path, and it is this perceived difficulty that causes too many leaders to avoid it in the first place. Their error will kick them hard in the future.

Making the Decision

Having already given yourself a deadline, the final step is to make and communicate the decision. Although each organization will approach these steps differently, we recommend that a report or presentation be compiled to summarize the following:

- The issue that required a decision
- Which stakeholders participated in various stages of the process
- The set of options and solutions that were considered
- The resulting solution to address the issue or opportunity
- The next steps to keep the issue moving forward

This information should then be communicated to the relevant team from which the need for a decision emerged. As simple as this sounds, this is the final point at which issues can be addressed that could help or hinder the proposed course of action. It is the decision owner's responsibility to communicate this information to those who would benefit from it.

There's nothing complicated about this process, but too few leaders and companies operate with such clarity. There are three complaints that are avoided by following a clear and consistent decision-making process.

Managing Speed

So far, we have discussed the need for leaders to more clearly define and articulate value creation over activity, to better manage the balance between thought and action, to develop intentional ways of generating more ideas, and to adopt a simple process for making decisions that involves reaching out and consulting more people. We now want to describe the factors that should have the greatest influence on the choices leaders make. Earlier we made two important points:

First, that leaders have a tendency to move to action too quickly, nearly always driven by a misplaced sense of urgency.

Second, that the most effective strategists don't start their thinking by reducing their options; rather, they expand them.

The logical outcome of these points is that decision-making may slow—a little—and that more ideas and possibilities will be identified. We don't accept that a slower speed is the price that must be paid for more effective thinking and consulting designed to produce more (and better) options. The reason people express concerns about moving more slowly is that they are thinking of developing options in the moment, and in the moment, that will certainly slow any move toward a preferred action. But our argument doesn't play out in the moment; it succeeds over time.

Any team that waits to the point when a decision is critical to do their thinking is certainly going to resist what might be a slower route. The question is how to do this thinking much earlier in the process so that when the time comes for the decision, the hard, cognitively demanding work has already been done. For leaders to be better decision-makers, they must also be better at looking further ahead and anticipating the issues that might knock them offtrack or delay them.

This can more clearly be defined as part of the simple decision-making process we just outlined—we allow enough time to consult and engage and produce more varied options, but we don't allow this time to progress without limit. We specify "when" up front. It might be a few months, weeks, or days. In extreme circumstances, it might be a half day. But it isn't without limit.

Purveyors of the "speed is king" approach are often the architects of their own urgency-driven mistakes—they don't take time to look ahead, think, and anticipate; they are living in the moment, calling balls and strikes based on the variables in front of them. This creates an illusion of leadership, but it isn't exceptional leadership. In rejecting the idea that deeper and more effective thinking and development of options slows you down, we believe the reverse: it actually speeds you up. Over the entire span of a specific project, from conception to implementation, planning each stage in the way that we describe is more efficient and effective. It is ultimately quicker. More importantly, it leads to better outcomes.

Diversity of Thought

Regarding outcomes, there is a significant current focus on the desire for teams to be more diverse, the assumption being that more diverse teams create value drawn from team members' different backgrounds and experiences and that this value translates to a commercial advantage. Current business parlance refers to this as "neurodiversity." Fueling this debate are two obvious facts:

> *First*, women and minorities are underrepresented in most leadership teams.

> *Second*, most leadership teams don't reflect the demographic makeup of their organizations, the communities where they are located, or the customers they serve.

While a credible sociopolitical-economic argument can be made on these issues, that is not our focus. Our focus is on efficacy—what produces the best results? To find an answer to this question, we have to expand how people traditionally define or talk about diversity beyond standard demographic identifiers (whether chosen or ascribed).

As desirable as demographic diversity is for many reasons (and you'll get no argument against it from us), the data on the relationship between more demographically diverse teams and performance (at either the team or organizational level) is mixed and often contradictory. Despite the claims of McKinsey & Co., their observation that the most (demographically) diverse teams achieve stronger performance outcomes fails to address the issue of individual leader Talent and simply draws a straight-line connection between two correlated pieces of data—the demographic "mix" of a leadership team and the growth of that company in its market.[53] If only it were that simple—and it provides an excellent example of the logical fallacy that correlation does not mean causation.

Our research has consistently found a complicating factor that leads us to question and then reject McKinsey's assertion. Women and minorities appointed to executive leadership teams tend to be stronger in measurable leadership attributes than their male and white peers, even as they significantly replicate them. This happens across industries and is consistent whether the company is small or large. It poses a huge problem for McKinsey (and other researchers), who failed to consider this possibility, but in McKinsey's defense, it isn't a "hardcore" research company and was not set up that way. More diverse teams might perform better than less diverse teams not because of having more women and minorities but because those women and minorities are much stronger and more Talented leaders than their white male counterparts.

The highest-performing teams we have studied are cognitively diverse—each member possesses a unique constellation of Talents that allows them to contribute their best thinking for the benefit of the team.

Diversity of Experience and Perspective

Several credible research papers have established that while demographic diversity addresses important social and political aspects of the work environment, diversity of thought has a stronger relationship to performance, especially at the team level.[54] This makes logical sense. While sex and race help define a person's identity, the experiences faced by women and minorities are not common. It is important to separate a perspective based on experience from the capacity to think differently (which is a consequence of cognitive variation).

Women don't think differently because of their sex; rather, their sex enables them to contribute a different and valuable perspective. To assume that these things are the same is a classic category error and will lead to the wrong conclusions. If you appoint more women to your team, you will get more diverse perspectives but not necessarily better performance.

The performance benefit is the consequence of assembling a team of disparate thinkers who could be men or women, or members of any minority racial group, for that matter. Our argument isn't against better representation of women and minorities in leadership teams—on the contrary. But the assumption that this will consequently lead to better performance outcomes is questionable despite McKinsey's claims. The ideal would be to appoint women and minorities with diverse Talents *and* perspectives. These traits can be measured and predicted, and we discuss broader issues of executive-level selection later in this book.

Cognitive Diversity

When we talk of diversity of thought—neurodiversity, if you will—what do we mean? We described this in outline earlier in the chapter when we described the three different elements that contribute to an effective thought process—breadth of perspective, configurative and contingent thinking, and upside or opportunity analysis. Being able to build a team comprising individuals who collectively exhibit these capabilities would make a significant contribution to the diversity of thought that can drive superior performance. But there is much more.

Here are just a few patterns of thinking that we have uncovered during our research, each of which contributes differently to the diversity of thought necessary in high-performing teams:

- Operational thinking—this describes the ability to think in a logical sequence of steps and to hold and manage significant amounts of data simultaneously.[55]
- Adaptive and agile thinking—this describes the ability to change course midstream and not become stuck on a particular idea or approach.[56]
- Convergent thinking—this describes the ability to see ideas in combination, contributing to a single outcome or approach.[57]

- Divergent and contrary thinking—this describes the search for different and broader perspectives that might contradict a preferred or chosen approach adopted by others.[58]
- Critical thinking—this describes careful evaluation and judgment that test the validity or reliability of evidence and proposals.[59]
- Creative thinking—this describes the ability to develop breakthrough ideas and new configurations that are beyond the vision of most people.[60]

This isn't a comprehensive list, and these types of thinking don't operate independently of one another, but they are distinctive and measurable. No one individual will exemplify all these types of thinking, yet their presence as a team deliberates over its options would be extremely helpful. The value created by the very best leaders comes from assembling teams that represent this kind of diverse thinking. We shouldn't need to explain that the presence of team members who are dominant in different aspects of thought processes ought to yield more varied ideas and approaches to address the challenges that the team faces.

The Intersection of Experience, Expertise, and Thought Process

When Francis Crick discovered DNA in 1953, he was a classical physicist dabbling in evolutionary biology, but more importantly, he thought differently than those who were grappling with one of the major problems in evolutionary biology—the standard theory predicted a replicable code that accounted for all genetic variation and predicted the form and function of every organism, from a piece of grass to a complex sea creature to modern humans. But no evolutionary biologist could make the breakthrough. They knew the code must exist, but they couldn't think outside their biological experience—they lacked the diversity of thought that comes from people who look at problems and issues in completely different ways.

Before finding the answer in the double helix in 1947, Crick worked out the general theory of X-ray diffraction by a helix, and it was only a matter of time before he realized that the alpha-keratin pattern was due to alpha helices being coiled around each other. It was this breakthrough in thinking that led to the discovery of the combined helix of DNA.[61] In retrospect, we see these developments as logical and predictable, but at the time, they were anything but. Crick could never even have conceived of this solution had not the standard theory predicted a specific genetic code and had it not been beyond the thinking of biologists of the day to conceive of a model used in physics with a clear application to their field.

In this example, it is the intersection of technical capability, experience, and thought process that produced the breakthrough, and this is the case for how teams can attempt to resolve their most intractable problems. Technical expertise matters, and so does experience, but they are less impactful than the capacity to deploy them in novel ways. This realization has led some team leaders to assign people based more on their dominant thought process than on their technical capabilities and experience. This is far-reaching and sophisticated leadership that is likely beyond the abilities of most leaders.

A Head of Strategy with No Strategy

One last illustration of this issue comes from my study of the head of strategy at one of the world's largest software/IT companies. This company was (and currently continues to be) the dominant player in its sector, larger in market cap and revenues than all of their competitors combined. If we considered strategy a "thing," they clearly had one, and it worked. But our focus is always on strategy as a process, as a way of thinking, and when I assessed the head of strategy and examined the results, I found very little evidence of strategic capability.

There appeared to be a disconnect. Here was a phenomenally successful company with a market-leading strategy (thing), yet the person leading that strategy had almost no measurable strategic capability (process). I certainly got his attention when I discussed his results. But the answer to this situation turned out to be quite straightforward and highlights the importance of hiring a team with diverse thought processes, where some team members might be stronger than the team leader.

The head of strategy turned out to be a masterful team builder with an eye for matching the Talents of a person to the projects they led and worked on and enabling them to contribute their capabilities to the team in a complementary way. He didn't need to be the "strategist in chief," as he had assembled people around him who were far better than he in this respect. His capabilities, and they were exceptional, were in drawing out the best in others and empowering them to develop ideas and plans, to challenge and stretch each other. His role was one of stimulation, coordination, and planning. He is one of the strongest leaders I have measured in this dimension, and his team loved to work for him.

Defining the Goal

To conclude this chapter, we must describe the most important task that lies at the end of every search for truth, every quest to find breakthrough ideas, every time we put teams of people together with the aim of coming up with a way forward.[62] It is to make the selection, the choice. To decide. Our starting point was arguing that leaders tend to do this too spontaneously based on a narrow, tactical focus driven by superficial plausibility and without acknowledging that our brains are lazy and that our initial ideas are rarely the best.

Our critique is of decisions being made too soon, not that they shouldn't be made at all. So how is decision-making best achieved? The simple answer is that leaders should choose the option most likely to take them toward their goals. Before you start to feel underwhelmed by this advice, it is important to think through its meaning very carefully. Many leaders struggle with this part of the decision-making process because they lack goals and objectives that are clear, sharp, and well-defined.

In describing goal orientation, leaders commonly express a preference for employees with a "take the hill" mentality. The origins of this phrase are military, and whether the hill was Little Round Top at Gettysburg or Hamburger Hill in Vietnam doesn't really matter. A hill is always of some strategic importance in battle and confers advantages on the force that controls the high ground. But what if there are many hills? The simple answer is to take all of them, which tends to be the prevalent response in business.

Rather than really thinking through the pros and cons of each hill, taking all of them means an army will naturally control the best hill. But at what cost in terms of time, resources, and personnel? This is where clear goal orientation counts, and a goal-oriented leader is known as one who makes the greatest progress with the least effort and most optimized cost. Such leaders operate with surgical precision and generate a great sense of achievement and progress. They recognize that the most important hill might not necessarily be the biggest and that the evaluation of options and possibilities contributes to selecting the right objective.

Focus implies the ability to discriminate, to make choices, to say, "Not this, but *that*." In the next chapter, we discuss the drive that compels many successful leaders to work hard and get things done. Rather than applying focus to their work, many adopt the "take the hill" mentality we have just described and see this as a badge of honor for the determination, perseverance, and work ethic it exemplifies.

The absence of focus in goal setting is evidenced by leaders who take on too much and can't let things go. We see it in project overload and employees feeling that nothing is ever decided or completed. The volume of critical tasks never seems to diminish, and leaders who lack focus contribute to this feeling of relentless overload by failing to make effective choices and trade-offs. Leaders must accept responsibility for creating this situation and then address it through careful choices and limiting the scope creep that gets in the way of quality work outcomes.

WHAT REALLY MATTERS

Effective direction setting is the product of distinct, related traits and characteristics that few individual leaders possess in full. Awareness of these traits and characteristics, along with the assembly of a team that can collectively accomplish each of them, is important in setting effective organizational and team direction:

- It begins with a recognition that leaders need to engage and motivate their teams with a compelling description of how value is created and how each individual role contributes to the effectiveness of the organization.
- It demands that leaders be more effective thinkers and rein in their more common tendency to drive quickly ahead to action and implementation with all the inefficiencies and frustrations that predictably occur.
- Having a clear and disciplined approach to decision-making prevents the confusion that has team members spinning in stress as

they battle project overload and their associated feelings of powerlessness. This requires clear objectives and goals and a leader's focus on defining both.

Setting the course is a critical function of leadership. You may be a leader who leads through the strength of your directional Talents if

- you tend to see the big picture and how complex issues are interrelated;
- you think about what is possible and can come up with new ideas;
- you enjoy learning about new ideas and approaches and see how these might add value in the future; and
- you enjoy identifying opportunities and solving problems.

No matter how good a thinker you believe yourself to be, a leader must hold their team to the highest standards for the quality of their thinking and how decisions are made. These questions can help when setting direction:

- Has the team identified at least two options for the problem we are dealing with?
- Are we implementing what we think is easiest and most obvious, or are we pushing ourselves to come up with the best and most impactful solution?

Once the goal is clearly visible, leaders need to push themselves and others to achieve and excel. The best leaders are both personally and organizationally driven, setting standards and challenging others to attain more. High expectations of outcomes are how leaders create performance and growth. It's important to understand that leaders are motivated by different things—and understanding these differences is key.

CHAPTER 6

Harnessing Energy

A DEMONSTRABLY HIGH WORK ETHIC HAS BEEN THE FOUNDATION OF MANY successful leadership careers. As Vince Lombardi once stated, "The price of success is hard work, dedication to the job at hand, and the determination that whether win or lose, we have applied the best of ourselves to the task in hand." It seems almost perverse to believe that hard work has little or low value because, throughout organizations, it is the primary means through which employee commitment and effectiveness is determined.

Contrasting a high work ethic with its counterpart—laziness—reveals its importance. We've never heard a compelling case for laziness in a work context, certainly not as a positive contributor to role effectiveness and career progression.

We have yet to meet an effective leader who is fundamentally lazy, so hard work is definitely the desired contribution. However, a person who is seen as under-reacting when situations arise isn't necessarily lazy. Just because we don't see or feel their determination to react quickly doesn't mean they lack commitment or can't make a contribution.

A lack of action or reaction may indicate a need for more analysis to understand what is required. A leader who disagrees with a proposed course of action may see that it is inadequate and poorly thought through and that accelerating toward implementation will have unintended consequences that will generate more problems in the future. If the urgency to act is partnered with a strong level of certainty and assertiveness from their colleagues, it's often easier to disengage and say nothing. It is therefore important, as we progress with a description of the importance of personal drive to an individual's success, that this drive be predicated on the effective thought and analysis that should precede it.

Every living thing, from prokaryotic cells (the simplest cells we have discovered) to the most complex creatures (such as mammals) requires a source of energy. Similarly, organizations and structures require a source of energy to build or maintain function. With respect to organizations, top-performing leaders know this all too well. They operate akin to the manager of a city's power plant, carefully calculating and predicting supply and demand, diligently balancing different sources of supply, operating efficiently to manage costs and optimize profit, looking ahead to predict variable demand, and reacting to demands for "cleaner" energy. They are sensitive to the most effective and efficient energy source. They need enough energy to power themselves and even more to power others. Not everyone is driven by the same amount and type of energy. The best leaders we have studied think and act flexibly, fully aware of the energy others need and how much they need themselves. They scan the dials and gauges that measure energy source, flow, and consumption, ever mindful of the need to never go into the *red* zone, with everyone's *red* zone set at slightly different levels.

As you consider this chapter, and the complex elements of top-performing leaders, keep the source-of-energy metaphor in mind. As a high-performing leader, you are really emulating the manager of a power plant.

Harnessing Energy involves

| Achieving and Competing | Aiming High and Taking Risks | Objective Measurement |

COMPETITORS AND ACHIEVERS

Research Definition: A strong self-starting nature that pushes a leader to do more and achieve more may be the consequence of an internal drive to achieve or an external focus on winning.

Individual leaders are driven and motivated by different things. They need and consume different types of energy. Understanding these differences provides insight into how a leader might productively engage in work that drives value and ultimate benefit to society. One of the biggest sources of confusion that impairs our ability to understand a person's drive is the assumption of competitiveness. Commitment not only is associated with determination, tenacity, and hard work but also is synonymous with a competitive instinct. This assumption is almost certainly wrong and can lead to mismanagement and disengagement.

To illustrate this more clearly, let's consider Olympic athletes who compete at the highest levels of their sport. These phenomenal specimens spend their athletic lifetime training to carve out a "competitive edge" in hopes of winning a medal. And yet, in postevent interviews, it's not uncommon for losing athletes to express a great deal of pride and satisfaction at having achieved a "personal best" in their performance. They reached a level not previously achieved in their own training and competitions and feel good about this despite having lost. A 1995 research paper explained the psychology of this phenomenon of some people

111

being happier when they don't win, even when they strive to. They termed it the "less is better" effect, and it perfectly describes the difference between a competitive drive and an achievement drive.[1]

To the true competitor, this represents a form of rationalization—a ready-made excuse for not winning. The defense in these situations is that the athlete never had a realistic prospect of winning—they are willing participants rather than competitors.

Satisfaction when measured against self is called an **achievement drive**.

Satisfaction when compared against others is called a **competitive drive**.

You would be well-advised to understand the difference. Many people are confused when evaluating themselves, and it takes some a long time to see the difference and understand how it applies to them.[2]

A Drive to Improve or a Drive to Win?

The behavioral manifestation of an achievement drive is almost identical to that of a competitive drive. Both individuals show incredible levels of determination and tenacity. They aspire to give their very best—to leave it all on the playing field. It's almost impossible to tell them apart except at the final reckoning. Take note of the athlete finishing fourth with a beaming smile because they did well against their own standards, contrasted with the athlete coming second weeping uncontrollable tears. The signs are visible, and they reveal dramatically different emotional states. This is why using the term "competitive" without understanding the underlying psychology can be wrong and inappropriate.

If your assumption of competitiveness is unchallenged, it can lead to potential mismanagement of an individual. This could apply to the way you set goals and objectives and how you determine discretionary, performance-based pay. An employee with an achievement drive wants to be held to the standard of their very best prior performance. A person with a competitive drive wants to do better than everyone else in their role. The difference is subtle but significant:[3]

- If you set a goal for an "achiever" that is based on beating everyone else yet doesn't build on their prior achievements, the goal could lack validity in their eyes.
- If you set a goal for a "competitor" that fails to establish them as first against their fellow employees, it might be considered a "soft" goal that is not worth pursuing.

And then there are those (fewer in number than you might think) who are both—driven by a strong sense of achievement and an unrestrained desire to come first. For these individuals, the competitive drive always takes precedence. For them, winning with a personal best is all that matters, and they need goal setting that clearly establishes these expectations. For such individuals, achieving a second-place finish is akin to being the first loser—not something to be celebrated. As a manager, you should be extremely careful before handing out rewards to employees with a competitive drive who fall short and come second. You might think you are motivating them, but deep inside, they find such actions condescending and patronizing. The best leaders know how difficult management really is.

How to Spot a Competitor
The competitive mindset is about a state of preparedness. Looking ahead to anticipate issues and events enables a competitor to optimize their response. This is why they tend to be very well prepared for meetings and think ahead to optimize their time and maximize their opportunities:

- Competitors, while waiting at a red traffic light, pay attention to cross-traffic stoplights in order to anticipate when theirs will turn green. Competition is therefore about a state of preparedness, maintaining a state of awareness that enables them to maximize all opportunities and to be efficient and effective in all things that they do.

- Competitors tend to walk just that little bit faster. As banal and puerile as this sounds, walking fast…and at least faster than others…is just one way competitors literally keep ahead. They tend to be early to meetings in order to maximize productive time. A competitor scratches their head at the sight of air travelers standing on a moving walkway in the airport. They see this as wasting time.

- Competitors reach their arm between closing elevator doors so they don't have to wait for the next. There are only so many minutes in a day, and competitors don't want to waste any of them.

- Competitors tend to count, and they use numbers as their standard of comparison. Competitors count the important business-tracking and performance numbers that matter, but they also play with numbers in their head all the time.

- Competitors who travel the same work commute by car each day hold a virtual stopwatch in their minds. They intuitively know how long it should take them to reach a specific intersection or landmark. Anything faster than the typical time feels good. Fall a little behind and it raises irritability by different degrees.

How to Spot an Achiever

If the competitive mindset is about a state of preparedness, with the individual ready to exploit any opportunity that presents itself, the achiever mindset is about a state of planning and sequencing. Achievers like to check off tasks and goals as part of a sequence of work activity.

- Achievers are serial list makers—checking items off their list builds satisfaction and further motivation. The list is everything, and as happy as achievers are at building their own lists, they don't hold back from building lists for others, whether they want them or not. Satisfaction comes from striking things off the list. It feels good.

- Companies make personal organization tools for achievers. Whether planners or calendars, achievers appreciate tools that make list-building easier and more ubiquitous. Franklin Covey built an entire business empire devising planning tools for achievers.

- Achievers are well equipped to plan the various stage gates in an implementation plan and drive themselves and colleagues to meet each of these requirements. With minds like a Microsoft Gantt chart, achievers forever mull over work sequences and how to build a plan that defines the critical path and coordinates complex activities that can be checked off en route to the outcome.

- If there are twelve steps in their implementation plan, then achievers will methodically and expeditiously work through each step in the sequence, checking off progress as they go. This kind of work can provide meaning for them.

Motivating Achievers and Competitors by Measurement

One differentiator between an achiever and a competitor is how measurement factors as a motivator. For an achiever, it is incremental and plays out on a scale. For competitors, it tends to be binary—win or lose. This fact highlights the most appropriate management tactic for getting the best out of each:

- **Create a scale (ladder, if you will) for achievers.** Use descriptive or numerical criteria and define a clear outcome. Achievers particularly value internal measures where they are able to compare their current achievement against what they did at a prior time.

- **Draw a clear winning line for competitors.** Competitors demand measurement, which implies numbers and scales. Competitors like to see how they are doing in comparison with their peers, but they are also driven by external measures if they are available, such as industry standards that they can beat or competitor companies whose published performance can provide a huge incentive.

Motivating Through Measurement

Achievers	Competitors
• Revenue Boost: 20% YoY revenue growth. • Efficiency Drive: 15% cost reduction, 25% efficiency increase.	• Market Dominance: Highest industry market share in 24 months. • Employee Engagement: Top-quartile engagement score in 12 months.

The performance management implications are clear, and we have often seen simple, progressive goals working for achievers but disincentivizing competitors.

"Who Sets the Higher Goal, You or Your Manager?"

Managers would do well to ask this question to understand who on their team is a real competitor and to manage them accordingly. It's rare to meet a strong competitor who doesn't look at the goal their manager sets without thinking they can do better. Their sense of accomplishment is influenced more by their achievement of the higher goal. Some of the best leaders we have ever studied see their goals as starting points—the minimum that should be delivered—and are driven by a moral and ethical obligation to meet and exceed that minimum.

It's worth reflecting on the fact that there are many more achievers than real competitors, but we tend to think the opposite because every time we see someone displaying drive and tenacity, we assume that they are competitive. Correcting this basic error is key to effective leadership and management.

Driving Blind at High Speed

I learned an important leadership lesson in 1988 when I was attending a development program at St. George's Hotel in Llandudno, North Wales. Thirty senior educational professionals gathered to be taught—and then to apply their learning—to understand how to construct educational timetables that enabled the best learning for school students. Complex scheduling has always fascinated me, and I was excited about this program. I was the youngest participant by some margin, and it was clear to me that I was in the presence of much more experienced professionals. It didn't unduly concern me.

To give you an idea of the task, think about the last airline flight you took and all the planning that had to go into achieving it successfully. The coordination of all the elements—aircraft, crew, fuel, passenger refreshments, gate crew, baggage crew, and so on. Then extend your thinking to an entire airline company and the complexity of scheduling everything that must happen to ensure that your aircraft is where it should be before it departs and where it goes next after you disembark. This schedule must be built months in advance and be sufficiently flexible to be varied due to bad weather or aircraft maintenance and breakdowns. It's the kind of complex mental work that I love, and this was the work facing me in Llandudno.

Instead of aircraft, we had classrooms of various sizes that could accommodate some groups but not others. Some of these rooms contained specialist equipment and resources that could be scheduled for only one purpose, such as science labs. We had teachers with different levels of expertise, some of whom taught in only one classroom while others were itinerant, a bit like having flight crew who are qualified to fly some aircraft but not others. Those teachers needed some "free time" scheduled across the week, and so on.

It was a five-day course, and on day four, we were given a fictitious institution and told all the constraints we would have to manage. Our test was to build a functioning timetable for one grade level. I thought this was too easy a task and committed to building the schedule for the entire organization—all seven grades (K5 through K12). In the time it took me to do this, some of my fellow attendees were still struggling to complete the one grade level they were assigned.

We were allocated six hours, and I finished with a flush of pride just before the clock timed us out. The supervising professors—most of whom were mathematicians—conducted their evaluation in real time with the whole class attempting to learn from their identification of mistakes or suggestions of how to improve the submitted work. As the group moved to my work, I realized that I had made a huge error just as the professor pointed at my submission and asked his question. I was so disappointed in myself. The mistake was significant, as it affected the entire schedule and meant that the work I had done on the grade we had been required to complete was also in error. I failed the assignment.

My competitive drive, my self-confidence, and yes, my arrogance, were my downfall. Rather than meticulously checking and cross-checking my work, pressure testing each sequence for error, I just blasted ahead, too sure of myself and too reliant on my natural intelligence and knowledge. I learned about the need to slow down, to be more modest in my goals, to curb my ego, to better appreciate that not every task is a test requiring me to prove myself. To show a little more humility. It was only after the accumulation of many similar examples when studying other leaders that I realized that the need for this lesson was more general and that many leaders hadn't yet learned it. It was a painful experience that I vowed never to repeat.

SENSE OF VALUE AND SELF-WORTH

Research Definition: High levels of self-confidence, self-assurance, and self-efficacy can push leaders to set high expectations for themselves and others.

The drive to achieve or compete isn't the only source of energy that can push a leader to succeed. Some individuals are driven by a sense of importance and significance—a belief that they can solve the big problems and achieve a level of success that lies just beyond the reach of others. These leaders tend to volunteer for the toughest assignments, in the most visible situations, where the potential for failure and reputational damage is extremely high, yet they are energized by a sense that they can succeed. We find that many competitive leaders are also strong in this trait, and the overlap should need no explanation.

The reason for such high levels of self-assurance is that these leaders have earned it through past success and achievements. They can recount multiple examples of having applied themselves to the most difficult problems and come through successfully. This fuels their belief that they can solve future problems. It shouldn't be too surprising that individuals who exhibit these characteristics earlier in life progress to positions of authority and leadership later in life. In his book *True North: Discover Your Authentic Leadership*, Bill George described in detail the early life experiences of many leaders who were thrust into leadership roles as young as seven years old.[4] When asked to describe when they first realized they had significant leadership capabilities, the vast majority talked about early school experiences that became more visible and accentuated throughout their teenage years. This isn't to claim that leadership is deterministic but rather to note that many of the most self-assured leaders exhibited these characteristics and traits at a young age.

Developing a Positive Self-View in Early Adolescence

"What Advice Would You Give to Schools Trying to Develop Leadership Qualities in Young People?"

In 2010, I spoke to an audience of school superintendents who asked this very question. Develop their self-confidence was my reply. Help them discover their strengths and capabilities, and then give them increasing opportunities to excel in those areas and affirm their achievements. There is no more important role for teachers and parents than to increase the confidence of young children and to affirm their capabilities to others.

Psychology researcher Barbara Fredrickson developed the "broaden-and-build" theory to describe her discovery that accentuating a young person's success in a specific area of achievement led to improvements in somewhat unrelated areas of activity and that encouraging more of this success created even more peripheral benefits.[5] A child who excelled in drama, for example, and who was affirmed for this capability and encouraged to build on their accomplishments could see a significant increase in their math scores in a way that was strongly correlated but clearly unrelated.

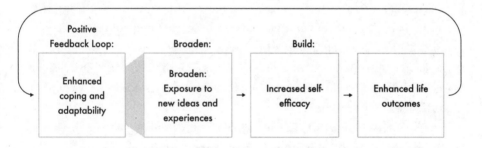

Fredrickson's research also established the pervasive influence of a negative focus. If you apply focused criticism to areas where young people don't do well, their performance in previously strong areas diminishes. Just as the beneficial focus on boosting self-esteem and self-confidence created a positive compound effect, the reverse created a broad and negative effect. Too little of her work has permeated modern management practice, and too often managers find it easy to catch employees doing the wrong things rather than catching them doing the right things and celebrating by affirming these.

If we take Fredrickson's research one step further, one prediction we could make is that highly assured leaders with a strong track record of success should be more likely to contribute effectively outside their area of competence and expertise. This is exactly what we find. Leaders fueled by a strong sense of self-efficacy are much more likely to contribute positively to areas unrelated to their specialist domain. The idea may seem counterintuitive, but helping to increase a leader's sense of efficacy and affirming their contributions may be a potential solution to demolishing the silos and trenches that keep people apart and drive more defensive and insulated functioning.

Owning Your Strengths

"What Do You Do Better Than Just About Everyone You Know?"
We ask all leaders this question, and the responses tend to be underwhelming. Even allowing for humility, and the tendency for people to play down their capabilities, the lack of specificity in response is stark. People genuinely struggle to talk about the things they do well and better than most, which highlights how poor a job companies do at describing a person's worth and establishing their expertise and value.

It is remarkable how quickly, when asked about their strengths, people pivot to describe a litany of weaknesses and failures. This is more than being self-effacing—it's a denial of contribution, and it has a strong cultural underpinning. We play down our abilities in order to avoid appearing as though we are the smartest person in the room, but this situation isn't in balance. It is heavily weighted toward a negative projection of self, and this is something we need to work collectively to address.

We often encounter people who, without really thinking, declare that a person's strengths can become their greatest weaknesses. It's ridiculous. Not only are people reluctant to own their strengths, but we also have a whole series of psychologist blowhards and cheerleaders—who should know better—taking the little positive reflection individuals have of themselves and turning it back on them as a potential negative detractor. A 2009 *Harvard Business Review* article by Robert Kaplan and Rob Kaiser titled "Stop Overdoing Your Strengths" (and their subsequent book, *Fear Your Strengths: What You Are Best at Could Be Your Biggest Problem*) is Exhibit A in this misguided characterization.[6] Oh, how psychologists like to revel in misery. We discussed this tendency in the first half of this book.

"What Do You Think Will Help You Improve the Most: Knowing Your Strengths or Knowing Your Weaknesses?"

Gallup has been asking this question for decades, and most people believe that knowing their weaknesses is the key to their success. This is completely wrong. Too many practices in organizations, from annual reviews to performance management, reinforce this negativity and act to suppress self-confidence and assurance. It requires very special individuals to be able to rise above this and create the impact they know they can achieve.

If companies and leaders are serious about drawing the best out of every employee, they need to build each individual's self-confidence. The best leaders do this intuitively. They celebrate the success of others. They position others so that their contributions shine. They distribute recognition and build people up. It is a relentless focus that weaker leaders regard as optional.

MEASUREMENT DRIVES GROWTH

Research Definition: Growth requires challenging goals and the clarity that comes from objective measurement in the pursuit of those goals. Growth is more the consequence of having the most Talented people in roles that fit them than of the products and services they sell or manage.

Some of the highest-performing leaders we've ever studied are nearly always driven by measurement that encompasses the breadth of their work contribution and value, and they tend to create these measures despite their organizations, not because of them.[7] These leaders look at their world through a dashboard that indicates how progress to the goals that are set is being tracked. It is a mindset that sets them apart from the vast majority of leaders, who see their value in terms of task and activity completion. To use our power source metaphor, their dashboard measures every critical activity and function in real time. Without these dials, leaders are "flying blind."

There are two elements that seem to be strong measurement principles for objective measurement and performance-oriented leaders:

First, they measure a broad range of indicators that capture how value is created beyond just financial terms.

Second, they use their dashboard as a base for setting goals that others believe might be just out of reach—the true definition of "stretch goals."

For these leaders, the drive to objectively measure performance is the essential ingredient in how goals should be set and how individuals should be held to account. They know that every employee in their organization needs to know whether the work they are doing this year is measurably better than the work they did last year or quarter to quarter, month to month, week to week, or day to day. Armed with data, high-performing leaders understand the diminishing returns that come from less Talented employees and focus their efforts on building teams where highly Talented individuals can contribute their best work. When this occurs, growth is the logical outcome.

Manager Ratings Are Not Measuring Performance

High-performing leaders establish objective measures of performance that help them evaluate the contributions of their people and whether their business is growing in meaningful ways. When we talk about "objective measures" with respect to how people perform, it's important to understand that this discussion has nothing to do with the manager ratings typically filed during the dreaded end-of-year performance reviews.

A mistake too many companies make is concluding that because one important aspect of a person's role is difficult to measure, then it makes an objective evaluation of their overall performance impossible. Very quickly, rather than doing the hard work we are about to outline in this chapter, companies default to a proxy performance measure—manager ratings. These are extremely problematic—so much so that an increasing number of leading companies are removing them from their performance management systems. We agree with these companies.

Before digging into the details of manager ratings, we should point out that top-performing managers and leaders dislike them and generally find them demotivating. Companies that do things that annoy their best performers should stop and take notice, but they persist in a state of denial and rely on the good nature and professionalism of top-performing managers and leaders to keep them quiet and playing the game. In most cases they do, but quite often they don't and silently leave organizations in "pursuit of other opportunities." We wish more would vote with their feet in this way.

Why do we state that manager ratings are a poor proxy for objectively measuring performance? The main reason is that in too many credible studies, manager ratings have an extremely weak or inverse correlation to the outcomes that are required—higher manager ratings don't relate to higher performance.[8] The main reason is that when managers are rating their employees, they are not accurately scaling their performance; they are scoring the likability of the employee. Companies that describe manager ratings as "performance ratings" deserve to be sued for false claims.

To repeat... companies should be strongly advised not to engage in practices that annoy and/or disengage their highest performers. The very best leaders know this, and as strongly as they might advocate for change to a more objective performance measurement, the HR systems in most companies (the endless paper chase of form filling and box checking) operate like a sponge and suck the life out of people, leaving these leaders to covertly develop commendably creative acts of subversion. If these leaders were to seek crowdsourced funding to support their efforts, we would be their biggest contributors. They might be fighting a losing battle, but it's one they can't afford to give up. Here are some research findings that have contributed to the move away from manager ratings:

- Managers intentionally distort their ratings of employees for three key reasons.[9]
  * Avoiding the negative consequences that could result from a more accurate rating motivates managers to produce inaccurate (usually inflated) ratings—it avoids them having to have a potentially difficult conversation with a low performer.
  * Managers wish to conform with organizational norms. For example, some companies require that no more than 20 percent of employees receive the highest ratings (or even specify the percentages for each score from 1 through 5). This also applies to negative scores when, if the manager gives a person a score of 1 (the very lowest rating), the company might ask

why that employee is still working for the company. Thus, managers know not to give anyone a score of 1 in order to avoid that difficult conversation.

* The self-interest of a manager could lead them to distort their ratings. Managers might believe that evaluations of their own performance are related to how they evaluate the performance of their team members—higher scores awarded to their team members might be seen to reflect positively on perceptions of their leadership.

- The way managers rate their employees is more a reflection of their own thoughts and beliefs about work performance than an objective evaluation of how the person being rated is actually performing.[10]

- There is a weak to negative relationship between manager ratings and objectively measured performance.[11] A research paper from 2002 concluded, "There appears to be little evidence that impression scales (manager ratings) predict job performance."[12]

- A 2003 research paper established that how strongly a manager rates an employee on a work characteristic depends on how well the manager also shows competence in that characteristic.[13] The same research paper showed that managers who displayed high discretionary effort were much more likely to rate highly employees who also showed high discretionary effort.

- For performance ratings to be accurate and credible, managers should use the full range of scores, yet they rarely do. A 2011 research paper found two biases that prevent managers from using the full scale.[14] One is "centrality bias," which accounts for managers' tendency to compress their ratings, typically to 3 scores—3, 4, and 5 on a 5-point scale where 5 is high. This bias was far more common than "leniency bias," which is the tendency of managers to inflate their ratings by a factor of 5.64, possibly to avoid some of those difficult conversations we highlighted in the previously mentioned first point.

- We found through our own research that the more socially sophisticated and positive an employee is, the greater the likelihood that their manager will rate their performance higher. Employees who might ask difficult questions or not show immediate compliance with their managers' wishes invariably receive lower ratings despite often being regarded more broadly in their organization as outstanding performers. We describe this as an "ease of management" problem, for obvious reasons.

- If manager ratings accurately reflect actual performance, then the aggregate of all ratings in an organization should closely correlate to that organization's financial performance. However, they don't. In fact, when aggregate manager ratings are compared, most companies fall in the range of 4.1 to 4.3, essentially the same across all companies, yet those companies show financial performance across a much wider range. The logical explanation is that even though we call them "performance ratings," the ratings have almost nothing to do with performance.

Sometimes We Find an Inverse Correlation

Our partnership with a large US-based retail organization revealed the fundamental flaw in pretending that manager ratings are an effective proxy for performance measurement. We studied all 132 of their retail stores and ranked and then quartiled them by their two main performance measures—conversion% and $spent per customer. Even though we were in possession of actual performance data, we asked the twenty-one district managers (DMs), to whom all store managers reported, to rate the stores based on their performance.

The DMs all had the same data we had. A cursory glance at this ranking would provide all the information they needed. What could possibly go wrong?

- The stores occupying the second quartile in the ranking received the highest average performance ratings by the DMs.
- The third quartile received the next highest rating and the fourth quartile the next highest.
- The lowest-rated stores were in the top performance quartile, and the overall correlation was slightly inverse when it should have been emphatically positive.

It was a puzzle. When we dug into the details to find an explanation, we found that the managers of the top-quartile stores were too much of a handful for the DMs to deal with. These store managers were pushy, demanding, and uncompromising in their relationships with the corporate organization. They used their insistence and assertiveness to secure benefits for their stores in terms of inventory and SKU availability as well as early access to promotional campaigns and employee training.

The DMs, when rating stores, weren't rating performance; they were rating ease of management. Their ratings were a reflection of themselves, not the store managers they were supposed to be evaluating. This was one of our first exposures to how weak managers can destroy organizations and why good people join organizations but leave bad managers.

It is for these reasons, among others, that many companies have stopped the practice of manager ratings.[15] We applaud them. Effective leaders often don't need confirmation from credible research studies to inform what they intuitively know to be true...but having research-based findings that expose the many problems with manager ratings is important in educating organizations, and particularly less performance-oriented leaders.

In this book, we also describe how the presence of positive characteristics in a job evaluation can influence managers to appoint those possessing strong relational skills and more favorably view candidates who are generally positive and upbeat over those who do not exhibit these characteristics. We not only have manager rating bias, but we also have employee selection bias—they are different sides of the same coin, and those seeking to address demographic imbalance in their organizations would be well-advised to evaluate their own manager biases before embarking on what could be a futile program of change.

Our conclusion—and this will be upsetting for some to read—is that organizations that rely on manager ratings as a proxy for measuring real performance are doing the opposite of what they claim. They are inherently lazy organizations.

Understanding Growth

Consider the two following graphs. They were created by two different leaders who were provided with the matrix and asked to "draw growth."

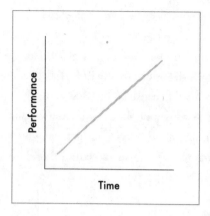

We're often invited to discuss ideas about performance management and growth orientation with groups of leaders. When we do this, we nearly always direct some members of the audience to a whiteboard and invite them to "draw growth." Now, there is no scale to this graph. Although the "Time" and "Performance" labels are understood, there are no objective measurement intervals or definitions. We are simply trying to understand what a person thinks when instructed to draw growth.

It's not a difficult task, but people approach it with some doubt and hesitation—no one wants to look foolish, and they are waiting for the catch. Usually, everyone succeeds in the task. Any line that starts low and ends up higher over time clearly represents growth, but each person approaches this in a slightly different way. Some people draw aggressive lines with a steep upward curve. Some draw wobbly lines that reflect the reality that growth over time isn't always consistent or linear. Some draw very shallow curves, perhaps in recognition that growth is hard to achieve.

The reason this exercise is important is that, alongside a drive to objectively measure performance, high-performing leaders are driven to achieve growth—they have an extremely strong growth orientation. But for too many leaders, their definition of growth lacks rigor. Boards and CEOs recognize this problem and attempt to define it in more objective ways. For example, if a company is to be regarded as a "high-growth" organization, it needs to deliver double-digit revenue performance consistently over time. This is a powerful statement, but only if the market is growing at a much slower pace.

Companies that struggle to achieve market-beating revenue growth look for other ways to describe their success, and the default is usually EPS. This becomes attractive when revenue growth is challenged because an internal focus on cutting costs is a little easier to achieve. Each company places a different emphasis on various financial measures to determine growth rates. Our general advice is this—if revenues outstrip prior performance while also exceeding the market, then that company can legitimately claim to be growing.

Highly Talented People Drive Growth

For high-performing leaders, the answer to "growth" questions is always *people*. Those who think it might be a combination of product, price, and service, important though they are, are completely missing the point. Every world-class element of your product/service offering will fail in the hands of a weak sales rep. Weak reps have a gift for making outstanding products sound tedious and destroying the idea that your company might be easy to do business with. It is the centrality of people to growth that unlocks the potential of successful organizations.

This doesn't mean that all people contribute equally. Consider how you would answer the following question:

You are leading a sales organization, and in the beginning of the fourth quarter, you are struggling to achieve your quota. In order to increase sales and achieve your annual quota, where will you apply the greatest focus?
- Your bottom-performing sales reps (who clearly have a big gap to close)
- Your top-performing sales reps (most of whom are already ahead of their quota)

Let's look at another question that will immediately reveal whether you got the answer to the previous question right or wrong:

All other variables being equal, which of the following would most likely result in higher growth?

* Trying to improve the performance of bottom performers
* Trying to improve the performance of top performers

If the answers aren't now obvious, this book wasn't written for you. Yet, for many leaders, this scenario seems counterintuitive and contradicts how they spend much of their time. Jack Welch made this precise observation in 2016 when he stated that "most managers find themselves in countless productivity-sucking meetings and sidebar conversations about underperformers."[16] We often attend leadership team meetings and talent reviews where leaders complain openly about how much of their time bottom performers consume. It's almost as though these leaders see wasted time as a necessary evil—it isn't.

Variable Talent Levels Impact Performance

For leaders who expend significant energy coaching bottom performers and rolling up their sleeves to ensure that commitments are met, the cumulative impact on the overall performance of the team is clear. Let's explore an example by looking at a hypothetical team with twelve members whose performance is plotted on an array.

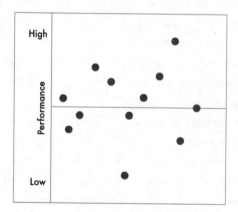

There is a range of performance in every team that reflects the varying level of Talent across all individuals. The horizontal line represents mean performance. Here, we see that five team members fall below this line, six are above it, and one is directly on the line. How do leaders and managers usually regard a performance array of this kind? First, leaders don't regard all individuals as equal. They make choices about where to spend their time and whom they want to see improve.

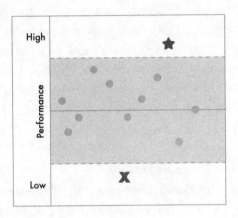

The shaded area around the mean represents an invisible band of "tolerance." Individuals performing just above or just below the mean don't tend to stand out. Their performance isn't outstanding or causing any obvious problems, and they get less attention from their leader as a result. The width of this tolerance band varies a little from leader to leader, but it is typically broader rather than narrower. In this example, one team member falls outside this "invisibility band" on the positive side (★) and one on the negative side (✖). They are outliers, and, more importantly, they are visible.

How might high-performing leaders look at this information in comparison with average- to low-performing leaders? A well-publicized 2012 study by Robert Half suggested that managers spend about one day each week trying to coach and improve poorly performing team members.[17] But this research conceals a much more important finding—that 89 percent of leaders are predisposed to focus (and spend the most time) on poor performers, and only 11 percent of leaders are predisposed to focus on top performers. Top-performing managers and leaders overwhelmingly focus and spend more time on coaching and developing top-performing team members, as we discovered from our database of over fifty-eight thousand leaders.

Focus on Improving Poor Performance

The interesting question is what the impact of this time focus achieves. If 89 percent of managers are predisposed to coach poor performers, does it have any impact? If so, is this an acceptable return on their time investment?

When we interview leaders who focus most of their time on bottom performers, they often claim that they are trying to turn these weak performers into top performers. The reality is that they are trying to raise these employees' performance to the point where they occupy the invisible band we previously illustrated, and then they can stop worrying about them. Put simply, they want the problem to disappear. Moving them up a little into this range solves the manager's performance variance problems.

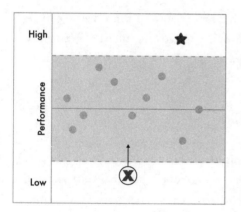 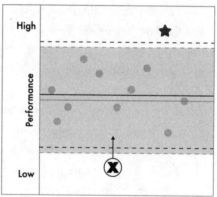

Calculating the impact of this "improvement" on the overall team performance (assuming all else remains the same) shows a negligible gain. The improvement in performance of that one individual barely impacts mean performance, but at least the improvement is positive. If 89 percent of managers in a company achieve this degree of performance improvement, what might the collective company benefit be? Returning to those "growth" curves we highlighted earlier, we can transfer the expected results—and they show a minimal improvement.

Before we begin to argue that all progress is good, we must recall that this is the product of managers spending 20 percent of their time, week after week, on a single task with diminishing returns. This explains why so few companies can

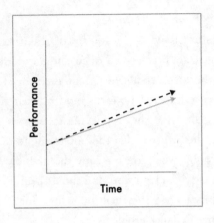

generate market-leading performance that separates them from their competitors. Rather than expect significant year-over-year growth, companies recognize the reality of their limitations, and phrases like "We win some, we lose some" justify their relative mediocrity.

Focus on Improving Good Performance

How different might these results look if more high-performing, growth-oriented leaders were the norm in organizations? First, we should point out that these leaders don't ignore poor performers. They apply minimal time working out whether the required amount of improvement is even possible, and they quickly reach the decision that in most cases, it isn't. They would rather act on this reality quickly to gain more immediate and sustainable performance gains with a higher-performing employee.

Poorly performing managers and leaders take too long trying to improve the poor performance of some team members and often never conclude that they should be terminated and replaced with more Talented individuals. Top-performing leaders act with a much greater sense of urgency, often bringing this focus to a close within three months. But even with a decision of this kind pending, they still spend most of their time coaching and developing those who have the capacity to achieve world-class performance.

In this example, the bottom performer exits from the company and is replaced with an individual whose Talents are a much better fit for the role and

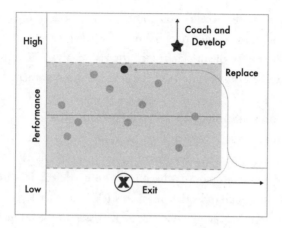

who has a greater capacity to perform. The focus on coaching and developing our high-performing outlier also contributes to better performance outcomes. A focus in this direction shows a significantly greater and more positive impact on the overall performance of the team.

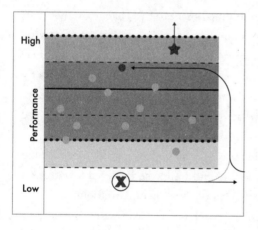

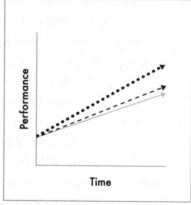

If more highly Talented, growth-oriented leaders were contributing performance improvements of this kind, we would see much different growth trajectories at the organizational level. The fact that this isn't happening tells us that companies employ too few leaders with this focus and that organizational performance management practices are too often rooted in popularity contests.

In these companies, the excellent outcomes of high-performing leaders are easily canceled out by the mediocre outcomes of weaker leaders. Not surprisingly, those at the very top of the org chart lack the vision, awareness, and capacity to change things. Their organizations are a direct reflection of them.

Goal Setting and Incentives That Drive Performance

High-performing leaders regard their goal as the minimum performance expected. This means that in sales organizations, everyone is expected to achieve their quota because the quota is the minimum expected. It logically follows, therefore, that financial and other rewards kick in at that level. The incentive should always target achieving quota as the first step in the reward process. But for organizations to grow and become more competitive in their market, incentivizing sales reps to perform above quota is required, and organizational leaders are best advised to spend their time and effort on determining how to build an incentive structure that drives sales reps to exceed the minimum expected by the quota.

Sales leaders who lack vision and who fear a negative backlash and possible sales rep attrition are the single biggest impediment to this change. Rather than setting quota achievement as the minimum level at which performance rewards kick in, they dispense emotional therapy and support and are happy to put their arms around sales reps who tried hard but didn't quite make it. They do this by granting financial rewards to reps for coming in just below quota at year end. This really raises questions about what "performance" means and the bar the quota represents.

Rather than building a reward ladder leading up to the quota, high-performing leaders use the quota as the bottom rung and build the ladder above it. It's a complete shift in mindset from what is typically seen in organizations.

The organizational benefit of this approach is that the overall company performance goal is more likely to be achieved or bettered, as reps exceeding quota hopefully outnumber those who don't. This almost never happens with systems that reward mediocrity. As you think through the implications of this approach, the idea of rewarding below quota achievement becomes challenging. If you want a high-performing organization, you won't build it by setting goals that reward average or poor performance—you will be much more likely to succeed if your expectations and management of performance require the achievement of exacting goals with strong incentives in place for those who exceed them at each level and with rewards that deliver exponential benefit.

Measuring Roles That Are Hard to Measure

Sales can be counted, plotted on a graph, and compared over time and between individuals and groups. Not only can quotas be set and used to drive performance, but absolute and percentage growth over time can be calculated. This objectivity is harder to define in roles that aren't typically measured by numbers or where performance is difficult to plot on a graph. High-performing leaders don't use this as an excuse, and we have seen some inspired and creative practices to address this problem.

The interesting thing about performance levels—even in sales roles—is that we can describe them with reference to criteria. These criteria can be descriptive of specific levels of performance. With thought and effort, it isn't difficult to describe poor (or great) sales performance by developing the criteria that indicate poor (or great) performance. This is true for all roles. Rather than just using timeliness or completion as binary output indicators (which typically ignore important qualitative criteria), high-performing leaders do the hard work of defining performance-level criteria and building a progressive, descriptive account of how performance should start with the minimum achievement expected (the goal) and progress to top performance. This scale or ladder might comprise three or five steps with the criteria becoming progressively harder to achieve at each level.

Starting by defining goals as "minimum acceptable performance" has the potential to transform the way leaders think of organizational success and growth, and moving toward this way of working is sure to create short-term casualties. Some people, to put it simply, won't make it. This inevitably happens when organizations shift toward a performance-based culture. Some employees won't be able to operate successfully with these raised expectations. High-performing leaders know this is not an excuse or a credible argument against change, but others will use it as a reason to try and prevent it. Those who have the most to lose from shifting mindsets about what is possible are below-average and poor performers, and they will kick and scream against change for as long as you allow them to.

The reason more poorly performing organizations are weak is because they have low Talent levels, and they are scared that raising performance expectations will lead to high failure levels, disengagement, and even higher turnover. They have this argument completely wrong, which is why they struggle to improve. You need to set the bar really high in order to expose the problem. Only by setting the bar so high will organizations understand who their great performers are.

Once these employees are visible and empowered, companies should build their recruitment policy around finding more of these Talented individuals. The difference between companies that initiate this journey and the failing organizations that don't is in the quality of the turnover. In aspiring companies where great leaders take steps to raise the bar and drive performance, poor performers leave and great people can't wait to join. In poorly performing organizations where weaker leaders are scared of the implications of change, poor performers feel secure and good employees, who join in error, quickly and quietly leave.

WHAT REALLY MATTERS

High-performing leaders are driven to succeed in different ways. Coupled with the direction-setting Talents discussed in the previous chapter, they are a formidable presence and force in organizations:

- For some, their self-starting nature might be the consequence of a strong internal drive to achieve or a more external focus on winning.
- Their success may be bolstered by high levels of self-confidence, self-assurance, and self-efficacy.
- The very best have objective measures of performance and the focus on Talent and growth to bring this about for the benefit of the company.

High expectations of outcomes are how leaders create performance and growth. You may be a leader who leads through an infectious motivation to perform if

- you have a knack for seeing the upside in most situations;
- you are never satisfied with your achievements and look to raise the bar even higher;

- you create scorecards and dashboards that drive you to be number one; and
- you are comfortable with risk and relish your role as leader in the most difficult situations.

Leaders need to apply objectivity to determine what opportunities have the largest upside—this applies to the business opportunities you pursue (and which ones you decline) as well as the people in whom you invest the most time. These questions can help ensure that your drive and motivation are focused in the right direction:

- What is the minimum level of performance that you are prepared to tolerate? Set your goal higher than this level.
- Nearly everyone knows the difference between good and bad. Define for every employee in every role the difference (using numbers or descriptive criteria) between the *minimum expected* and what constitutes *good* and *excellent* performance.

In the next chapter, we address one of those aspects of leadership without which change is very difficult—the capacity to challenge and influence the thinking and actions of others. To the disappointment of every motivated and self-driven leader, despite their very best efforts, they can't do it all on their own. They must bring others along, preferably on the same journey, in the same vehicle, heading in the same direction.

CHAPTER 7

Exerting Pressure

WHILE THE SCIENTIFIC COMMUNITY HAS ALMOST UNANIMOUSLY EMBRACED Darwin's evolutionary theory—that humans and apes descended from a common ancestor and evolved into separate species over time—nearly 60 percent of Americans take a creationist view and believe humans were created exactly as they are today—or if they believe humans have evolved, they believe this evolution was guided by God, specifically the Christian God.[1] This disparity between the overwhelming scientific consensus and public opinion is attributable largely to Christian fundamentalists, who have attempted to discredit established scientific theory since the late nineteenth century. Read about Galileo and his death sentence from the Catholic church and you'll understand that the battles between religion and science have been going on for centuries.

In 1925, Tennessee legislators passed the Butler Act, which banned public school teachers from teaching any theory that contradicted the story of human creation as it is presented in the Bible.[2] Upon hearing the news, the American Civil Liberties Union (ACLU) began advertising that they would defend anyone prosecuted under the Butler Act.[3] A young high school football coach and science teacher was recruited to challenge the law, thus catapulting *The State of Tennessee v. John Thomas Scopes* to the Tennessee court dockets. The trial played out over an eight-day period in front of a packed courthouse and was the first hearing to ever be broadcast live over the radio. Millions listened.

Ultimately, the jury sided with the prosecution and found Scopes guilty of violating the law, a misdemeanor offense that carried a $100 fine.[4] The verdict (which was later overturned) did very little to detract from the broader debate about academic freedom and whether religion had a place in public education. In the years that followed, antievolution laws were defeated in twenty-two states until the opportunity arose to argue the issue in front of the Supreme Court. In 1968, the ACLU filed an amicus brief on behalf of an Arkansas schoolteacher, which led to a unanimous decision that these bans were a violation of her First Amendment rights.[5]

Through litigation and advocacy—and effectively balancing reaction and proaction—the ACLU has exerted tremendous influence on the policies that have shaped American life over the past century. The Scopes trial highlighted three critical aspects of influencing that high-performing leaders, emulating the ACLU, know too well:

1. *First*, testing the constitutionality of the Butler Act provoked an impassioned debate about the separation of church and state and served as a catalyst for progress. The best leaders know that challenging popular and widely held beliefs is essential, even if people strongly hold on to those beliefs.

2. *Second*, well-reasoned arguments and expert analysis throughout the trial successfully persuaded the public of the importance of academic freedom. The best leaders know that eventually data and evidence will win the day.

3. *Third*, the ACLU's commitment to defending civil liberties, in the face of backlash, opposition, and the potential consequences of losing a high-profile trial, required steely resolve and a heightened level of

assertiveness to challenge the law head-on. The best leaders know that when you are right, you must take a stand, even if it means challenging those who are stronger and have more power than you.

This is what we mean when we say that top-performing leaders "exert pressure."

Exerting Pressure involves

Catalyzing Change

Persistence and Persuasion

Direct, Assertive Challenges

CATALYSTS FOR CHANGE

Research Definition: High-performing leaders fight against complacency in their teams and wider organization. They solve difficult problems and challenges and are willing to destabilize and then rebuild parts of their organization that are currently suboptimal but have the potential to be world-class.

When the English reformist politician William Cobbett wrote, "I defy you to agitate any fellow on a full stomach," he was providing insight into the cause of riots and rebellions in early-nineteenth-century England.[6] As rapid industrialization and factory labor caused alienation and enormous poverty, Cobbett was stating a clear truth—if you address perceived deficiencies that disproportionately affect the lives of poor people by providing affordable food, shelter, and the ability to subsist, they will be grateful for their lot in life, abide by the law, and be productive members of society. He was arguing that if the rich establishment wanted an easier time, they needed to do a better job of looking after workers and the poor. His message fell on deaf ears.

Cobbett was the political precursor to Abraham Maslow and a full century ahead of his time.[7] Cobbett saw the light, and his philosophy influenced philanthropic business owners looking to carve out a competitive advantage with a more motivated and productive workforce. What most business leaders today understand and take for granted was a rarity only one hundred years ago.

If It Isn't Broke, Why Fix It?

The relative absence of such hardship and strife today, when the primary demands of working people one hundred years ago have largely been addressed and met, has shifted expectations to the point that organizations now operate with an appropriate focus on employee health, safety, and general well-being. The battles being fought in the modern workplace are entirely different from the beatings and maltreatment dished out to workers in the past.

As leaders and employees seek more collaborative work practices, the benefits of these approaches can also lead to complacency and a lack of drive for excellence unless leaders can find ways to encourage this attitude among those beneath them in the organizational hierarchy. All the gains and improvements in organizational relationships and functioning should not bring us to the point where the dominant attitude is "Why change?"

Although it's difficult to comprehend this attitude in modern times, when the demand for change and improvement seems dominant, I worked with a leader who espoused this very attitude. While experiencing particularly difficult times under his leadership, he promised employees that a "plateau of stability" would be just around the corner. All this turbulence would eventually dissipate, and the status quo would resume. It was a statement of such jaw-dropping stupidity that I still bristle at the implications thirty-five years later. It's as though, in the times since Cobbett, the workplace has evolved to such an extent that all change is to be resisted, that what everyone needs is peace and calm...a quiet life.

The biggest problem with this line of argument is that it is never true. However undesirable and turbulent the present is perceived to be, pretending that the future will be more balanced and less pressured is a lie. It might be an attractive idea for some, but high performers reject its very essence, and most others can see right through it. To the best leaders, comfort equals complacency. When

141

things are going smoothly, these leaders inject highly targeted disruption into the mix to bring about change and improvement.

In Cobbett's England, our high-performing leaders would have used poverty and housing conditions as agents of change. They would have harnessed the forces of anger and injustice in the hope of agitating people to drive more fundamental change that would improve everyone's lot and then pushed to extend these improvements. They would have fomented disagreement and dissent in order to upset the established order—in the modern case, they would seriously unsettle those complacent organizations that have the capacity to be much better. They would be a handful to manage. And if you are a reader with a long career ahead of you, there is much to be said for being a handful to manage, especially if you are achieving top performance.

"If it isn't broke, why fix it?" is the prevailing attitude our high-performing leaders are fighting against. This puts them in the minority of company leaders, and it takes an extremely strong and self-assured organization to live with and manage their incredible but disruptive impact. Yet this impact is often the ingredient that makes excellence achievable. The object might not be broken, but an act of targeted vandalism could lead to excellence. That's an attitude more leaders should exemplify. If established executives are reading this book and balking at this idea, there are pretty coloring books they should buy instead in every airport bookstore.

Leaders as "Agents Provocateurs"

The role of "agent provocateur" has an important purpose. High-performing leaders not only understand its value but also impatiently exploit it. To use another historical analogy, it is like Catherine the Great saying of Peter the Great, the last of the Romanovs, in 1720, "He acted on Russia like nitric acid on iron." The reforms of Peter the Great were doubtless corrosive to aspects of Russian society, but without them, Catherine's work and reforms would have been almost impossible.

High-performing leaders see the phrase "If it isn't broke, don't fix it" as the sham it is. For them, improvement can come only by breaking some things. In contrast to all the mediocre leaders complaining that they have enough problems to solve without creating more, high-performing leaders strike at the heart of their organizations and drive meaningful change and improvement. For those employees (and inadequate leaders) looking for an uneventful life at work, these high-performing leaders represent a real threat to an otherwise peaceful existence.

Whether emulating the effect of Peter the Great on Russian society, the agitators for higher wages and better food in nineteenth-century England, or the "agents provocateurs" who stirred ordinary citizens to revolt in the French Revolution, high-performing leaders seek out change and then agitate and influence others to bring it about. John Kotter, in his 1999 book *John P. Kotter on What Leaders Really Do*, argued that it is the role of leaders to create change and of managers to resolve the ensuing disruption.[8] While this is simplistic, we don't fundamentally disagree. Kotter used some real-life examples to describe this characteristic, such as Lou Gerstner's transformation of American Express in 1979—an act of destruction followed by subsequent rebuilding that enabled the company to address its challenges and grow into the modern powerhouse it is today. Few inside American Express supported him at the time.

Playing Down Performance

The value of leaders as catalysts for change is clear, but they are an intimidating presence in more complacent organizations that would rather protect and defend what they have built than address their deficiencies and shortcomings. We recall attending a leadership team meeting of a large company comprising seven divisions, ranging in size from $200 million to $18 billion. The company was struggling, and there was a legitimate feeling that if things didn't improve quickly, some of these leaders (including the CEO) would lose their jobs.

The meeting was a business performance review of each of the seven divisions, and six of these were depressing. The leaders all seemed shell-shocked, and confidence ebbed out of them with each line in the financial spreadsheet. Yet there was one bright spark...one business that seemed to defy all logic. Unlike the other six, this was a thriving business significantly outpacing its market. The woman running this division spoke confidently and assuredly about the state of her business, its pipeline, and future expectations, and how she was leading it. It was an outstanding performance.

Unfortunately, the success of this business wasn't sufficient to cover the losses of the other businesses (a fact the CEO relayed as a point of criticism and expression of disappointment). He then proceeded to state that it would be best if this incredible leader suppressed talk of her success—played down her results—so that other leaders sitting around the table wouldn't feel so bad about their poor results and lagging performance.

We never worked with this company again. They remained in business only due to some smart divestments over the following few years that resulted in the loss of about seventy thousand jobs, a casual act of self-inflicted pain that destroyed the livelihoods of too many honorable employees who were oblivious to the incompetence of those above them.

This event taught us that you should never apologize or feel bad about outstanding performance. The complacency of leaders playing victim to the circumstances they should have sought to control is anathema to high-performing leaders. This example perfectly illustrates what can happen, and the attitudes that take root to drive it, when there is an absence of catalysts at the leadership level. There was certainly no room for them in this company, and too many disillusioned employees paid the price. Far too many more that we don't know about still do.

PERSISTENCE AND PERSUASION

Research Definition: There is an art to persuasion, and high-performing leaders show extraordinary patience and persistence in their attempts to influence the thinking and actions of others.

If one form of pressure comes from high-performing leaders acting as catalysts and agents of change, another form of pressure comes through the more subtle, and typically softer, acts of persuasion. Persuasion, as practiced by high-performing leaders, requires persistence over time and, ultimately, the intent to change a person's mind. Effective persuasion isn't about answering the question "What should I do?" but "*Why should I do it?*"

Former AlliedSignal CEO Larry Bossidy once said, "The day you could yell and scream and beat people into good performance is over. Today you have to appeal to them by helping them see how they can get from here to there, by establishing some credibility and by giving them some reason and help to get there. Do all those things, and they'll knock down doors."[9]

Here are nine rock-solid pieces of advice to help leaders enhance their persuasive capabilities.

Build Your Credibility

Leaders with a track record of consistent behavior and strong performance are generally seen as credible, trustworthy, and worth following.[10] In behavioral terms, the critical criteria include perceptions of a leader's fairness and balance and whether they display emotional maturity that prevents them getting so excited about an idea that they lose all objectivity, become immune to alternative perspectives, and display extreme emotional swings.

Having achieved a level of success in the past, a leader can usually advocate from a position of confidence and assurance that calms doubters and encourages people to work more effectively together. For a follower to really commit and be persuaded to a course of action, the level of trust between the two parties becomes extremely important. This trust is relationally driven and helps answer critical questions:

- Has this leader achieved good outcomes previously?
- Do they have a record of doing exactly what they said they would do?
- Have their advice and guidance been right before?
- Do they seem to be in command and demonstrate a comprehensive understanding of the issues they are dealing with?
- Even though we might disagree, do they seem to have my best interests in mind?

The problem and challenge in establishing credibility is that it is difficult for a person to determine this about themselves. Few organizations have successfully built feedback-rich environments, and it is often difficult for a leader to truly understand where they stand with others and how they are perceived. A 360 assessment can help, especially when a leader has been leading a team for some time and true perspectives have not already been drawn out. But the problems with 360s, and the "noise" they amplify, is that they rarely lead to accurate outcomes. At a time when "feedback" is attracting much more attention on business bookshelves, the difficulties in providing feedback are not easily addressed.

Kim Scott's answer in her 2019 book, *Radical Candor: Be a Kick-Ass Boss Without Losing Your Humanity*, is to focus on shooting straight, cutting through the BS, and saying exactly what you feel.[11] But rather than cutting through the BS, this idea creates piles of its own. Saying something more directly doesn't help anyone if it has no objectivity. It's a little like believing, when traveling through a foreign country where we don't speak the language, that shouting loudly and waving our arms around will make it easier for the other person to understand us. Marcus Buckingham and Ashley Goodall, in their excellent 2019 *Harvard Business Review* article "The Feedback Fallacy," skewer, fillet, and completely demolish this line of reasoning in a way that we approve.[12]

They explain in simple and powerful terms that too few companies have developed feedback as a dominant area of expertise. We have encountered too many individuals in our work who, in answer to the question "What feedback have you recently received about yourself?," talk in ways that suggest that few conversations of this type take place in the organization, or the ones that have taken place focused on negative, unrealistic expectations of how a person can legitimately improve. "Well, I haven't ever been given feedback" is a common and disappointing response. This perspective is a bit hit-and-miss, and this is why individuals struggle with objective self-appraisal and the level of trust and credibility this justifies. Buckingham and Goodall argue that the best advice for individuals to learn about their credibility is to ask each of their individual colleagues in turn, because this is the only valid perspective.

Frame Issues Appropriately

Assuming a high-performing leader has passed the credibility test, the next step is to establish common elements around which there is collective agreement.[13] Outlining areas of agreement, whether around principles, practices, or facts, shows that agreement (at least on some things) is possible and that this isn't about "doing battle" with others in order to defeat them.[14]

High-performing leaders also understand the power of framing issues in a way that people are more receptive to. The late Daniel Kahneman, in his outstanding book, *Thinking Fast and Slow*, outlined research that he had conducted with Amos Tversky that established the "framing effect" as a psychological bias and heuristic that led to flawed reasoning in many humans, with the potential to drive a wedge between them on important issues.[15] They discovered that how issues were framed—the language that was used and whether it was positive or negative—has a significant impact on what people think and the decisions and choices they make.

If you focus on all the negative characteristics and how you propose addressing these, it might not work as effectively as presenting how your proposal will improve things and make work lives easier or more fulfilling. This isn't a form of deception, just careful and thoughtful use of language and an essential ingredient of effective persuasion.

Build a Series of Steps

High-performing leaders build common ground and shared perspective by establishing a clear decision-making process and defining the exact steps that need to be followed to reach a final decision. They deal up front with the relatively simple issues that typically lead to confusion and disengagement:

- Who will be involved in each stage of the discussion?
- How will the discussion progress from one stage to the next?
- When will the final decision be reached, by whom, and with respect to what criteria?

Argue Like a Scientist

The most effective persuasive approach follows the scientific method and ensures that everyone is aware of how the method works, how it contributes to more effective decision-making, and how it can be applied to navigate and resolve differences between people.[16] In general terms, the scientific method is a process that we follow to consider the evidence (what is known), establish a hypothesis (or hypotheses) that points to a potential solution, and testing to see what works before a conclusion or resolution can be reached.

The most important question a scientist asks as they go through this process is "What evidence, if it showed up, would prove me wrong?" If you want to build common ground with those who oppose your arguments, you have to ask them to identify the evidence that would lead to them changing their mind and offer this up in your own argument.

Focus on Objective Data and Evidence

One of the worst logical fallacies when presenting a case is the argument from authority. This involves one party asserting technical or experiential superiority in an attempt to declare victory. High-performing leaders steer clear of this temptation. It isn't perceptions of expertise and superiority that sway the decision but the strength of the evidence and data.

This doesn't mean experts don't count or that their arguments should be given equal weight as everyone else's; rather, it means that best contribution comes from amassing the data and evidence that validate their position. High-performing leaders keep emotions calm and lay out the evidence as a means of inching the protagonists a little closer together and highlighting the right direction for a possible solution.

Tell Stories

Data and evidence don't often win the argument on their own, and this is sometimes where our experts should be kept in the background. High-performing leaders use the power of storytelling, which involves building a compelling narrative from the data and evidence, but in terms that people can understand. Numbers don't typically make a strong emotional impact, but a story can.[17]

In a 1998 *Harvard Business Review* article, "The Necessary Art of Persuasion," Jay A. Conger recounted how two Microsoft marketing managers used storytelling to persuade the executive team to invest in new software technology.[18] Rather than amass data and evidence (which they certainly had), they decided to tell a story that captured the essential elements:

> Imagine you want to cook dinner and you must first go to the supermarket. You have all the flexibility you want—you can cook anything in the world as long as you know how and have the time and desire to do it. When you arrive at the supermarket, you find all these overstuffed aisles with cryptic single-word headings like "sundries" and "ethnic food" and "condiments." These are the menus on typical computer

interfaces. The question is whether salt is under condiments or ethnic food or near the potato chip section. There are surrounding racks and wall spaces, much as our software interfaces now have support buttons, tool bars, and lines around the perimeters. Now after you have collected everything, you still need to put it all together in the correct order to make a meal. If you're a good cook, your meal will probably be good. If you're a novice, it probably won't be.

We [at Microsoft] have been selling under the supermarket category for years, and we think there is a big opportunity for restaurants. That's what we are trying to do now with BOB: pushing the next step with software that is more like going to a restaurant, so the user doesn't spend all of his time searching for the ingredients. We find and put the ingredients together. You sit down, you get comfortable. We bring you a menu. We do the work, you relax. It's an enjoyable experience. No walking around lost trying to find things, no cooking.[19]

Karen Fries and Barry Linnett, the marketing managers who made this pitch, succeeded in persuading reluctant executives to invest. Of course, behind their story were all the data and evidence you could imagine. They just didn't lead with them.

Connect to Emotions

Using storytelling to connect data and evidence to individuals can help nudge reluctant people toward being more accepting of proposals for change. But the appeal based on emotion can have an even more powerful effect. Emotions describe how people feel and are essential to the human experience:[20]

- "Let me tell you how this would make me feel..." is a powerful way of connecting to others and inviting them to share your positive emotional state.
- "Imagine how our people would feel about being able to do things this way..." forces the externalization of positive emotions and helps break down resistance to an idea or approach.

- "Imagine how this would make you feel…" is an appeal that rises above the specific argument to describe and imagine a future state where positive things might happen.
- "Imagine customers expressing their appreciation to you for…" is another form of emotional appeal.

High-performing leaders don't shy away from declaring their own emotions, although they are careful not to sound too emotionally driven. The importance of a discreet emotional disclosure and appeal is to prevent others from viewing you as an automaton—someone so driven by facts and data that you project no sense of what it really means to be a person with feelings and aspirations. The whole purpose of this approach is to develop a shared emotional approach, to feel and experience similar things, and to communicate the positive and uplifting benefits of a proposal.

Play the Long Game

Those who approach the art of persuasion with short-term intent and perspective will always be disappointed. Imagining that you can address all concerns and make converts of participants in a single meeting is completely unrealistic. Persuasion is a long-term game played out over a timescale that leaves sufficient room for influence to occur. In a business world dominated by perceptions of speed and immediacy, the art of persuasion could become a lost art.

We often disappoint leaders who, looking to move forward quickly with their proposal, are told that change of the required magnitude could take a year or more of hard, persuasive endeavor. If you need a decision in two weeks, don't pretend that you are engaging in an act of persuasion. Just tell people what you are going to do and let them "like it or lump it." Engaging in an act of persuasion when the timeline doesn't allow for it or when you have already made up your mind is disingenuous.

Co-create

We have defined persuasion as getting a person to agree with something they originally disagreed with and to do something different than what they originally intended. It is difficult work, and it takes time—time that too many leaders pretend they don't have. But there is another way that involves no persuasion at all.[21] We call it co-creation, or the act of building something together.

We frequently express frustration with leadership teams who make all their decisions behind closed doors and ask themselves, "How are we going to sell this to our organization?" Identifying the need to persuade at this point in the process is entirely the wrong approach. At the start of their discussions and deliberations, someone should have asked, "Whom do we need to involve?" in order to bring dissenters into the fold and apply more persistent influence to their thinking.

The opportunity to co-create gives everyone "skin in the game." Defining the vision as a collective endeavor helps frame how future discussions and arguments will progress and be resolved. High-performing leaders know this all too well—it is always preferable to build something together, to help each person see the value they contributed, and then to help each of them describe this new approach with enthusiasm to the rest of the organization.

As we have developed our discussion regarding influence, we have described a complex process of back-and-forth between parties, where the agitating party seeks multiple ways to get another person to change their perspective. Simply telling another person what to do is an ineffective way to apply influence and persuade them to follow a new course of action. A leader who uses their position to assert authority might achieve short-term "wins" but will surely pay a long-term price.[22]

DIRECT, ASSERTIVE, AND CHALLENGING LEADERSHIP

Research Definition: Being assertive, without being aggressive, is extremely important, and leaders who get this balance right are more highly regarded by others, who are then more likely to accept their argument and see them as leaders who operate with integrity. The self-confidence that can cause assertiveness can also lead to higher levels of leadership courage and the ability to make difficult decisions.

A third aspect of leadership pressure has been less well studied, and we found this characteristic in many high-performing leaders. It is based on a leader making an argument with an authoritative tone or style. It typically involves forceful assertiveness and is a characteristic, trait, or disposition found in some but not all individuals. It's a natural capability that, when present, demands attention from others. This capability is associated with an insistent feeling. It's difficult to ignore.

There is a fine line between assertiveness and aggression, and to keep on the right side of this line, a leader needs to pay careful attention to others' views and not behave in a way that closes people down. Leaders who possess this capability have no problems asserting their presence in a way that captures attention and demands that others pay attention. They draw considerable authority from their self-assurance and make their argument firmly, fairly, and with sensitivity to others. This enables them to establish control during a contentious discussion or to calm people down if they become too argumentative.

A major benefit of assertiveness is that it leaves others in no doubt where a leader stands on issues, which is important in establishing clarity and removing politics from the equation. Assertive leaders stand their ground and are rarely bullied. They just have to be careful not to bully others. When navigating disagreements, they focus their attention on the issue at hand and are careful not to attack or demean the person. Far from being bullies themselves, assertive leaders are very good at dealing with instances of poor or unacceptable conduct.

Regulating Our More Assertive Tendencies

When some form of negotiation is required, whether due to disagreement, the consideration of options for implementation, or balancing competing resource needs, high-performing leaders show sophistication and sensitivity in deciding how hard to press for what they want. An excellent 2017 research paper defined "interpersonal assertiveness" as playing out on a scale, with low assertiveness leading to passivity, withdrawal, and avoidance of disagreement and high assertiveness bringing about resistance to yielding, competition, and coercion.[23] The researchers argued that people judge themselves and others along this scale, which reflects the degree to which a person "stands up and speaks out for their own positions when they are faced with someone else who does not want the same outcomes."

The authors concluded that "too little" and "too much" assertiveness can be problematic, but this was an argument about quantity, not effectiveness. They found that assertive behaviors can be highly effective, provided individuals show a high level of "self-regulation." They saw the most effective examples of assertive behaviors during negotiations where leaders were able to make precise offers to appeal to the disagreeing party, along with developing compelling rationales that were supported by data rather than just allowing the data to make the case for itself.

In our own research on high-performing leaders with more assertive characteristics, we rarely saw these leaders stray into more aggressive, bullying behavior. These leaders tend to be quietly confident without being arrogant. They appear relaxed and make clear eye contact during conversations. Their spoken word is well modulated, neither overexcited nor subdued. Most importantly, they never try to be the smartest person in the argument—they simply speak openly and directly until the negotiation reaches a conclusion. Consequently, these leaders tend to be seen as more honest and forthright, with a greater degree of integrity.

Assertive and Effective Communication

In his 2020 book, *The Keys to Being Brilliantly Confident and More Assertive: A Vital Guide to Enhancing Your Communication Skills, Getting Rid of Anxiety, and Building Assertiveness*, Richard Banks argued, "If you can be assertive at work, you will feel confident knowing that you can handle any situation that presents itself to you throughout your workday."[24] Banks identified several obstacles to assertive communication, and these highlight how difficult it is for a dispositionally nonassertive leader to acquire this capability (adapted by psychologist Jeremy Sutton):

- They don't know what they want.
- They aren't sure of their emotions and assume that everything is anger.
- They feel as if their needs don't matter.
- They want to be liked at all costs.
- They become flustered and cannot communicate effectively.
- They are uncertain or insecure about their abilities, skills, and Talents.
- They have experienced excessive criticism in the past.

- They fear saying the wrong thing.
- They worry about hurting or offending others.
- They are afraid they will be "found out" (imposter syndrome).
- They are afraid of being challenged.
- They fear retaliation.
- They are afraid of what people will think.

A leader's degree of anxiety in each of these characteristics is a good indicator of where they sit on the assertiveness scale. The more extreme the self-analysis, the more difficult it will be for such a leader to show effective assertiveness at work. If a leader looks at these fears or anxieties and doesn't feel the same degree of concern, this doesn't make them naturally effective at assertive communication. There are several elements that positively contribute to assertive leadership:

- Context is important. Some companies do a good job of stamping out disagreement and assertive conduct, usually because the CEO and leadership team feel threatened by this behavior. This context requires careful reflection by the leader to determine what level of assertiveness is productive. These considerations are never easy, yet it is essential to get them right.
- Be prepared to say no. This is important with respect to the boundaries a leader feels are important. A leader might say no for a number of reasons, but a primary one is that what is being asked or considered requires them to compromise their ethics or beliefs. In these situations, "no" is followed by careful reasoning.
- Speak for yourself. Arguments claimed to be made on behalf of others use collective language: "We believe…" Assertive leaders make sure to speak for themselves, and their arguments are "I think…" to ensure that people are absolutely clear about where they stand.
- Address the best argument being made.[25] A temptation of weaker leaders is to argue against a "straw man" rather than against the very best points being made. This can generate negative reactions and leads to others believing the leader lacks integrity. Addressing

a strong argument head-on establishes a leader's credibility and seriousness.

- High-performing assertive leaders don't let emotion cloud their judgment when the stakes are high. They maintain control and moderate their voice. By remaining calm but insistent, they are able to listen better to what others are saying and respond directly to their arguments.

- Recognize how assertive you are.[26] In 2011, Murphy, Ackerman, and Handgraaf developed a measurement scale of what they called "social value orientation" that captured aspects of assertiveness strength and awareness in individuals. This was amended slightly to produce this self-assessment:[27]

  * Do you look people in the eye when you are talking to them? Can you recall their eye color or what their glasses looked like?
  * Do you project your voice clearly? Are you asked to repeat yourself or speak up?
  * Do you speak with confidence? Are your sentences full of "um"s and "uh"s?
  * Do you stand up tall? Are you slouching?
  * Do you feel comfortable around others? Are you relaxed or uptight?
  * Can you express how you feel?
  * Do you feel anger, annoyance, or frustration? Is this obvious to others?
  * Do you offer your opinion even when it may be unpopular?
  * Do you defend yourself when incorrectly blamed for something?

A series of negative responses to these questions might suggest that a leader will struggle to be sufficiently assertive at work, which might limit their overall effectiveness.

Assertiveness and Gender Stereotypes

Our final point on "assertiveness" in leadership is with concern to gender stereotypes and how these differ for male and female leaders. In their excellent article

"From Aggressive to Assertive," Mary Maloney and Patricia Moore recounted the biased and contemptible treatment of tennis star Serena Williams when she played at Wimbledon in 2018:[28]

> We watched with mounting concern as Serena Williams challenged the chair umpire in the 2018 Women's Final of the U.S. Open this past September. "Stay cool," "Walk away," "Don't get him mad," we said to ourselves and the television. But she did not take our advice. She firmly disputed the warning that she was being coached from the sidelines, which is a violation women get called for more than men in tournaments.[29]

> Soon after, she broke her racquet in frustration at missing a point, for which she was then penalized a point. She vigorously challenged that penalty, accusing the umpire of "stealing" from her and treating her differently than men. For that, she was penalized a game, which is a rarity in Grand Slam matches. Serena lost the match, later dissolving into tears.

> Outrage followed, and not just from women. The crowd at the U.S. Open booed the officials. Billie Jean King and others took to the airwaves and social media to call the umpire sexist.[30] Even tennis "bad boys" John McEnroe and Jimmy Connors agreed that the umpire behaved in a sexist way toward Serena. They reminded us that they name-called, broke racquets, and even swore at tennis officials during matches and, while sometimes fined, they were never docked a whole game.[31] The chair umpire and other U.S. Tennis officials stood by the decision to go by the book.

Assertive women are judged in very different ways than assertive men. "Aggressive behavior in men is seen as decisive, forceful, ambitious, and leader-like; it is often commended and even rewarded. Aggressive behavior in women is seen as hysterical, domineering, bitchy, and certainly not rewarded."[32] It is highly likely that both implicit and explicit (unconscious and conscious) bias are at play, creating a clear double standard that discriminates against women.[33]

There is no easy answer to this predicament. Leaders should pay careful attention to who talks in meetings and for how long. Research consistently finds that men occupy more meeting time than women, and in more competitive teams, where people seem to talk over each other and some team members are more interested in trying to make their point than in listening to the person who is speaking, women do less well.[34] It seems that men exhibit a greater sense of their own power in these situations, which correlates strongly to volubility (the amount of time they talk). Women tend to feel that the more they speak, the less favorably they'll be viewed.

We've been fortunate to study high-performing male leaders who effectively manage gender dynamics on their teams and have identified a number of positive patterns that certainly help address these perceptions:

- Don't allow individuals to talk over each other. We have seen examples of leaders requiring a direct comment or question about what was just said before they can advance any argument or opinion of their own. This seems to help place the contributions of female leaders on an equal footing with those of their male counterparts.
- Rotate team leadership responsibility. Rather than the team leader managing every meeting, the responsibility is rotated across all team members. Again, this enables female team members to contribute on equal terms.
- Choose neutral territory when planning social events. High-performing leaders show great care in choosing activities that draw team members together. Museum tours, escape rooms, and community volunteering are just a few examples of activities that more inclusive teams might pursue.
- Make sure that quieter (less voluble) team members' voices are heard. We have seen some very good examples of leaders who actively seek the opinions of quieter team members (often women) in meetings.

They prime these individuals in advance of their intent to do so and give them time to prepare and deliver their opinions with appropriate thought and confidence.

Courage to Make Difficult and Unpopular Decisions

Our final point is with respect to leadership "courage." Courage is an extension beyond assertiveness. We define "courage" as a leadership characteristic, trait, and disposition that enables a leader to make a difficult decision or take action that is unpopular and/or strongly resisted by others. It is typically seen in ethical situations where a leader clearly perceives right or wrong behavior, but others see shades of grey. These are nearly always related to acts of omission or commission.[35]

Leadership courage is highly correlated to leadership integrity.[36] In our research on high-performing leaders, we observed leadership courage in the following scenarios:

- Terminating a high-performing employee for ethical misconduct
- Terminating a moderately performing employee
- Articulating a restructure that leads to their own job disappearing
- Suggesting the sale of the business unit they are leading
- Resigning rather than implementing a proposal they disagree with

Courage isn't just a direct challenge of others, although this can certainly happen. It is more a challenge of self. Courage requires leaders to face up to the most serious perceptions of risk and to make the right decision when easier options might be available. So, while assertiveness is clearly visible in the way a leader engages with others, courage is what helps a leader face the most challenging opinions and attitudes. These might involve others, but they are typically indicative of a leader's internal fortitude. Perhaps the best test of leadership courage is this question: "Could you terminate your best friend if their performance was subpar?"

WHAT REALLY MATTERS

Effective influencing plays out over a longer period to change hearts and minds and influence the thinking and actions of an entire organization. Awareness of these traits and characteristics, along with the assembly of a team that can apply them to the appropriate situations, is essential in ensuring that leaders can meet the expectations they've set:

- High-performing leaders fight against complacency in their teams and wider organization. Although they solve difficult problems and challenges, they also cause some of their own by applying pressure to parts of the organization that might not be showing negative symptoms but could be much better.
- High-performing leaders deploy an array of different persuasive techniques and processes designed to effect their desired change. They are driven not by competitiveness, or a desire to "win" the argument, but by their view of the benefits to the organization and what is required to bring these about.
- Speaking up and standing their ground, while balancing these attributes with sensitivity in interactions with others, enables high-performing leaders to exert influence. Without this balance, more concerning elements of typically male leadership dominate, which can silence the opinions of others, particularly women and minorities.
- Being assertive, without being aggressive, is extremely important, and leaders who get this balance right are more highly regarded by others, who are then more likely to accept their arguments and view them as leaders who operate with integrity. The self-confidence that can cause assertiveness can also lead to higher levels of leadership courage and the ability to make difficult decisions.

Inspiring others to action is a critical function of leadership. You may be a leader who leads through the strength of your influencing Talents if

- you know your mind and speak with authority and confidence;
- you like to reason things through with others and help them understand the issues around them;

- you like to "stir the pot" and enjoy challenging others to think differently; and
- you like to take charge and manage and lead others.

Here are key questions to keep asking yourself:

- Do I take the time to really listen to what others are saying?
- Do I struggle to deliver direct, honest, and challenging feedback to others who might not be performing very well?

CHAPTER 8

Increasing Connectivity

THE POWER AND IMPACT OF SOCIAL NETWORKS, BOTH INSIDE AND OUTSIDE work, was first discovered by researcher Nicholas Christakis and popularized in his 2009 book with James Fowler, *Connected: The Surprising Power of Our Social Networks and How They Shape Our Lives*.[1] They found that "with every step away from an individual in a social network we take, the number of ties to other humans, and the complexity of the branching, rise very, very fast."

In their paper from 2011, Rand, Arbesman, and Christakis established that more fluid, dynamic social networks promoted cooperation and provided insight into some of the ways work silos might be breached.[2] In these dynamic networks, bonds are formed with cooperators and selectively broken with detractors. A "rewiring" of the network occurs, and an interesting phenomenon emerges—detractors tend to change their behavior so that ties can be reestablished, and more stable cooperation results.

In the book *The Social Instinct: How Cooperation Shaped the World*, Nichola Raihani made the point that our social instinct and need to build networks are part of our evolved state and that although all humans have this characteristic and need, only a few possess these capabilities to an exceptional degree.[3] Through our own research, we've studied leaders who intentionally build and cultivate their network because of the benefits this produces. They build relationships with people who will challenge their ideas and delight in picking holes in their thinking. They establish relationships before specific work projects demand it in order to accelerate the progress of a newly formed team. They seek out relationships across the breadth and depth of their organizations to more firmly establish two-way communication between leadership and frontline employees. This becomes both a source of advice and a means of extended influence. They constantly seek to expand their relational network as a potential source of candidates for future recruitment efforts. The very best leaders we have studied hold a relational map of their organization in mind and consistently seek to add connections that strengthen this network. At the very top levels of leadership, many of these new connections are external—outside the organization.

There are three critical issues for leaders when forming relationships that matter:

First, high-performing leaders display elevated levels of self-awareness as well as the ability to read others. They are sensitive to conditions that might compromise cooperation across the network, picking up on pockets of negativity and resistance that require careful engagement.

Second, the best leaders build close relationships and make targeted investments in their best performers. They are highly selective about which nodes in the network require reinforcement in order to increase the organization's chances for success. They spend much more of their time with their best performers.

Third, high-performing leaders know they are accountable for the overall integrity of the network. They hold themselves and others to the highest ethical standards and understand that some ties must be severed in order to add new connections that allow the organization to strengthen and grow over time. Ties with those who fail these ethical tests are nearly always severed and never rehabilitated.

Increasing Connectivity involves

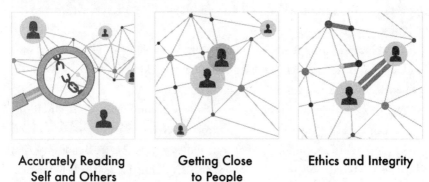

| Accurately Reading Self and Others | Getting Close to People | Ethics and Integrity |

AN ACCURATE READING OF SELF AND OTHERS

Research Definition: High-performing leaders are constantly curious about the subtle differences between people. They read individuals extremely well and vary their approach to issues such as praise and recognition and performance management.

In our study of high-performing leaders, we identified a capability that was such a natural feature of how they operated that they had little conscious awareness of its strength and how it helped them build and manage the relationships they developed. The term we coined to describe this capability is "Individualized Perception," which boils down to two main elements:

First, a high level of self-awareness. This describes an elevated sense of self and how these leaders' personal traits and capabilities helped them interact positively with the people around them or sometimes got in the way.

Second, an extraordinary ability to "read" other people and see their emotional and psychological state alongside a deep and accurate description of their personal traits and characteristics, particularly their predispositions and emotions.

Self-Awareness Fuels Authenticity and Self-Efficacy

Self-awareness is leaders' conscious (rather than unconscious or assumed) knowledge and understanding of themselves related to how they perceive their character, feelings, motives, and desires and how these affect their interactions with others.

Psychologist Philippe Rochat described self-awareness as "arguably the most fundamental issue in psychology, from both a developmental and an evolutionary perspective."[4] Even this might be an understatement.

We discussed in an earlier chapter how self-confidence and self-efficacy intersect in enabling superior outcomes from early career through life, and self-awareness is another component that contributes to this. Albert Bandura (1977), who developed the modern theory of self-efficacy defined it as "the belief in one's capabilities to organize and execute the courses of action required to manage prospective situations."[5] To paraphrase his work, a person's belief in their ability to succeed sets the stage for how they think, feel, and behave:

- Someone with strong self-efficacy views challenges as mere tasks to be overcome and is not easily discouraged by setbacks. They are aware of their flaws and abilities and utilize these qualities to the best of their ability.
- Someone with a weak sense of self-efficacy evades challenges and quickly feels discouraged by setbacks. They may not be aware of these negative reactions and therefore may struggle to change their attitude.[6]

Having a strong and, more importantly, accurate perception of self is required for high-performing leadership. Self-awareness enables a person to judge how frequently they contribute to meetings, how strongly they assert their position, and the types of questions they might ask. If you meet a leader who struggles with feedback and becomes defensive or dismissive when they receive it, they are likely lacking self-awareness.

How many times have you encountered people who are both blind and insensitive to these issues? Like a bull in a china shop, they lack finesse and say things that prolong conflict rather than resolve it. A realistic sense of self helps a leader calibrate in real time to ensure that the right balance is struck to achieve goals and move issues forward.

Accurately Reading People

"When You Hear the Term 'People Person,' What Comes to Your Mind?"

When you hear someone being described as a "people person," is this enough for you to know what is meant? Does it contain all the complex code you need to understand what kind of person you'll be dealing with? Leaders with an elevated ability to read people see each person as an individual with unique talents and capabilities. As if peeling back the layers of an onion, they get to the core of what makes people tick.

In his excellent book *How to Know a Person: The Art of Seeing Others Deeply and Being Deeply Seen*, David Brooks described this capability very clearly, although he stated that humans aren't wired to do this well.[7] He noted that people who are great at reading others ask very different questions and focus very clearly on the stories they tell. Brooks made the same observation that we make about high-performing leaders: they are driven by an insatiable curiosity about the people who are important in their lives.

Listen carefully to your peers and colleagues describing people and situations. Their use of superficial generalizations and category labels indicate someone who lacks a more sophisticated ability to read people. If they find these broad categories helpful, they are less interested in people as individuals. Their assumptions will lack depth and sincerity, and so will the relationships (if any) that are subsequently built. They will simply put people in broad boxes and make similar assumptions about what each box means.

This satisfaction with broad category labels is anathema to our high-performing leaders. Seeing people as individuals requires a leader to be attentive to subtle and unique aspects that describe the individual. High-performing leaders are fascinated by these differences because they might influence how individuals can be positioned to make their best and strongest contributions.

We interviewed a high-performing leader who provided an excellent account of this. Her response to the "people person" question was as follows: "What do you mean by 'people person'? Do you mean selling to people? Listening to people? Challenging people? Persuading people? Spending social time with people? Changing people's minds? Coaching and mentoring people? Helping people? Beating people? Arguing and debating with people? Sharing ideas with people? Brainstorming? Whiteboarding? Being a people person isn't just one thing."

Knowing What's Going On

A friend of mine from many years ago made a career choice to join the local police force in their traffic division. Although he could drive a car, he went through the police driver training school, and it completely opened his eyes, literally, to what was expected.

He described a full week of high-speed training. There would be three supervising officers in the police car observing him, giving instructions, and asking random questions. The first request was for him to maintain a speed of 50 mph along twisty country roads with many blind bends and corners. The pressure to maintain speed and concentration was intense. While my friend was going around a sharp corner, maintaining speed, an officer in the back asked, "What was the registration number of the red truck you passed five minutes ago?" My friend had to answer. "How many occupants are there in the car three vehicles behind?" His answer needed to be exact and correct; otherwise, he failed the test that day and had to repeat it. "What was the telephone number on the ad billboard for the Ford car dealership we passed twenty minutes ago?" "How many pedestrians are waiting at that bus stop on the opposite side of the road? How many were wearing brown shoes?" And so on.

It was intense and required phenomenal observation skills and perfect recall under considerable pressure. It requires extraordinary Talent to be able to pass this test, and my friend did so. Learning that being a traffic cop was more than just being able to drive fast cars safely and issuing traffic tickets was an eye-opener for me. It was only when I studied high-performing leaders that I saw similar characteristics of observation and recall, but this time with respect to people in companies.

Accurately Reading Situations

The capacity to read people is distinct from the ability to read situations and events, and high-performing leaders can typically do both.

We have observed countless meetings in organizations, from the boardroom to the executive suite to business and functional reviews. One common and predictable pattern is that individuals become engaged and animated when an item on the agenda related to their specialty comes up for discussion. But when the moment passes and the discussion shifts, you learn a lot by watching how these leaders subsequently behave.

Most are paying vague attention to the contributions of their peers (we call this "passive listening"), and in some cases, they check out in order to check missed messages on their phone—under the table surface, of course. A small number stay dialed in and attentive to everything happening in the room. They scan for subtle changes in body language, taking note of comments that elicit a positive or negative emotional reaction in others. They are actively reading the room and the situation, and the insights they glean will influence their future behavior.

"Do You Always Seem to Have a Good Sense of What Is Going on Throughout Your Company?"

High-performing leaders with this sensibility seem to always maintain a good feeling for the "pulse" of their organization. Keeping their antennae switched on gives them an excellent ability to detect variance in perspective. As they walk the corridors and converse with colleagues, they show great intuition and pick up on signals that demand further investigation. In subsequent meetings, these high-performing leaders are the ones most likely to highlight pockets of negativity they encountered on their travels and help the team determine how best to engage and turn this around.

This behavior is nearly always not a matter of conscious choice; it is automatic. It is their natural Talent and a phenomenal way to manage the variable elements that drive team effectiveness. They never switch off.

Reading People
Seeing subtle differences that make
each person unique

Reading Situations
Maintaining a good sense of the
pulse of the organization

GETTING CLOSE TO TEAM MEMBERS AND PARTNERS

Research Definition: The very best leaders build highly effective relationships that don't compromise their objectivity. They are powerful coaches and mentors, and they help their most Talented players perform to their highest potential. They intentionally seek to expand their network and influence.

While completing the research for *Strengths Based Leadership*, Tom Rath and I paid careful attention to the factors that caused followers to feel so positively about the leaders they most admired. While "stability," "trust," and "hope" (three of the four Follower's Needs we identified) might top the list in the opinion of most intelligent observers, and we found strong research evidence supporting their importance, "compassion" (the fourth Follower's Need) was viewed as more surprising.

Following the book's publication, many commentators questioned how strong the research evidence for compassion really was. People were puzzled that other factors—like strategic direction—weren't seen as more valuable. It turned out that compassion was the strongest of the four Follower's Needs. So much for expert opinion.

We used the term "compassion" to describe the very deep and genuine affection that followers felt for their high-performing leaders—many used the term "love" in the affectionate sense. They felt a deep relational connection with the leaders they most admired, who showed tremendous insight into and empathy for those they led.

The breadth, depth, and strength of relationships built and developed by leaders helps employees identify powerfully with the organization, what it stands for, and the importance of their contribution in working there. However desirable or important you believe this identity to be, it figures in just about every credible measure of employee engagement. Where data links identity to organizational performance outcomes, it should certainly attract your attention.

Although evidence for the importance of relationship building in organizations is compelling, significant numbers of leaders are cautious and sometimes negative about its value and impact. Gallup researchers have tracked this phenomenon through their engagement survey, which includes the statement "I have a best friend at work." Respondents struggle to score this statement "high" for reasons that seem to contradict its intent, and their opinions are certainly at odds with Gallup's research findings.[8]

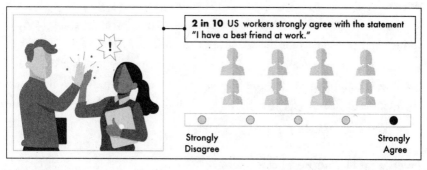

Source: Patel and Plowman, "The Increasing Importance of a Best Friend at Work."[9]

Less effective leaders who question the value of having a best friend at work equate this to playing favorites, which could negatively impact team morale and functioning. They go a step further to say it crosses an invisible, but very real, line that might compromise a leader's decision-making in difficult situations. This is more of an argument about their limitations than a principled argument about the importance of close relationships between a leader and those who follow them. The best leaders we studied, and continue to observe, simply don't see this line, and their close relationships don't limit their ability to make difficult decisions regarding those closest to them, including termination where necessary.

There Should Be No Line

"Should a Leader Help Their Employees, No Matter What the Circumstances?"

We regularly ask this question of leaders, and the same people who struggle with the "best friend" question invariably say "No." They worry that helping an employee who might have committed bad acts or behaved illegally, even criminally, might reflect on them if they offered help. Those who keep their distance don't see the sad indictment of their leadership that this attitude reveals.

"Help" doesn't mean agreeing with a person's actions or unconditionally supporting their perspective or behavior. It is about a more fundamental duty of care from one human being to another. Should a leader help their employees, no matter what the circumstances? "Yes" is the resounding answer from a high-performing leader who is highly invested in the success and well-being of others.

In countless cases, we have heard terminated employees speaking of their respect and admiration for the actions of these leaders: "They were right to terminate me, but they helped and cared for me as they walked me out the door." While it is certainly true that you learn a lot about a company, their values, and the quality of their leaders by the way they hire people, you learn even more about them through the way they let people go.

Investment in Your Best Performers

A major concern of many CEOs is that individuals who remain in their role for a long period can become "blockers" who prevent the upward mobility of Talented employees occupying roles that could serve as good developmental pathways to high-level executive positions. We described a "blocker" in our Preface—a weak, white, male leader who suppressed the potential of a female Aborigine leader. This problem disappears when leaders take significant professional and personal pride in helping elevate Talented individuals to roles directly above them without feeling slighted, overlooked, or undervalued themselves.

This is precisely the focus and drive of high-performance leaders. They actively invest their time in the growth and development of others because building the leadership capabilities of Talented individuals across the company is the right thing to do. Furthermore, our high-performing leaders know that this task is much easier if they appoint strong leaders to their own teams—individuals who are stronger than they are.

What does this investment look like? What are our high-performing leaders doing to develop and nurture the Talents and capabilities of rising stars?

The answer is counterintuitive, yet it is better understood these days than it was twenty years ago, when I first wrote about this issue. Quite simply, they spend the most time with carefully selected individuals who represent the best chance for success in elevated roles in the future.[10] Yet they manage the act of selection and focus investment in ways that are not immediately obvious and still allow other team members to feel cared for, supported, and important in their leader's eyes.

Fairness Doesn't Mean What You Think

Time and again, we hear leaders who struggle to build high-performing teams say, "I am diligent in conducting one-on-one discussions with each member of my team each week."

As a measure of effectiveness, this is hopeless; as an indicator of impact and value, it contributes nothing. It's as though these leaders see fairness and equal time as evidence of their effectiveness—each employee gets their fair and equal share. This concept of fairness runs counter to the more effective approach of high-performing leaders.

In his book *Moral Minds: How Nature Designed Our Universal Sense of Right and Wrong*, Marc D. Hauser argued that fairness was a highly developed and evolved concept in humans that elicited formalized and standardized behavioral responses.[11] He quoted George Lakoff's ten types of fairness to illustrate this:[12]

Type of Fairness	Specific Example of Fairness
Equality of distribution	Every person gets one meeting
Equality of opportunity	Everyone is eligible to apply for a job
Procedural distribution	Benefits are rules-based
Rights-based fairness	You get that to which you are entitled
Needs-based fairness	Those who need more get more

Type of Fairness	Specific Example of Fairness
Scalar distribution	Those who work harder get more
Contractual distribution	You give based on what you promised
Scalar distribution of responsibilities	Those who can do more have greater responsibility
Equal distribution of power	Everyone can vote, and each vote is equal

This just goes to show how evolved concepts of fairness really are and how ingrained they are in most people's psyches. However, from the perspective of the high-performing leader, one element of fairness is missing from Hauser's list that needs no explanation:

Type of Fairness	Specific Example of Fairness
Fairness by differentiated performance value	Those who perform the best deserve the highest reward

Lakoff's work does provoke a broader question—have humans evolved to be more sensitive to issues of fairness than to the achievement of outcomes and performance? We argue that as strongly as some individuals believe that the concept of fairness implies "equal," the concept of fairness based on differentiated performance outcomes is also strongly felt, but by much fewer people.

For instance, how did you feel participating in group projects during college, where everyone received the same grade regardless of how much or how little effort they contributed? Did this seem fair and right to you? Lakoff seems to have missed the importance of this type of fairness, yet it is fundamental to the approach of the high-performing leader.

Focusing a Leader's Investment

The primary development focus of high-performing leaders when investing time in their rising stars is on two areas as a starting point:

First, challenging thinking and raising the bar regarding elevated thought processes.

Second, helping employees build a constituency to grow their visibility and influence across the organization. Other important leaders need to know about them—to at least know they exist.

Some of the very best leaders we've studied focus their coaching and mentoring on challenging a person's ideas and improving the process of how they think. This is not unlike the proverb attributed to Maimonides that highlights the difference between giving a person a fish and teaching them to catch it. The business equivalent, well understood by high-performing leaders, is that you can point out a solution to a problem, or you can teach and develop the skills that enable a person to do it themselves.

The focus on the process of thinking explains why the second area of focus—building a constituency—is also important. Growing connections and establishing credibility across the organization provides our developing leader with a broader consultative pool against which their ideas and suggestions can be tested and challenged. It sets the expectation that collaboration and consultation are two sides of the same coin and that both are important in developing resilient ideas and plans.

It's not always easy for an emerging leader to get the attention of other leaders across the organization. High-performing leaders see their role as helping break down doors and barriers to access and ensuring that emerging leaders are learning and growing from their association with other high-level leaders and experts. They introduce their protégés in important meetings and showcase their Talents through their presentations and discussions. By the time succession planning and performance review discussions come around, the vast majority of top leaders in the company can match a face to a name and are able to talk intelligently about the person's capabilities and qualities.

ETHICS AND ACCOUNTABILITY

Research Definition: Ethics and accountability are effective partners, and high-performing leaders exhibit both. Their clear, enduring values and beliefs about how to treat people and doing the right thing set the standard that others want to follow.

One of the most important factors contributing to effective relationship building—especially the deep proximal relationships that tend to engender trust—are the ethical and moral values of the leader. This is a complex area, but the concepts are not difficult to grasp. The baseline expectation that provides a foundation for trust to develop is transactional compliance, where commitments are made and then met consistently and without exception.

"Do You Do Exactly What You Say You Will Do?" Is a Critical Question, and You Learn a Lot from a Leader Through Their Response

Leaders who say, "I try to," are leaving the gate wide open for all those occasions when they don't, and these are typically the leaders who struggle the most when trying to build trusting relationships. A surprisingly large number of leaders fail this basic test of their integrity yet still regard themselves as ethical by their own, somewhat dubious standards. For high-performing leaders, meeting commitments is a basic requirement that should never be breached. And they never do.

Doing What You Say You Will

Some commentators are puzzled that we define ethics and accountability within the broader category of relationships and building connections rather than execution. Surely, they argue, accountability is about what you deliver, and delivery is definitely about execution. I had a mild argument about this in a podcast interview in which this criticism was laid out in precisely this way. Our response is very simple—you make commitments to people, not things.

Accountability, and the ethics and integrity that underpin it, is 100 percent about the relationships built between transacting parties. This is why consideration of what it means and why it is important is so critical to effective leadership.

"How Do You Feel When You Let Someone Down and Can't Do What You Committed To?"

This is a horrible situation, and we have yet to talk to a leader who is on the fence on this issue. Everyone detests it. To avoid this, many leaders exercise extreme caution over their commitments. They make few promises and commit only to what they know they can achieve. We suspect these leaders may be difficult to work with, as they are willing to commit to only a small number of things when our expectations likely require much more.

Other leaders have the appetite to devour a large volume of work but lack the capacity to deliver across many fronts simultaneously. Without strong leadership to help them say no, they become overstretched and overcommitted, working all hours of the day and night. These leaders exhibit such strong personal accountability that when things do fall between the cracks, it has a punishing effect on their sense of self-worth and professionalism and makes it even more difficult for them to effectively delegate and let some things go.

The ideal situation is one in which a leader can make extensive commitments and still experience little difficulty in achieving them all; this is where high-performing leaders excel in comparison to their weak or mediocre peers. It is a natural Talent, whereas others have to work much harder and still fall short.

Doing the Right Thing

"Do You Always Need to Do Things Right?"

The broader, and more important, question for leaders is how the judgment of individuals influences current and future behavior in terms of not just doing things right but doing the right thing. High-performing leaders excel in this area.

When we ask leaders if they always try to do things right, their default response is typically yes. The more interesting question is why they behave this way, and there are three variations in response that leaders typically give when we ask them to explain:

Response 1: Doing things wrong might create other problems and would be inefficient and ineffective.

Response 2: There may be personal or professional consequences to doing things wrong.

Response 3: I don't see a choice. I have to do things right; it's just how I'm wired.

The similarity between the first two responses stems from a consequential argument. Leaders who respond similarly to responses 1 and 2 are weighing up the consequences for not doing things right and deciding that this is the least desirable path. They are doing things right to avoid negative repercussions for their professional standing and self-esteem.

We call this an "outside-in" argument, as if some external supervisor or arbiter were imposing negative consequences on the leader should they step out of line. Instead of an intrinsic drive to do things right and do the right thing, these leaders need an external framework and guardrails to keep them on track and point them toward the right outcomes.

High-performing leaders who possess a strong and principled framework for doing the right thing invariably give response 3. They see no choice, no other option than doing things right. Ethics and morality are intrinsic features of who they are and what they stand for. These qualities lie within them and arise to guide their behavior toward doing what is right rather than what might seem more advantageous in the short term.

We call this an "inside-out" approach, not moderated by external perspectives or perception. These leaders do the right thing in circumstances where their actions may go unseen and unacknowledged or, conversely, where they need to make an undesirable and unpopular decision.

Companies that are "rules-based" and attempt to legislate against every potential misdeed completely buy in to the "outside-in" approach to managing their employees. The logic of this mentality is that if the guardrails weren't there or the sense of personal reputational damage wasn't real, individuals would commit all manner of offenses. This is why legal and HR departments in companies write rules and limitations about employee conduct—by telling people what they shouldn't do, they attempt to prevent them from making bad decisions.

High-performing leaders, while they understand the reasoning regarding the setting of behavioral rules and see why this might be necessary, quietly feel offended that this might also apply to them.

Responses of Ethical Leaders with High Accountability:

	Never				Always
Do What I Say	○	○	○	○	●
Do the Right Thing	○	○	○	○	●
Do Things Right	○	○	○	○	●

Leaders with strong accountability are clear, crisp, and definitive in their assessment of right and wrong. They are a consistent and stable presence in their organizations, and others know they can be relied on.

Telling White Lies

Societies have evolved rules that punish lying and cheating, and it is the same for organizations, companies, individuals, and teams. Any group of individuals, aside from actual criminal enterprises (which also have their own rules about the type of behavior they permit), expresses an aversion to dishonest conduct. However, there are some exceptions in the form of what we typically call "white lies," where someone might express a perspective that isn't strictly true but is offered in protection of another person—the truth is stretched as a favor to the other person.

Examples of white lies are making excuses for why you won't be attending a social occasion or offering a response to a child's question that is designed to stop subsequent inconvenient questions. Finesse in telling white lies is learned early by children and reaches levels of sophistication in most adults. In their 1994 research paper "What Makes Strategic Deception Difficult for Children—the Description or the Strategy?" James Russell, Christopher Jarrold, and Deborah Potel argued that deceptive behavior is based on two foundational cognitive skills:[13]

First, knowledge that it is possible to plant false beliefs in the minds of others.

Second, suppressing what is known to be true while expressing what is known to be false.

These behaviors in both children and adults depend on a judgment of whether they are likely to be caught...or get away with it, another classic "outside-in" perspective. It is interesting that most research on lying and cheating by developmental psychologists focuses on this negative behavior rather than trying to figure out why some children—and the adults they become—reject this behavior. It seems that some children, and some adults, choose to behave ethically without needing the fear of being watched to encourage them to do the right thing.[14]

The Wells Fargo Story

There are countless examples of ethical confusion in companies playing out in real time.

One recent, and very public, implosion forever tainted the reputation of one of America's largest and most respected banking institutions. How was it even possible for so many Wells Fargo employees to open so many fraudulent checking and savings accounts for customers without the collusion of those around them, including managers and leaders at several levels? How could these practices be hidden?[15]

To put it simply, they weren't hidden. As leaders in Wells Fargo set aggressive "cross-selling" goals, they unwittingly encouraged the highly unethical behavior that they must have known was happening in the company. This went on for years, with those who knew either turning a blind eye or, even worse, deciding they wanted to join the fast track to easy money and rewards. To this day, as I consider the egregious acts that ruined this once great company's reputation, I cannot understand why no one spoke up.

When the board finally acted, it removed several senior leaders, including the CEO, because it recognized that when trust is so badly broken, it is impossible for those tainted by this activity to ever recover. Too few leaders, knowing what was happening, were prepared to take a stand. Many lost their jobs (too few and too late, in my view). Those that didn't will be forever tainted by their association with these acts.

The ethical lesson is clear—act to protect those responsible for ethical wrongdoing and you will pay a significant price. I feel a profound sense of sadness for the many outstanding employees and leaders (completely in the dark regarding this behavior) who carry the stain of that appalling behavior as they try to salvage what is left of Wells Fargo's credibility.

Is It Possible to Recover?

"What Does It Take for a Person Who Has Ethically Transgressed to Recover with You?"

Too many leaders begin their response to this question with "It depends." They attempt to play the role of "honest broker," parsing the nature of the transgression and what a recovery might mean. The idea of giving people a second chance is appealing. After all, who hasn't made a mistake from which they are determined to recover?

But we aren't talking about the everyday, run-of-the-mill mistakes a person might make in the course of their work. In these situations, individuals deserve an opportunity to recover, or else they might learn that errors aren't tolerated in their organization and risks are to be avoided.

We're talking about ethical transgressions that constitute intentional acts to deceive or defraud. Leaders with a strong ethical grounding, who operate from the "inside out," see no recovery from behavior of this kind. Even if the perpetrators somehow escape termination, their behavior will never be forgotten. Everything that person does will be carefully checked and no assumptions made with respect to its accuracy or efficacy.

Giving free rein to those who ethically transgress is a failure of leadership, as everyone now knows the standards that you hold. Lying, stealing, cheating, defrauding, falsifying, and various acts of deception may be forgivable offenses to some. Highly ethical leaders who deserve the trust of their organizations supply an easy answer to the previously posed question.

Recovery? *No.*

Ethics Aren't Measured on a Probability Scale

At the conclusion of this chapter, we want to return to ethical conduct and its importance to effective leadership. But rather than recapping our earlier arguments, we want to highlight how language about ethics lacks precision and invites some unfortunate assumptions. Consider how you would answer this question: "As you consider the promises you make, how well do you keep them?" It's an intriguing question and one we have asked a lot in our work with leaders. We think it's a relatively straightforward question, and when we started our research by asking it, we never expected the variable responses that resulted. For example, consider responses on a 5-point scale where

5 = Always

4 = Mainly

3 = About 50/50

2 = Rarely

1 = Never

With a forced choice, we would expect the overwhelming majority of leaders to respond 5, with some possibly scoring 4 (who either didn't fully understand the question or suffered a mental aberration while doing so). But we didn't anchor the responses to a scale like this; we asked an open-ended question. The implications of the responses we get are staggering. Relatively few people are so clear and emphatic that they say "Always" or "Without exception."

As challenging as rating scales are, we fare little better when using descriptive language. As you weigh responses to questions about ethics, what does the phrase "almost certainly" mean? How does this compare to "highly likely"? Which is the stronger response? At the other end of the scale, we encounter language like "chances are slight" and "highly unlikely." Which of these terms is a more negative response? Is "probable" the same as "probably"? And where do these two terms stand alongside "likely"? As difficult as rating scales are to interpret, understanding how they operate psychologically is extremely important.

The common feature of responses that aren't definitively *yes* or *no* is the acceptance that leaders won't always keep their promises and that they regard this as an acceptable state of affairs. "I try pretty hard to keep my promises" indicates that you don't try too hard. In terms of ethics and their consequent impact on behavior, the responses should be binary: you either keep your promises or you don't. High-performing leaders understand this distinction very clearly, and weak and poorly performing leaders live life with a constant struggle. We call questions like these "pregnancy questions." Reflect on the number of times a woman has described her newfound maternal state as being "somewhat pregnant."

The Universal Language of Ethics

- There is no such thing as "business ethics," although the *Stanford Encyclopedia of Philosophy* disagrees with us.[16]
- There is no such thing as "legal ethics," although Cornell Law School disagrees with us.[17]
- There really shouldn't be something called "government ethics," but apparently there is... and it seems to be needed.[18]
- There's no such thing as "finance ethics," although the Securities and Exchange Commission (SEC) disagrees with us.[19]

If you take time to read these various versions of ethical standards and conduct, they largely describe and value the same thing—ethics. Just like mathematics, ethics is a universal language, and ethical conduct plays out in different contexts and situations. The fact that some people struggle to speak this language doesn't change this finding. There's no such thing as French algebra or Indonesian double-slit experiments. Ethics requires judgment and deciding to do the right thing, not just when everyone is watching but when no one is watching.

WHAT REALLY MATTERS

Effective leaders find multiple ways to impact the performance, development, and growth of others. They invest in their people, care about them, and genuinely want them to succeed. Fundamentally, leaders know that any organizational success rests on the successes of each person within it.

Building the relationships that help individuals and teams succeed is the product of distinct, related traits and characteristics that few individual leaders possess in full. Awareness of these traits and characteristics, along with the assembly of a team that can collectively accomplish each of them, builds engagement that positively impacts performance:

- High-performing leaders see subtle differences that influence their approach to each person. They remain constantly curious about people. They observe carefully and adjust their behavior in real time. They read people extremely well, which helps them vary their approach to issues such as praise and recognition and performance management.

- The imaginary line that some leaders and managers like to build between themselves and their team members is invisible to high-performing leaders. They build highly effective relationships in a way that doesn't compromise their objectivity. They are effective coaches and mentors, they help team members perform to a high standard, and they hold them accountable for achieving those standards.

- High-performing leaders have clear, enduring values and beliefs about how you should treat people and see clear differences between what is right and what is wrong. Their ethical filter is natural, strong, and a fundamental aspect of how they show up as a leader. They set the bar regarding ethical conduct the highest for themselves and hold similar expectations of others.

Building and cultivating strong ties across your organization is a critical function of leadership. You may be a leader who leads through the strength of your relational Talents if

- you are drawn to more personal and deeper relationships with people who are important to you;
- you feel high levels of sensitivity to how others feel and show empathy;
- you connect with others on different levels and are interested in their growth and development; and
- you tend to consult and be effective at getting others involved.

No matter how close you think you are to people, a leader needs to be intentional about the network they build and the contributions they make to developing the capabilities of those within it. These questions can help increase your effectiveness:

- Am I consciously seeking to expand my constituency and grow my network?
- Am I so focused on achieving goals that I fail to take into account how others might feel?

CHAPTER 9

Controlling Traffic

Keeping the trains running on time" is a phrase typically used in business to describe individuals who manage systems and processes that lead to effective execution. It's a poor metaphor. Trains run on tracks, and we often talk about the need for people to think outside the tramlines. We all know what this means, and the train metaphor fails—please stop using it.

Air traffic control, however, is something all leaders should understand and hold in awe. It is the perfect metaphor for effective execution, and we'll explain why.

The rules and regulations regarding the control of aircraft on the ground, taxiing between gate and runway, and in the air are not difficult to understand.[1] Keeping safe distances between aircraft in all scenarios is key—these are measured in feet on the ground and miles in the air. These rules must never be breached, and on the rare occasions when they are, "near misses" hit the news headlines. Firm rules exist that must never be varied. For example, westbound flights around the world must fly at even-numbered altitudes (like thirty-eight thousand feet), while eastbound flights fly at odd-numbered altitudes (like thirty-nine thousand feet). As long as horizontal spacing rules are maintained, then no aircraft should collide with another. All air travelers reading this can breathe a sigh of relief.

But air traffic controllers need to deal with the unexpected, like poor weather, delayed flights, medical emergencies, and mechanical malfunctions. This can affect flight routes as well as airports and requires deft management. Sometimes these issues happen so quickly that air traffic controllers have no time to prepare. Our scientist meteorologists are often our air traffic controller's best friend. They work hand in glove. The astrologers we talked about earlier aren't much use, and if you hear a pilot mention that he's consulting the almanac to determine whether the moon is entering Sagittarius before changing flight levels, then it's already too late to start praying.

LEADERS AS AIR TRAFFIC CONTROLLERS

The best leaders see effective execution in the same way that air traffic controllers see their work. They manage phenomenal complexity through a framework of rules and guidelines and then have to be incredibly flexible and adaptable when things change in real time. The bottom line for air traffic controllers is probably that, even on the very worst of days, no one dies. All the planes take off and land safely, preferably on time and in the right places. There are no near misses or close escapes. Drastic actions might be taken to reduce load during pressured times—flights do get canceled, for example—but the main goals regarding safety and effective service outcomes are met.

The very best leaders are like air traffic controllers. As you think of effective execution from an executive leadership perspective, keep air traffic controllers firmly in mind. This metaphor perfectly describes your role and accountability. Now that this point has been made clear, every reader will readily understand that not everyone can become a high-performing air traffic controller. It's simply beyond their capabilities. It's no different thinking about execution for high-performing leaders. There is little value in reducing daily plane crashes from 9 percent to 8 percent when the absolute and only goal is 0 percent. It takes a special talent to achieve this level of executional performance.

Our study of high-performing leaders uncovered two often contradictory traits and characteristics that defined effective execution. Navigating these dialectical states is part of what differentiates high-performing leaders from everyone else. For them, execution is more about a way of thinking and planning, adapting, and changing than it is about pure transacting:

First, the high organizational and structural precision that enables effective forward progress in a logical and systematic way. The systematic and structured framework through which work activity is transacted ensures that progress toward goals remains consistent and doesn't deviate. Air traffic controllers are diligent in following rules and procedures that keep everyone safe. These rules have been developed over many years, and as incidents occur that stretch safety margins to their limit, new rules and procedures are developed and implemented to handle them. In work, as in the air, we learn from experience with a constant focus on improvement.

Second, the capacity to manage pace and complexity in an unpredictable, sometimes volatile, environment. The spontaneous, agile, and adaptable characteristics of high-performing leaders enable them to quickly change to meet current and future circumstances. They are air traffic controllers dealing with unpredictable weather, among many other things. They have to predict and react quickly.

Controlling Traffic involves

Structure and Process   Orchestration and Complexity

THE ACTIVITY DRUG

The term "execution" with respect to business has become associated with the implementation of plans—that part of business activity where work is done and things happen. It is unfortunately and unhelpfully seen as distinct and separate from strategy, as we discuss below. All those impatient leaders out there, drumming their fingers on the desktop, anxious for discussions to conclude and meetings to end, can barely restrain themselves from initiating activity and creating the forward momentum that leads to tasks and goals being completed. This need to act is visceral, and many individuals describe the huge satisfaction they receive from just getting things done.

Getting things done satisfies a strong kinesthetic need to be physically busy and active. This becomes visible when observing those individuals who have a hard time just sitting at their desks and working with high levels of concentration—it doesn't take long for them to be up and about, talking, discussing, engaging, and debating, excited by what lies immediately ahead. When the phrase "rolling up your sleeves" is used, it usually means exactly what it states. As dominant as this feeling is at lower levels of an organization, where its value is obvious, there are still significant numbers of leaders at the executive level who feed on the activity drug and can't shake off its all-consuming allure. It's enjoyable. It's fun. But it's problematic.

Execution is synonymous with action. Action makes a lot of people feel good—a surge of adrenaline, a flush of dopamine, a pulse of serotonin driving their sense of concurrent and reflective pleasure in achievement. It's a vindication of their personal and professional effectiveness. A glow of pride in their association with a successful outcome. A job well done. Yet in earlier chapters, we established that speed of response and the inclination to act can be problematic without the right thinking guiding a clear direction. Activity needs to be guided carefully lest problems that could and should be anticipated knock a team or organization off course and lead to inefficient execution, stumbling and meandering, increased costs, and frustration.

Measure Twice, Cut Once

"Measure twice, cut once." My grandfather taught me this principle nearly sixty years ago in his garden shed, which I thought was the most exciting place on earth. He was teaching me how to make a small wooden car. Even though I was unable to hold a saw or chisel, he would show me how to mark pencil lines on scrap wood, and I would practice sawing. When I didn't get it right, he would always say, "Measure twice, cut once."

It has stuck with me through life, not just when making furniture or the guitars I love to build but also when applied to important decisions in completely unrelated areas. It guided me when buying my very first car—was I absolutely sure? It taught me to be cautious and less impulsive. I didn't always remember to apply it when I should, and I sometimes regretted decisions I made when I didn't. I've advised many leaders about this principle to help them to slow down and think of a more effective response or decision—pause, think, check, act. It seems to be an important principle to apply to business execution, and it lies at the heart of what every air traffic controller does.

ELEMENTS OF EFFECTIVE EXECUTION

If diligent thought and careful consideration of ideas and future obstacles are essential in shaping teams and organizations and applying energy to issues in the right way, it is also essential for effective execution to balance the systems, resources, and structures that will most likely lead to successful outcomes. At the leadership level, where the direction for work is set, effective execution demands the creation of guardrails and processes that focus actions in the most productive ways and prevent action-oriented employees from deviating from the preferred path to pursue interesting, nonessential diversions that lead to "dead ends."

Here are the main points of what we learned about execution from researching highly effective leaders.

Execution Is About What You Manage, Not What You Do

To avoid a category error and ensure that our discussion of "executing" adds value to our evolving concept of leadership, it is important that the activity of execution—the "doing"—be attributed to the "drive" of individuals and their source of energy (Chapter 6).

When we discussed the "achievement" drive or the "competitive" drive exhibited as a source of energy by so many leaders, we were describing these traits in terms of how people behave and the actions they are driven to perform. All the practical steps taken by individuals to ensure that work gets done are a product of their drive to act and their determination and tenacity to see things through.

As we talk about "execution" in this chapter, we are more concerned with how leaders manage the process of execution—setting the framework and structure that guide all those actions toward productive outcomes. The distinction isn't subtle, yet too many individuals fail to understand it and will forever experience executional failures.

Execution Sits on a Continuum Alongside Strategy

A mediocre strategy well executed is better than a great strategy poorly executed.

*—Roger Martin, former dean of
the Rotman School of Management*

I'd rather have a first-rate execution and second-rate strategy any time, than a brilliant idea and mediocre management.
—Jamie Dimon, former JP Morgan Chase CEO

Strategies most often fail because they aren't well executed.
—Larry Bossidy and Ram Charan,
Execution: The Discipline of Getting Things Done

In his thought-provoking article "The Execution Trap," Roger Martin, former dean of the Rotman School of Management at the University of Toronto, raised valid questions about the strategy-execution divide.[2] He made three telling references and rightly questioned how a strategy can be described as brilliant if it ultimately fails:

1. Strategy and execution aren't neatly divided functions—one developed by leaders and the other carried out by minions (or lemmings, as one inadequate CEO unhelpfully described his employees). The detailed consideration that goes into deciding how things are done is a way of thinking that connects the initial ideas to the specific actions that will be taken to ensure that progress is made toward goals. A strategy that ultimately fails because it avoids important executional considerations can never be described as "brilliant."

2. For strategy and execution to succeed, it is important for organizations to blur the divide that traditionally exists between the two and make them bidirectional. Rather than dividing responsibilities—we get to choose; you get to do—the best strategies are nearly always the product of judging what is possible. This judgment requires the perspective of those who are implementing and those who are affected by those choices applying their influence early in the process to prevent bad or unrealistic ideas from gaining steam and then to ensure that there is a dynamic flow of information that enables strategy to be recalibrated in line with executional realities.

3. A "bad idea" is one that requires the organization to do what intelligent observers recognize can't be done. An important caveat here is to acknowledge that sometimes strategy needs to force an organization to evolve its systems and processes to be able to transform its performance. Understanding this distinction is extremely important to ensure that potentially groundbreaking ideas aren't strangled at conception through the resistance of an unimaginative and resistant organization. High-performing leaders see this distinction and challenge very clearly.

Execution Requires More Than Alignment

What if many organizations achieved excellent alignment along the strategy-execution continuum? Would this heal the strategy-execution divide? One possible indicator would be the way important objectives were developed, understood, and implemented. One approach to strategy-execution measurement—Peter

Drucker's management by objectives (MBO)—attempted to achieve this. The good news for Drucker is that many organizations (based on survey data) seem well aligned on these measures and how the work of teams and individuals is commonly directed. And yet, despite this apparent alignment, strategies still fail to deliver on their promises. Sull and Spinosa offered six main obstacles to effective execution:[3]

1. Too many organizations have "silos" that get in the way of effective coordination.
2. Employees are disengaged and don't work effectively together.
3. There is no clear accountability for when things go wrong.
4. Organizations lack the agility to respond to change.
5. There is a lack of trust between stakeholders and executives, with lots of finger-pointing.
6. There is an organizational fear of moving from the status quo.

The solution to these obstacles is always people, and typically managers, where the problems take root and where negative attitudes develop and propagate. The "solution" is clear—hire effective managers. The managers who created these problems are unlikely to be the ones who will solve them.

High-Performing Leaders Dispel Five Common Execution Myths

It has also been argued that the reason for the strategy-execution problem is managers and leaders holding beliefs that are completely untrue, and the ubiquitousness of these beliefs explains why strategy execution is such a major issue for so many organizations. In their article "Why Strategy Execution Unravels—and What to Do About It," Sull et al. identified five unhelpful myths that get in the way of more effective practice.[4] Their work, based largely on survey analysis and observations, led to the following definitions of these myths.

Myth 1: Execution Equals Alignment

Further to the aforementioned point we make, having consistent metrics to measure outcomes doesn't address the suspicions that can lead to poor cross-functional behavior. While employees within a function expressed confidence in how a project was being managed by them, they tended to be extremely negative about their cross-functional partners. Yet most employees would say they were aligned on goals.

Myth 2: Execution Means Sticking to the Plan

No Gantt chart survives contact with reality. As we will discuss shortly, the capacity of leaders to make real-time adjustments in response to rapidly changing conditions reflects a capability to adapt and show executional flexibility. Sometimes it requires revisiting strategic assumptions and reframing the organization's entire approach. Too few leaders exhibit this capability. The psychological basis for most resistance to adaptation is Kahneman and Tversky's "sunk-cost fallacy."[5]

Myth 3: Communication Equals Understanding

Consider this question: "Is learning the inevitable consequence of teaching?" The answer is definitively *no*, to the annoyance of pretty much everyone in the educational and development industry. Receiving great evaluations from students after that class you taught simply suggests that they liked and appreciated what you shared. To assume that learning occurred, we need to see evidence of an altered brain state and better outcomes, which requires us to observe what level of consistent behavioral change occurred afterward. We have already outlined that there are as many identified strategic priorities in a company as there are executives on the leadership team, suggesting how much of an uphill challenge communication work is.

Myth 4: A Performance Culture Drives Execution

While a weak performance culture can certainly kill many strategic-execution challenges, defining performance in binary terms can lead to poor decision-making and short-term accountability. A binary focus and emphasis on getting things done leads to limited outcomes that fail to optimize the capabilities of an organization.

Consider the answer to this question as you evaluate the strength of your performance culture: "Who gets the big annual awards (rewards, recognition, and praise): those who solve problems or those who prevent them?" If your performance metrics favor activity and reaction, you are causing some serious strategy-execution missteps. We have yet to encounter a company that rewards problem preventers over those who, because of many failings in the organization, fought overnight through snowstorms and hostile creature attacks to deliver that important package to a customer that someone failed to mail the day before. Yes, we are talking about your company.

Myth 5: Execution Should Be Driven from the Top

Execution should be seamlessly interactive and bidirectional rather than the "handoff" from thinkers to doers that we typically see. High-performing leaders understand the need to involve a broad constituency in the development of strategic choices and to maintain this collaboration through implementation so that the right adjustments and flexible responses can be made. Why is it that organizations understand the value of keeping close to their customers but not their frontline employees?

Frontline Employees Should Influence Strategic Choices

A determination and drive to uncover more strategic options and possibilities is essential to effective execution, and there should be a serious intent to engage as broad a range of constituents (employees) as possible in all stages of the strategic development process. It remains a puzzle to us why leaders believe strategy to be exclusively their domain. Even worse is the condescending attitude that leads those leaders to think that they understand all the issues relevant to effective implementation. They don't. Nor have they consulted sufficiently with people who do understand these issues.

The reason companies continue to struggle with the strategy-execution problem is that they see strategy and execution as separate and operate on that assumption. We set strategy; you implement. If our strategy fails to deliver the expected (hoped-for) outcomes, it was a failure of execution, because the strategy was developed by important and smart people. The problem is obviously failings in execution. Versions of this perspective permeate most organizations.

So what are the key traits, dispositions, and characteristics of high-performing leaders who manage effective execution? What did we learn in our study of these leaders? It turns out that to be brilliant at execution, two main naturally occurring capabilities need to be present—structure and orchestration.

STRUCTURE AND PROCESS

Research Definition: High-performing leaders work extremely hard to determine an organization's strategic direction and apply the right thinking and planning to projects, ideas, and proposals that both involve team members and help them execute work effectively.

One of the fundamental characteristics of leaders who excel in operating along the whole strategy-execution continuum is structural thinking. This has long been identified as one of the best means of managing systems with the high levels of pace and complexity typically facing most business leaders.[6] Structural thinking helps a leader navigate all the organizational complexity that tends to lead to poor scheduling, ineffective decision-making, bloated inventory, and outsized operating costs.[7]

To make sense of their world, leaders who are strong structural thinkers build a mental map of all the complex variables they are dealing with. The map analogy is interesting because maps contain a tremendous amount of "messy" information that is exact and precise in its description. This exactness can enable pinpoint navigation and the ability to see things from on high that are invisible at ground level. Maps tell us where we are in relation to specific destinations and the broader world around us, probably more so than the GPS we discussed earlier. A leader who thinks structurally can hold an ordered and complex set of information in their mind—information that actually represents the reality that people encounter at ground level—and to provide a big-picture perspective on their world.

When doing separate research on leadership behavior in 2004, I identified a parallel characteristic that I named "making sense of experience."[8] This describes the way leaders make sense of the world around them and communicate that understanding to help others appreciate why their own role and purpose are so important. Structural leaders achieve this clarity by building and communicating mental maps of their organization. These high-performing leaders take a clear and structured approach to thinking through strategy-execution challenges and establish clarity regarding how the interrelationship really works.

This was captured by Cabrera, Cabrera, and Gibson in their 2021 paper "Leapfrog Leaders," which identified four patterns of structural thinking that draw leaders to a more integrated approach to the strategy-execution challenge:[9]

1. **Make Distinctions:** Highlight how one thing might differ from another,
2. **Organize Systems:** Require that ideas be grouped together into defined systems,
3. **Identify Relationships:** See the action and reaction relationships between and among ideas, and
4. **Take Perspective:** Look at ideas or systems of ideas from different points of view.

Elements of Structural Thinking

While these patterns are helpful, we need much more specificity to capture the real value and focus of structural thinking. Evidence from the evaluation of high-performing leaders suggests five granular elements that are important to effective structural thinking.

Systems Thinking

Also described as "connected" or "holistic" thinking, this requires leaders to look at their organizations as a whole so that all the various connections and interdependencies are clearly visible. Understanding the interplay among the components of a system allows them to be reconfigured into something new so that novel approaches and procedures can emerge. As these are implemented, the systems thinker establishes early feedback and information flow to enable small-scale adaptations and adjustments.

Researcher Linda Booth Sweeney, in her article "Systems Thinking: A Means to Understand Our Complex World," defined nine discrete components of systems thinking:[10]

1. See the whole picture rather than single events or snapshots.
2. Understand how the various components of a system interrelate and work together.
3. See how the relationships between elements in a system influence the patterns of behavior and events to which we react.
4. Understand that business (like life) is always moving and changing.
5. Comprehend how one event can influence another—even when the second event occurs a long time after, or far away from, the first.

6. Know that what we see happening around us depends on where we are in the system.
7. Challenge our own assumptions about how the business (or the world) works and be aware of how these limit our thinking.
8. Think about the long- and short-term impact of actions.
9. Ask probing questions when things don't turn out as expected.

While analytical thinking is extremely important and goes deep, systems thinking is the fundamental basis for problem-solving, which itself involves diagnostic and hypothetical thinking. It is a holistic approach to organizational flow based on analysis of how different parts of the system interrelate, communicate, and drive function—played out over time and within the context of ever larger systems from which value is produced.

Systems thinking enables high-performing leaders to target four types of critical issues:

- Issues that lie beyond the expertise or functional focus of any single part of the organization
- Chronic issues that persist, along with their negative effects
- Familiar problems with a known history and effect
- Persistent problems where earlier attempts at resolution were unsuccessful

Effective systems thinking can provoke negative reactions as truth is uncovered. Where a problem or issue is the result of functional or operational failings and errors, attempts to engage and resolve can provoke feelings of inadequacy, blame, and fear as layers of the onion are peeled back. This can sometimes generate defensive and disruptive behavior in employees attempting to cover up or conceal their efforts. Persisting through these negative phases typically leads to breakthroughs and increases in the flow of information.

Despite the multiple directionalities of systems thinking at the whole company level, systems thinkers tend to be linear or sequential when it comes to thinking through the steps toward implementation. Although the holistic perspective guides how attention is directed and focused, implementation is built through a series of interactions and handoffs. This is one reason why we believe companies compartmentalize the strategic development process and keep operationally minded individuals from "tainting" the evolution of strategy—it's back to "we think; you do." The implementation process feels separate and distinct from consideration of possibilities and choices. Of course, too few people think of strategy and execution as *one* process, so the perception persists, and companies reinforce this separation through the way functional responsibilities are allocated and determined.

Process Mindset

How you do things can be as important as the outcomes you achieve, and leaders who are obsessive about getting the process right will typically achieve superior outcomes. While performance is the ultimate arbiter, process excellence is one of the best predictors. Edwards Deming (the Total Quality Management guru) famously said, "If you can't describe what you are doing as a process, you don't know what you are doing."[11]

Our research on high-performing leaders, especially those with strong operations, logistics, or supply-chain backgrounds, shows that the drive to build and develop scalable processes dominates much of the strategic and tactical focus of their work—strategic in the sense of choosing where to focus and tactical in terms of the specific processes to develop. At the most fundamental level, processes attempt to eliminate variation through standardized steps and decision gates.

The important thing about process thinking is that it has relatively little value when considered in isolation from the broader systems thinking of which it is an integral part. We strongly argue that without overarching systems thinking, process thinking will lead to problems being identified in isolation from the systems that produced them. "Solutions" to these isolated problems will fail to take into account the interdependencies that flex throughout a system, and lead to that most undesirable outcome: a problem being "solved" in one part of an organization in a way that spawns six other problems in other components of the system. Without broader systems thinking, a process mindset can create greater inefficiencies than it is designed to resolve.

Process thinking, although it is deployed with the aim of scaling behavior to reduce error and variation, is rarely static. Rather than feeling a sense of smug satisfaction at solving a problem or developing a process, high-performing leaders always wonder what could be improved. A whole field of process improvement and process engineering has evolved to capture and codify these contributions. They enhance process thinking in important ways and raise questions such as the following:

- Is this the best we can do?
- How robust is this process to anticipated and unanticipated change?
- Can changes be made to the process that accelerate achievement of the end state?
- Can changes be made to the process that produce better outcomes?

These questions assume that nothing (even elements that are currently functioning well) is perfect and that everything can be improved—even the things that no one is complaining about. Rather than basking in the glory of their perceived brilliance in solving a problem or developing a process, high-performing leaders always wonder what could be improved and what might be next. We discussed how important this attitude is in Chapter 7 when we described leadership catalysts—people who agitate for change when things seemed to be progressing perfectly well. Process improvement is a different side of the same coin.

Causation

If process thinking starts at the beginning and identifies all the necessary steps that lead to a successful outcome, causal thinkers look at an outcome and consider "How did we end up here?" If only we can understand the antecedent variables, we'll be able to look at outcomes with explanatory clarity. It's a very logical way of thinking, but causation is extremely difficult for most people to understand.

I recall as a young student being fascinated by causation, and when attempting to answer the question of why the World War of 1939 (1941 for Americans) began, I found that causation had many layers. Causation has a macrolevel where the existence of themes creates the overarching conditions for an event as catastrophic as a world war. For example, the conflict in 1939 was actually rooted in the Treaty of

Versailles in 1919 and the severe reparations demanded of Germany that enabled Hitler to leverage the resentment necessary to subvert German democracy. But causation also has microelements, such as the invasion of Poland by Germany and Germany's subsequent invasion of Belgium, by which time war was inevitable.

How we think about causation is extremely important in determining how we understand issues and go about solving problems. If we identify the wrong variables, we might end up with unworkable solutions. Causation is important because it forces us to dig down to the root cause—the trigger event that led to the consequences we are now trying to resolve.

When high-performing leaders conduct root cause analysis, to be sure that they are focusing their energies in the right place, they recognize that roots are complex structures with many interdependent parts shooting off in many different directions. Root cause analysis is an attempt to untangle complex structures to determine how the dominoes lay before they were toppled. This isn't always clear or obvious.

The Agency for Healthcare Research and Quality (AHRQ) determined the following areas of analysis that might shine a light on causal factors, and leaders should systematically work through each one:[12]

- **Institutional/Regulatory:** Whether external, statutory factors put pressure on the system
- **Organizational/Management:** Whether internal, strategic, or policy changes were a factor
- **Work Environment:** Whether budgetary or goal changes created a causal chain
- **Team Environment:** Whether changes to team composition or roles created systemic pressures
- **Staffing:** Whether levels of employee engagement or stress-inducing expectations created tension and pressure on work activities
- **Task-Related:** Whether changes to how tasks are to be completed were not supported by parallel training, leaving employees unsure of protocols
- **Customer Behavior:** Whether changes in customer needs and expectations caused short-term pressure on systems and services

This is a useful framework of demarcation that helps leaders think through the focus of causal disruption and how they should explore the factors that stress system functioning. In each case, it is recommended that leaders develop a hypothesis to test through data gathering and evidence sifting. For example, if the organization made changes to compensation structure that affected how employees are paid, then this should be examined to determine whether affected employees were positive, neutral, or negative about the proposed changes and whether there was any subsequent impact on their performance.

Some authors have argued that root cause analysis should be based on certain principles or assumptions.[13] Tableau, the data-driven online consultancy, outlined the following principles that it follows for effective root cause analysis:

- Focus on correcting and remedying root causes rather than just symptoms.
- Don't ignore the importance of treating symptoms for short-term relief.
- Realize there can be, and often are, multiple root causes.
- Focus on *how* and *why* something happened, not *who* was responsible.
- Be methodical and find concrete cause-effect evidence to back up root cause claims.
- Provide enough information to inform a corrective course of action.
- Consider how a root cause can be prevented (or replicated) in the future.

These "principles" are more guidelines and watch-outs, but they provide a useful checklist to ensure that root cause analysis hits the target and causation is determined accurately. We can imagine valuable work being achieved by following these recommendations. They are useful areas of focus to supplement root cause analysis and provoke the right kind of balance to influence decision-making. But it still takes Talent to operationalize the responses.

Detail Orientation

A detail-oriented person can give a task their undivided attention and catch mistakes, errors, and changes before they become much bigger problems. The value of this is self-evident and extremely important in information exchange and business accountability. Information that progresses from executive levels to the board of directors and the investment community comes to mind as critical reports requiring exact accuracy. Inaccurate or sloppy documentation can be the death knell for how a company's brand is perceived externally.

Because detail orientation is a character trait, it is not something that can easily be developed. This makes it an extremely important team consideration for leaders who struggle with details—do you have someone doing this work on your team? Are they well positioned to operate that way? Every CEO of a publicly traded company knows this requirement immediately, as aspiring leaders should.

Our research has revealed that a relatively small number of people are detail oriented about almost everything, whereas a great majority of people are detail oriented only in specific areas due to a particular interest or need. Leaders should think about and reflect on their personal characteristics to determine their level of detail orientation, especially in relation to the types of situations and information that are more difficult for them to detect.

Here are some typical signs of high detail orientation:

- Double- and triple-checking work before it's handed over
- Having a great memory for numbers and/or events
- A preference for methodical and sequenced work where tasks are completed one after the other
- A satisfaction with the quality, rather than quantity, of work achieved
- Picking up typographical, formatting, syntax, and punctuation errors as you quickly scan a document or send emails
- Finding yourself checking the work of other people, particularly team members, likely without them knowing
- Digging for more data or information before you feel able to start a project

As desirable as some of these characteristics are, some forms of detail orientation extend to less obvious areas—areas that arguably add little value and represent a form of obsession:

- Being unable to sit in a room with a painting out of alignment on the wall without getting up and straightening it
- Constantly shuffling and then squaring papers and documents to align with the corners of a table surface
- Deploying a classification system for books on a bookshelf beyond arranging them by size or color
- Alphabetizing a kitchen spice rack
- Organizing, storing, and retaining an email inbox with at least two designated subcategories for every main organizing category
- Maintaining an immaculate indexed filing system to aid document storage and retrieval
- Organizing clothes in a closet by color, season, formality, length, and so on

Some of these characteristics can indicate a strong "gestalt" tendency, which likely reflects a desire for perfection that can sometimes get in the way of actions because the requirements for precision aren't met...and might never be met.[14] These tendencies can lead others to see highly detail-oriented leaders as inflexible or intransigent despite being supremely well organized. The psychological basis for gestalt predicts that an individual will exhibit a strong desire to group or organize information in four different organizing types:

- **Similarity:** Where things/information/data are sorted because of similar characteristics
- **Proximity:** Refers to information that is adjacent to or physically interdependent on other information or data, such as periodic business performance data for a specific business quarter
- **Continuity:** Where patterns of similar data or outcomes are visible and are perceived to belong together to aid future retrieval

- **Closure:** Where the detail-oriented leader sees gaps in data and where grouping similar items is suggestive of a closure of the gaps

Contingent Thought

Contingent theory claims that there is no best way to organize anything, not least an organization, because the optimal path forward is dependent on changing circumstances and variables that are difficult to predict and control. In 2016, researchers Esponda and Vespa defined contingent thinking as "a form of 'what-if' thinking that entails reasoning about events without knowing whether these events are true or will occur."[15]

The most fundamental question that contingent thinking addresses is "What could go wrong and what are our options for dealing with this?"

Given that "contingency" is in large part the balance of probability of future events, this makes it beyond the reach of many individuals. In their excellent 2019 paper, "Failures in Contingent Reasoning: The Role of Uncertainty," Martínez-Marquina, Niederle, and Vespa argued that contingent reasoning is so difficult because of the amount of uncertainty inherent in every future-state analysis.[16] They described this as follows: "When moving from an environment with one state of known value to one with multiple possible values, two changes occur. First, the number of values to consider increases. Second, the value of the (future) state is uncertain."

Let's look at a practical example to show how hard contingent thinking can be. This scenario was first developed by Samuelson and Bazerman in 1985:

When deciding to acquire a company, a leader has to decide whether or not to purchase a firm with a value of $500m. The leader knows there is an equal chance the firm's value could either be lower than $500m (let's say the lower value is $400m), or higher than $500m (let's say the higher value is $600m). So, although she believes the value to be $500m, she also knows that, with equal chance, it could be $400m or $600m. Without knowing the realization of $500m, the leader submits an offer of P. The leader acquires the firm when P = ≤$500m and her payoff is 1.5 × $500m − P, otherwise she doesn't buy the firm and has a payoff of zero.[17]

In 2009, Charness and Levin showed that even in such a simple version of the problem, with only two contingencies to think of, a large proportion of leaders fail to select the profit-maximizing price.[18] They shoot low and miss, believing they stand a greater chance of maximizing the asset's value. But without the asset, there is no value. Contingent thinking seems to be beyond the reach of many leaders.

What do our high-performing leaders do with respect to contingent analysis? We initially discussed this as an element of strategic thinking, and it has cropped up again as we consider effective execution. They dig for information and data that might disprove their hypothesis. They ask questions about the kinds of obstacles and setbacks that were previously encountered and how unanticipated problems were solved in the past. When researching and observing the best contingent thinkers, their thinking and considerations were anchored around five important areas:

1. **Expect Failure:** High-performing leaders anticipate future problems and develop a plan to deal with each situation. If the negative events they identify don't occur, but some other unidentified issue crops up, the discipline of already having developed detailed scenario planning better equips them to develop plans in real time. A muscle has been built that can now be flexed.

2. **Define Responsibility in Terms of a Person:** A team should never be responsible for a process or action; a person always should be. This person involves and engages others in the contingent analysis, but they take full ownership of the process. They are the ones who ensure that three to five scenarios have been identified and that plans have been developed to deal with each of them.

3. **Obsess About Checks and Balances:** Who else is pressure testing plans and actions? Who is reviewing and monitoring how the plan is shaping up and whether contingencies are being targeted at the right areas? If you fail to detect and control the small things, the big things will become too big to take on. Being obsessive about details ensures that the right focus is brought to bear on emerging issues.

4. **Refine the Plan in Response to Changes in Circumstances:** Weaker leaders cling too long to failing plans in the hope that they might eventually work. Contingent thinkers are agile thinkers who react carefully as circumstances change. In the next section, we develop the idea of agile and flexible thinking as a critically important element of execution.

5. **Keep Close to Your Customers and Frontline Employees:** These are the people for whom problems will create an initial, and potentially significant, impact. Listen to what they say and be attentive to the issues they are talking about. Frontline employees and customers are the early-warning antennae of your business. Whatever is going wrong will typically be felt here first.

These five areas of focus ensure that contingent thinking is taken seriously and that the ability of the organization to adapt to change isn't compromised. Contingent planning inspires confidence and ensures that risk can be managed in a way that frees people to experiment. Far from being the restrictive and limiting force that some people believe it to be, contingent thinking can have uplifting and positive effects in business. If you are trying to build a learning, innovative organization, the liberty afforded by effective contingent thinking is sometimes what is needed in order to remove the blinders and ideate more aggressively. For our top-performing leaders, contingent thinking of this kind comes naturally.

We encourage you to think deeply about the challenges of structure and process in terms of your own traits, dispositions, and characteristics. We are sure some of these descriptions will resonate with you, and others won't. This awareness may be key to becoming an effective leader guiding excellent execution.

ORCHESTRATION AND COMPLEXITY

Research Definition: Things change, sometimes unexpectedly, and leaders need to know when to change, and how quickly, to maintain forward momentum and ensure that teams remain productively engaged. High-performing leaders understand how to manage complex projects and communications so that everyone is aware of what needs to happen next.

Have you ever watched an orchestra playing a piece of music guided by a conductor? All the components that contribute to a musical performance are there… people, instruments, sheet music (a plan)…but none of these matters unless the conductor can control who plays what and when. The conductor is there to create music—beautiful symphonies of coordinated sound that bring the best out of each section and each player individually, keeping the whole ensemble to plan.

The essence of orchestration is the blend of activities, executed with speed and precision, factoring in extreme complexity without dropping a ball or missing a beat.

The fundamentals of business orchestration require leaders, like air traffic controllers and orchestra conductors, to manage a diverse range of complex variables, with their central focus being people. People are generally organized in clearly defined process or functional groups that are responsible for specific activities. Different workflows, overlaps, and handoffs help each functional entity achieve its goals and the overall organization achieve some bigger objective.

The Tension and Complementary Nature of Structure and Orchestration

If structure and process anchor one element of execution, the leadership trait of orchestration, alongside the ability of leaders to manage complexity, anchors the other. These two parts—structure and orchestration—seem to be in tension, almost as though they contradict each other. Our argument, though, is in the power of how they complement each other.

"How Do You Feel When, Just After You've Sorted Out What to Do, Everything Changes, and You Have to Start Over?"

This is clearly a question that highlights the balance between an assumed "steady state" and change. Responses to the question bifurcate dependent on how one feeling dominates the other. The leader who expresses frustration finds change annoying, even though they know it is inevitable. It's annoying because all their meticulous planning now needs revision or a complete start-over. All that wasted time and effort. It is for reasons like this that some leaders cling to their plans and avoid making changes for too long. When they eventually make the change, the cost in employee morale and efficiency is negative—they waited too long, and the process of change became even harder.

The leader who finds change stimulating and exciting can sometimes make changes so quickly—before all the external change has manifested—that they then have to make a series of subsequent changes and adaptations as events continue to evolve. They moved too soon. There is a happy medium, but this isn't easy to determine. The excited leader will tend to act earlier than they should; the planful leader will tend to act later than they should. How risk is calculated in both scenarios will determine which is preferable.

Evidence of Effective Orchestration

The best orchestrators are big-picture thinkers who see the totality of the world in which they operate, much like the systems thinkers we described earlier. All the interlocking parts are visible, and the flow of activity is managed to ensure no disruption. Of course, this is rarely achieved to perfection, yet this is exactly the aim of our high-performing leaders. While unattainable goals, such as perfection, drive leaders to orchestrate activities as well as they can, certain indicators suggest that progress toward perfection is being achieved:

- **Increased Collaboration:** This should be evidenced in two specific areas. First, in teams, with individual team members attempting to help each other and solve problems together. Second, between teams, where workflow handoffs occur, and the attitude of each team is to be as helpful and constructive toward the other as it can be in collectively solving problems. Ineffective orchestration nearly always leads to silos and trenches—artificial but real divisions that prevent work being done.
- **Higher Employee Engagement:** The social and relational dimension of work matters, and as relationships develop and deepen, it tends to increase employee engagement. This leads to more productive relationships and higher levels of confidence in what others are doing. To the extent that teams are customer-facing, this has a big

effect on how positive customers feel about their relationship with the company.

- **Increasing Customer Engagement:** Happy employees don't guarantee happy customers, but they certainly help. Customers are rarely satisfied after interactions with negative and angry employees who gleefully throw their colleagues in other parts of the organization under the bus.

- **Objectivity in Decision-Making:** Numbers represent our only common language because they establish objective truth—or try to—whenever we use them to guide our thinking and actions. Evidence of teams sharing numerical analyses suggests that they are beyond the typical posturing that can be a feature of one immature team attempting to assert its superiority over another. Evidence of shared data suggests that teams are willing to meet where data and truth intersect.

- **Operating at Scale:** When workflows and handoffs are smooth, fewer people are needed to pick up the pieces left behind by inefficiency and compensate through adding more head count to solve what existing teams can't. We worked with an organization that had recently introduced the Workday human resources management system and still found itself hiring more employees because some departments were unwilling to share data due to a fear of losing control. The one thing that people can do is run manual workflows where disruptions to the system prevent this from being done automatically.

- **Reconciliation, Adaptation, and Adjustment:** Orchestrators tend to meddle. They have their fingers in many pies (if not every pie). They tinker and tweak, cajole and encourage. The best orchestrators recognize that there is no such thing as a steady state and that variability can provide a short-term stimulus to drive improvement. Orchestrators are constantly balancing supply and demand and assessing capabilities to adjust and improve.

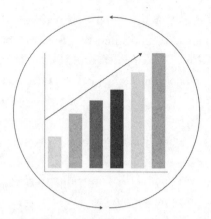

Indicators of Effective Execution
- Increased cross-functional collaboration
- Higher employee engagement scores
- Increasing customer engagement scores
- More decisions made on the basis of objective analyses
- More efficient operating at scale
- Continuous reconciliation and improvement

Orchestration as a Thing or a Process

Just like strategy, orchestration can be defined as a thing or a process (way of thinking). As a thing, orchestration is

- reducing repetitive tasks;
- reducing operating costs;
- improving task completion times;
- reducing errors through validation, standardization, and eliminating duplication;
- improving workflows and handoffs;
- connecting isolated systems to ensure that they add combined value;
- driving the right metrics and dashboards; and
- implementing standardized processes to establish excellence but preparing to develop customized solutions.

As a way of thinking, orchestration is about flexibility and adaptability, which are essential indicators of a mind that is continuously learning. High-performing leaders with this particular Talent reframe typical business questions in a way that builds on the strong platform of consistent business process execution:

- How can we profitably serve emerging market customers at the bottom of the pyramid?
- How can we break out of the commodity trap?
- How can we grow outside our core market?
- How can we provide an integrated customer experience across all areas of our company?
- How do we grow revenues on a low-cost product?
- Why should we automatically accept that growth products will eventually decline?
- Why doesn't every product we sell meet our minimum expected contribution margin?

When it comes to execution, the very best leaders exhibit an ability to raise the questions that require high orchestration and a flexible mindset to see and take advantage of less obvious opportunities. It is the process of orchestration that brings about this focus. High-performing leaders, like orchestra conductors, keep the energy flowing through the resources at their disposal, which in turn generate ideas and responses to important business questions. Flexibility and adaptability in thinking are key executional capabilities for leaders.

Learning Agility

Central to questions and discussions about leadership flexibility and adaptability is whether a specific leader is open to new ideas and approaches. We regularly hear questions like "Do they have an open mind?" which usually means "Is this person open to new ideas and approaches?" Being open to new ways of thinking and developing ideas and plans based on new ways of thinking are two completely different things.

What people really mean by a person who is open to new ways of think-ing isn't the specific idea itself but whether those different ideas drive effective outcomes. The term "learning agility" is often used to describe this capability. Learning agility is typically defined as "a set of complex skills that enables us to learn something new in one place and then apply what we learned elsewhere, in a wholly different situation."[19]

Although this definition is common, we don't like it. In 1852, the British politician Benjamin Disraeli described the then prime minister, Sir Robert Peel, as being "the burglar of others' intellect, trading on the ideas and intelligence of others."[20] He went on to say that Peel's entire political life was "one great appropriation clause." It seems to us as though learning agility is just a nuanced version of idea plagiarism, and this is much too narrow a construct.

For learning agility to be real, it must take place at the level of the brain. This means that when evaluating whether a leader has learning agility, we need to assess whether they can reconfigure old information into something new or identify a better and more effective way of doing something that positively impacts performance. For learning agility to have meaning and value, it needs to be more than just taking an idea from one situation and applying it to another.

Reconfiguration lies at the heart of learning agility to prevent it from being a mere matching process where an existing idea is simply lifted from one loca-tion and installed in another. Our definition of learning agility is "to be able to disassemble and reassemble components into a completely new configuration that has a positive, compound impact on future performance."

Learning Agility Isn't Revealed Through Sandwich-Making
Korn Ferry CEO Gary Burnison believes that learning agility can be deter-mined by asking an unusual question (his preferred example is "How do you make a tuna-fish sandwich?") and seeing how people react.[21] I don't know what Gary thinks he is learning by asking questions like this, but the need to come up with an answer on the spot that he is satisfied with is unlikely to produce supremely agile learners.

However, he does clearly state that "learning agility is so important, our firm views it as the number one predictor of success." We don't want to spend our limited time and cognitive resources picking holes in such a target-rich environment as the post we previously referenced, but as important as learning agility can be for an operationally astute leader, it is certainly not the most important predictor of success. There is zero research data to support this conjecture.

Learning Agility Is Not a Skill

The Center for Creative Leadership (CCL) has distilled some sensible suggestions for how leaders might develop learning agility.[22] They provide a good set of indicators:

- Be a Seeker—this is further defined by the following suggestions:
    * Embrace the challenge of the unfamiliar.
    * Take on a new challenge that scares you.
    * Don't get stuck on first solutions.
    * Make a habit of pushing for new ideas.
- Hone Your Sense-Making:
    * Really actively listen to understand what others are saying.
    * When you find yourself feeling stressed, pause.
    * Find another way to understand a problem.
- Internalize Experiences and Lessons Learned:
    * Ask for feedback and be open to criticism.
    * Don't defend.
    * Reflect, both alone and with others.
- Adapt and Apply:
    * Learn to rely on your intuition.
    * Don't overthink.

Alert readers will see some overlap with the suggestions we made in Chapter 5 regarding our description of strategy as a process and a way of thinking. But the mistake made by the CCL is to assume that these tips are things that everyone can do. It isn't that simple. For example, "Find another way to understand a problem" seems to be a good thing to do. But some people struggle to transfer learning this way. They might understand a concept in one situation but fail to see its relevance to another context or situation. Defining learning agility as a series of actions that everyone can take rather than a more innate capability of a person at the level of the brain is to turn leadership into a series of light switches. It is much more complicated.

Learning agility is an important characteristic to which leaders should pay serious attention. For leaders who struggle to think in agile ways, our best recommendation is to partner with other leaders who have strong natural capabilities in this area and position them to make this contribution to your thinking. This is the approach taken by high-performing leaders. The timing of this contribution comes in the early stage of strategic thinking, when options and possibilities are still being identified.

Complexity

A final characteristic that helps define orchestration as an important contributor to effective execution is complexity. Not only is the present complex, but few people would argue that the future is trending toward simplicity. Most people believe that complexity is here to stay and that the future will be even more complex in ways that are difficult to predict.

So what is complexity, and what role does it play in helping leaders manage increasingly complex environments and problems?

Complexity isn't just about managing an increasing number of variables; it's the ability to do so at increasing speed. Consider a circus performer keeping ten plates or various other flat objects spinning on poles. In order to keep adding more spinning objects to their act, they need to perform a greater number of small and rapid movements to keep pace with the increasing complexity of managing fifteen objects versus only ten. Quantity and speed are therefore two important components of complexity. Our air traffic controllers go to work each day expecting increasing and unpredictable levels of complexity.

Despite the voluminous evidence of complexity in the world, it has received serious study for only about thirty years. Gary Grobman defined complexity as "situations that exhibit uncertainty and non-linearity."[23] Grobman based this definition on the work of Plsek, Lindberg, and Zimmerman, who argued that a complex, adaptive system is "a system of individual agents, who have freedom to act in ways that are not always predictable, and whose actions are interconnected such that one agent's actions changes the context for other agents."[24]

Grobman believed that new approaches in the natural sciences (particularly physics and biology) could be applied to organizations and leadership to identify different ways of engaging with problems and opportunities. In his paper "Complexity Theory: A New Way to Look at Organizational Change," Grobman summarized several management principles that conflict with the more typical, top-down, command-and-control approach of some companies:[25]

- View your organization as a complex system rather than an assembly line or machine.
- Provide minimum specifications and avoid overly scripting plans and procedures.
- Recognize situations when "going with your gut" is more appropriate than "going with the data."
- Maintain a healthy level of discomfort and discontent to promote creativity.
- Recognize that there is a limit to the number of relationships a person can handle, and limit the size of work teams.
- Let unstable situations simmer until a solution emerges rather than jumping in to resolve it.
- Build in some information and skills redundancy to ensure the longevity and security of the system.

We don't disagree.

Complexity and Social Interactions

It is important for leaders to understand that complexity breeds much unpredictability. The more complex the system, the more importance should be attached to social interactions so that complexity can be harnessed for positive effect. In their 2009 paper, Uhl-Bien and Marion argued that leaders need to manage complexity through the following three areas:[26]

1. **Social Interactions:** Change can be stressful. Leverage the strength of social relationships to bring people together to share experiences and

interact more productively rather than seeking to control, standardize, and exhibit more autocratic characteristics.

2. **Shared Leadership:** Complexity is best managed through shared leadership, where authority is not vested in one person. Rather, anyone in the organization can make a telling leadership contribution through the strength of their social capital.

3. **Everyone Has Influence:** Recognize that, if correctly engaged, each person can have influence and positively impact organizational outcomes.

There is nothing fundamental about these areas of focus, but as leaders engage with increasing levels of complexity, the approach to help organizations navigate through this involves core principles around relationships and the level of engagement and involvement expected of each individual.

WHAT REALLY MATTERS

This chapter has highlighted that a relatively simple concept, such as execution, is more complex and challenging than we might think. Rather than being simply an expression for things just getting done, it is a way of thinking that starts with the strategic formulation we highlighted in our chapter on sense of direction.

Execution is the consequence of structure and process with orchestration and complexity. While individual high-performing leaders may struggle to excel in each of these areas, they build teams and organizations around them that ensure that each of these elements is effectively managed:

- A lack of continuity and flow from strategy to execution is a problem that leads to much stop/start implementation in organizations. High-performing leaders work extremely hard to determine an organization's strategic direction and build the most appropriate structural framework to ensure that it can be effectively executed. This is invariably built around people with high levels of Talent in complementary areas.

- Being able to handle fast pace and work complexity is important in leadership. Things change, sometimes unexpectedly, and leaders need to know when to change, and then change quickly, to maintain forward momentum and ensure that teams remain productively engaged.

Effectively balancing both components of execution is a critical task for leaders striving to solve the strategy-execution problem. You might lead through your ability to see how things get done if

- you are effective at organizing your thoughts into action and then driving hard toward your goals;
- you want to meet your commitments and arrange your work in a sequence of logical, manageable steps;
- you tend to work hard with a lot of stamina and be tenacious in your pursuit of goals; and
- you are effective at considering and mitigating risk if you can control your visceral need to act.

Effective execution isn't just about getting things done. It demands careful consideration of all the variables that could affect your planning before you act. These questions can help ensure that you don't miss critical details or fall victim to barriers that should have been anticipated:

- Am I moving too quickly from thought to action and failing to plan each step effectively?
- Am I effectively managing my workload and avoiding taking on too many tasks?

This chapter concludes our research findings that describe the dispositions, traits, and characteristics of the highest performing leaders. Five powerful chapters—The Five Talents That Really Matter—that dispel the confusion, distraction, and obfuscation that shrouds most work on this subject. No aspiring leader should persist in their career growth and professional development blind to these important findings.

PART FOUR

TRANSFORMATIVE QUESTIONS, HARSH TRUTHS, AND OUR INVITATION TO YOU

CHAPTER 10

Transform Your Organization's Selection Process

INTRODUCING OBJECTIVITY TO YOUR COMPANY'S SELECTION PROCESS MAY seem daunting given the effort required to build an assessment that has predictive value and one that has a good effect size and is statistically valid, fair, and reliable. Part of the challenge is that leaders want immediate solutions to processes that can take years to get right. We are well aware that hiring managers are rarely statisticians, but don't let that discourage you from introducing components of scientific methodology into your approach to selection. What you can achieve on your own is remarkable. There are various steps that any organization can take to increase the reliability of hiring without having to invest significant resources. This section highlights some of these steps and the benefits they can bring, but all will be enhanced by using an assessment like one with the characteristics we have previously described.

So far, we have used the Executive Leadership Assessment to demonstrate the application of scientific methodology to selection. It predicts outcomes beyond what humans can achieve using their wit and wisdom. But leadership isn't the only role we have researched; we have focused our methodology on many other functional and commercial roles.

The same approach can likely be extended to every role where performance can be measured. We have created assessments for dozens of generalized roles, including frontline managers, sales reps, customer service reps, and financial analysts. Our findings on the validity, reliability, and fairness of these assessments as predictors of future success are comparable to those that we described for the Executive Leadership Assessment. Sales and revenue growth is an obvious pain point for many organizations, and it should be no great surprise that sales became an early focus for us.

INSIGHTS FROM STUDYING THE VERY BEST SALES REPS

Sales representatives are remarkable individuals, not least because the revenue hopes and dreams of entire organizations rest on their shoulders. We've studied them extensively. We've learned how different combinations of sales Talents predict high performance in one situation but not in another. Along the way, our results have helped us dispel some myths about what makes a great salesperson.

A common belief is that a great salesperson can successfully sell anything. It's held by many people, including sales reps themselves—even the exceptional ones. It isn't true except in a small number of cases. When you ask sales reps the right questions, they quickly concede that many conditional factors apply to their sales Talent. We've asked reps currently selling health care products whether they could sell tobacco products—"Absolutely not." We've asked reps who sell complex service propositions B2B whether they could sell low-priced consumable products B2C—"Probably not." These conditions matter because they change the entire context of selling. We've even discovered that within the same industry, where the brand values of competing companies differ significantly, it's difficult for a rep for one company to successfully transfer to another company and sell its products, because they struggle to adapt to the new brand values. It's as though the brand values of the company and the values of the rep become inseparable.

Sales reps are an ideal study population because in most cases, their performance is easy to measure. Commercial leaders equipped with spreadsheets can rank their entire sales force. They can tell you how good some reps are at selling a broad product mix, they can tell you who has achieved the greatest revenue growth over last year, and they know who is at (or over) quota as the year draws to a close. The more sophisticated sales forces can correlate all this financial data to customer engagement and satisfaction to increase (or decrease) confidence in the current sales trajectory and improve forecasting accuracy. Sales reps really are a research dream.

What makes studying sales groups fun is that individuals are rarely short of an opinion and will tell you exactly what they think. This directness creates clarity, and differences in perspective are easier to detect. Sales reps tend to be confident around people, and they aren't overly concerned about being wrong because in their minds, they rarely are. It was our study of sales reps that accelerated our approach to the development of effective selection questions, and we were able to validate the findings in short order based on how performance tracked over time. Defining critical aspects of a sales rep's role, developing questions targeting these behaviors and characteristics, and measuring the effect on sales performance over time was how we proceeded. We learned a huge amount about high-performing sales reps through this structured interviewing approach. Here's a summary of some of our findings:

- Managers with higher sales leadership Talent terminated poorly performing reps almost twice as quickly as managers with lower sales leadership Talent.
- Managers with higher sales leadership Talent hired reps with consistently higher sales rep Talent—the exact opposite of what we found for managers with weak sales leadership Talent, who consistently appointed weaker reps.
- Sales reps with higher measurable sales Talent sell more and grow their accounts more quickly than sales reps with lower measurable sales Talent. It's that simple. It's this point that drives revenue growth.
- Sales reps with higher measurable sales Talent, who sell more, tend to stick at companies longer provided they also have a manager with higher sales management Talent. If they have a manager with lower sales management Talent, they leave quickly.
- Sales reps with higher measurable sales Talent are adored by their customers.

- Sales reps with higher measurable sales Talent aren't always easy to manage.
- Most companies are so influenced by the performance of their own sales organization that they have little clue what excellence or "world-class" status looks like—in every sales Talent benchmarking project we have conducted, only 5–15 percent of internal reps reach the top quartile for their industry.
- The best sales reps exhibit different traits and characteristics on a sales assessment. This is different from what weaker sales managers desire or expect. Weaker sales managers have unfounded preferences for certain dispositions that they value, regardless of whether these correlate to high sales performance.

Few leaders would argue against the value of these discoveries. We were able to uncover these findings through developing our questioning capabilities to match the sales environment. We applied what we learned from studying teachers and other roles to sales organizations with similar, sometimes much more dramatic effects. The same approach can be applied to almost any role; the only requirement is that high and low performance in the role can be adequately defined and measured. This is a stretch for many companies.

Building a fully validated, predictive assessment is not simple, but it is possible. Many companies might not immediately recognize the significance of investing in such a tool, however. If that is the case, leaders and hiring managers can effectively increase selection efficacy by incorporating some of the following methods. We recommend that any organization incorporate as many of these methods as possible and continue to refine them over time until you can benefit from the value of reliable predictions. We have advised dozens of companies during their efforts to do exactly this. The following recommendations are processes that have high impact without much overhead.

SELECTION CHARTERS SET CLEAR EXPECTATIONS

A Selection Charter explains, in no uncertain terms, what candidates can expect when participating in a company's selection process. Such a document can help organizations establish a more consistent approach to interacting with candidates in a way that eliminates confusion and maintains the integrity of the overall process.

Codifying and enforcing these tenets can be a first step toward improving a selection process otherwise mired by biases. It sets expectations both internally and externally about the appropriate steps that a fair and balanced process should follow.

As you read through the following statements, consider your current process and what gaps need to be addressed in order to meet these expectations. Also consider the principles that your recruiting and hiring teams might follow in order to show this degree of professionalism. As a rule, candidates should feel cared for and that their time was valued. They should feel that they were given fair and appropriate opportunities to showcase their Talents. Whether they are successful or not, candidates should be treated with a high degree of respect so that they will recommend your company as a great place to work—even if they don't join it themselves:

- The job description and role requirements will form the basis of the company's evaluation of candidates, and the candidate deemed to most closely match, or exceed, these requirements will most likely be appointed to the role.

- We evaluate many different sources of evidence when determining whether a candidate is the right match for a role. Decisions made are balanced against that evidence, whether it be a candidate's experience, knowledge, skills, or other characteristics that would help them succeed.

- The company could well be talking to multiple candidates as part of this process.

- All candidates (whether internal or external) will be given the exact same opportunities to showcase their capabilities.

- While we may express our thanks and appreciation to candidates as they go through the various aspects of our selection process, no specific feedback will be given until after the final decision.

- While candidates may feel more or less positive about different aspects of our process, they should not assume any favor or disfavor because of discussions with representatives of the company.

- Unsuccessful candidates will be informed of the outcome once a successful candidate has been appointed and employment terms and conditions agreed upon. Unsuccessful candidates will be informed of how they might expect to receive feedback on their application and the form that feedback will take.
- Not being appointed to this position should not be viewed as a negative decision against a candidate. We sometimes interview a candidate for one role and then later realize they may be a better fit for a different role in the future.
- Experiencing rejection for a role is never a great feeling, but this doesn't imply that a candidate is deficient in some way. It just means we believe we found a candidate who is a much better fit for what we are looking for. Our serious interest in a candidate indicates that we view them as highly credible and capable.

HIRING MANAGERS CAN BE EFFECTIVE RECRUITERS

We believe that search firms can be valuable partners to hiring companies in sourcing multiple plausible candidates that meet their requirements. But we also assert that too many companies are overly reliant on the opinions and recommendations of their search partners and that the conflict of interest inherent in a search firm sourcing and assessing their own candidates is too great to ignore. Our recommendation is that search firms be engaged with a more limited scope regarding the sourcing of candidates and that assessing and evaluating the quality of those candidates be done internally or through a reputable third party.

There are many different avenues to explore when sourcing candidates—they might come from a search firm, an employee referral, or even a current employee looking to make a lateral or upward move in their organization. Some of the best candidate sourcing we have seen is by managers who never stop working their network in search of Talented individuals who might join their teams. Regardless of where a candidate comes from, they should be evaluated by the same means as every other candidate, and no decision or commitment should be made until all the evidence is collected and the process concludes.

STRUCTURED INTERVIEW QUESTIONS INCREASE THE FAIRNESS AND RELIABILITY OF CANDIDATE EVALUATIONS

Introducing structured interviews is the primary step to building a resilient selection process. We made a key distinction between structured and unstructured questioning in Chapter 2 when describing how most companies approach face-to-face interviews. Unstructured questions are those that have no predefined assessment criteria. There is no correct answer; the candidate needs only to say something that the interviewer likes. Structured questions have explicit criteria, whether in the form of a multiple-choice question or the interviewer listening for specific key words and phrases in an answer. Using structured questioning in an interview introduces a measure of fairness and is the first step toward being able to track the predictive value of questions:

- The questions you ask should aim to uncover the candidate's innate characteristics—their Talents. This can be difficult to achieve. For our Executive Leadership Assessment, it took years of observing leaders, running focus groups, and administering barrages of psychometric tests, but don't get caught up on this. Initially it will be enough to simply ask questions that you think will reveal the candidate's Talents. This will be an iterative process. As time goes on, your questions will invariably improve and enable your insight into an individual's natural capabilities.

- Bifurcated questions are those that delineate between two groups based on a response. Ideally your structured questions will be able to separate whether the candidate does or does not possess the Talent you are probing for. Again, this is iterative. A good bifurcated question has answers that may all seem appealing, but the correct answer predicts the candidate's Talent. Be sure to avoid asking questions that have obviously correct and incorrect answers, as these are effectively useless.

- Interviews should ideally be conducted over the phone or Internet (with cameras turned off). This will reduce the biases prevalent in face-to-face interviews. Additionally, you must spend time training interviewers to ask questions and score responses consistently with each other using the same criteria. Without this step, the whole process falls apart. The data will produce meaningful patterns only if there is agreement on what each item of the interview means. Interviewers should also be trained to avoid helping the candidate in any way. This is the part that most interviewers struggle with— when the candidate is almost saying the right thing but left out a key part of the criteria. The interviewer must resist the urge to push them to the correct response.

Coming up with questions that meet all these criteria can be difficult, so we've provided some examples of good questions that accomplish these three features.

Questions About Setting Direction

Question: *"How Would You Describe a Great Team Meeting?"*
The most effective, high-performing leaders hold themselves back from making immediate, superficial decisions. They test the various options they see and then plan a course of action. This question tests whether this thoughtful approach is something they naturally gravitate toward to the extent that it is a clearly stated preference in, for example, team meetings. When team members might be hungry for action and impatient to make progress, do leaders resist the temptation to jump in and instead drive more thoughtful consideration of issues?

Answer
The response should always start with the exploration of ideas and associated argument and debate about the best way to achieve something. Words like "debate," "exchange," and "dissent" should be present. If all you hear is effective agenda management and a sense of checking each item off the list—a "readout" of activities—then this candidate may perpetuate a problem you already suffer from.

Question: "How Would You Describe the Risks That You See When Making Important Decisions?"

Too many leaders place high value on quick decision-making in the belief that doing so enables them to realize success sooner. They place higher value on speed than on effectiveness, convincing themselves that they are achieving both. They aren't. This question is asked to test whether leaders are as aware of the different types of risk as they should be. For example,

- Making decisions without having all the information to hand or having consulted enough people
- Placing too much weight on past experiences
- Assuming the current problem is like one you have faced in the past
- Experiencing "analysis paralysis," where the need for even more information and data holds you back from even the most basic decision

Answer

We want to hear candidates describe a balanced analysis with the emphasis on the extensiveness of thought and evidence. It is better for a leader to be able to judge the risk inherent in every decision, even the smaller, less significant ones. The aim is to be "right" rather than "wrong," and balancing risk is more likely to achieve this. Leaders who fail to balance risk are destined to face a lifetime of situational and reactive problem-solving. One thing to be cautious about is a leader who struggles to articulate meaningful risks, even as they claim to evaluate risk carefully. If leaders are in the habit of calculating and balancing risk, they should have no problems coming up with multiple illustrations in a short period.

Question: "After Making a Decision, Do You Sometimes Find Yourself Coming Up with Better Ideas?"

One of the interesting characteristics about naturally ideating leaders is that there is no "off" switch. Ideas swirl constantly. This question is designed to identify these leaders, as the capacity to generate more and different ideas and options feeds the strategic thinking process. There's a clear downside to this capability, as revisiting decisions after the fact creates false momentum and constant stop/start activity that sucks energy out of people and can cause significant disengagement. But this is why the question is smart. If you are a naturally ideating leader, you will be confident in the likelihood of this approach being more successful because it usually achieves a better solution or outcome.

Answer

This is one of those questions where the response will separate those who are effective ideators from those who would rather decide, move on, and not revisit earlier assumptions. Of course, coming up with better ideas doesn't mean we turn the clock back and start again from scratch—nothing would ever get done that way. But having such thoughts is a sign of constant creativity, and this can bring value as ideas are implemented and ways to improve initial suggestions are identified.

Questions About Harnessing Energy

Question: "Which of the Following Is Most Worthy of Your Attention?"

- A complaint from one of your biggest customers
- News that a key employee has just resigned
- Shipping issues that will affect product availability to your customers
- News of local tax incentives to encourage mid-price-range apartment building

Many leaders are driven to achieve "growth" while lacking an understanding of concepts that drive growth. One of these is the ability to see opportunities and to prioritize them over other issues that might seem more urgent in the short term. High-performing leaders do both—they address short-term urgent issues, but not at the expense of detracting from real growth opportunities. By presenting a series of difficult choices, we can learn in real time how a leader balances "urgent" and "important." Few get this right. The question doesn't imply that you deal with one situation and ignore the others; it asks which is most worthy of your attention. If you are a growth-driven leader, then only one of these issues highlights a real growth opportunity. If you read this explanation and struggle to understand how news of tax incentives is a growth issue, or, even worse, you look at issues such as customer complaints as opportunities to drive growth, then you likely have growth challenges of your own.

Answer

A very good answer would be to delegate the first three issues to competent team members so that you can spend time ruminating over the implications of those tax incentives for local business growth. Does the influx of new people provide recruitment opportunities, maybe customer sales opportunities? Maybe your suppliers are growing and hiring? There will be some candidates who see this question as an "in-tray" exercise where you do the most urgent thing first (maybe shipping issues, followed by the customer complaint) while missing the real opportunity. You really want to hear leaders engaging with unusual ideas and opportunities in order to establish opportunities for growth. They might not materialize this time, but someone with a constantly searching and questioning mind will see more of them than someone less intellectually engaged.

Question: "Which of the Following Is the Riskier Appointment to You, and Which Candidate Would You Most Likely Appoint?"

- **Candidate A:** young, inexperienced, arrogant, highly talented, could be divisive on a team
- **Candidate B:** more mature, strong experience, congenial, moderately talented, will fit in well with a team

Questions like this aren't especially difficult, but they do place the candidate in an awful dilemma. It seems that either way they choose to go, there are traps and minefields. This is the whole point of the question, and what makes it a good one is that both options could be attractive depending on the circumstances—circumstances that won't be provided and that candidates will have to determine themselves. The candidate's response will help you understand where they stand with respect to business growth. The risk with Candidate A is that their Talent comes with less experience and the potential to be difficult to manage (as Talented people sometimes are), which might cause friction with other team members. Yet their promise seems high. The risk with Candidate B is that you will get a steady, congenial team member but with moderate Talent that suggests a struggle to achieve great results. The "ease of management" response would suggest picking Candidate B and settling for steady behavior and unexceptional results. The performance and growth-oriented response would be to select Candidate A and be prepared for a wilder ride. The question involves trying to tease out a candidate's risk tolerance and where they would rather spend their time— managing the behavioral challenges of a potential high performer or coaching better performance out of a congenial team player.

Answer
You should listen carefully to how the interviewee balances the risk of both candidates. To which of the two candidates does the interviewee feel more naturally drawn? Hearing reluctance toward Candidate A suggests that they are more concerned about the potential negative impact of their behavior on others than they are about achieving higher levels of performance. Hearing them express a strong preference for the behavioral maturity of Candidate B suggests that they would prefer someone who might fit in well but who might not move any needles on key measures. Believing you can coach someone with mediocre Talent to be a high performer is one of the fallacies that plagues attitudes toward effective management. While Candidate A might be a riskier appointment, they should definitely be the preferred appointment. As you consider this reasoning, you might find it challenging and counterintuitive. Rather than question whether you agree with the recommendation for Candidate A, you should first reflect on what this might say about you.

Question: "Have You Ever Felt Overstretched at Work—Too Much to Do and Too Little Time to Do It? How Did You Feel?"
Everyone at some point in their career has had that feeling of being so busy and so overwhelmed that it is sometimes hard to work through and achieve success. This is why quite a few highly responsible people, who are driven to achieve, work long hours. They made commitments they intend to keep. But if everyone feels this at some point in their career, why ask the question? There are two reasons. First, how frequent are these feelings: weekly, daily? Second, as an interviewee describes working through these occasions, do they mention feeling miserable, stressed, overburdened, motivated, or energized? This question

is essentially an attempt to find out whether the reality of feeling overstretched disengages or engages a person.

Answer
You want to hear a person increasing their effort in the face of challenge or resistance. For high achievers, work is fun, and they seem better able than many people to look at this in a positive light and more effectively manage their time and personal resources. Those who focus on the negative aspects of being overstretched will tend to lack the ability to push through to a successful conclusion and the good feelings that result from it.

Questions About Exerting Influence

Question: "If It Isn't Broken, Why Fix It? How Do You Feel About This Statement?"
This question taps into a common attitude at work—we have plenty of problems to deal with without you creating more; if it seems to be working, then stop meddling. You will find that many people agree with this sentiment, using an argument that places greater emphasis on fixing "real" problems than self-inflicted ones. Yet the real value in a leader is how they apply pressure to functioning parts of the organization that, while not broken, are capable of much-improved performance and better outcomes. Sometimes this requires that something be dismantled in order to be rebuilt to a higher standard.

Answer
It's sometimes necessary to break things to achieve superior outcomes. Those who reject this concept or place too many caveats on how to do it effectively are likely satisfied with the status quo, which will always lead to suboptimal performance.

Question: "What Circumstances Would Cause You to Step In and Intervene in Your Team?"
Highly responsible managers find it hard not to influence how their team members go about their work, even though allowing them to try and fail is a valuable

lesson. Believing it to be preferable to keep close to their team, they are ready and waiting to step in with advice, guidance, or firmer direction. Experienced managers who have seen similar problems before feel the need to guide and influence in real time. Few have the concept of delegated leadership clearly in mind, and they intervene before they should. The key to effective management and leadership is to do two things. First, hold off all the time. Allow the team to discover and learn by making their own mistakes. Second, keeping a distance from your team allows you to keep impediments and obstacles from knocking them off track. Clearing away blockages or future obstacles and then allowing a team to press ahead and accept ownership is one of the most rewarding behaviors of a manager.

Answer

You will hear a lot of leaders struggling to hold back, but the successful ones tend to win this battle. Those who can quickly identify reasons to step in and act are the ones who will constantly struggle to develop and grow future leaders. Rather than exemplifying the heroes they believe their team will appreciate, they will, instead, struggle with the temptation to micromanage while denying that this is their intent. The best leaders learn to let their team fail a few times.

Question: "When You Think You Are Right, Are You Most Likely to Argue Your Case or Seek to Compromise?"

This is a very difficult question to receive in an interview because it looks as though you have strong options whichever way you go. The critical phrase is "when you think you are right." Many people believe themselves to be right a lot of the time, but those who are right most frequently have seen this borne out by evidence and experience. Those who claim to be right, but subsequent evidence shows them not to be, also learn from experience, and these experiences predict the best response.

Answer

You should always prefer a leader who stands and argues their case over one who moves to compromise, precisely because of how experience has played out in the past. Asserting that you are right when evidence then forces you to compromise suggests that these leaders will seek to compromise sooner. A track record of digging in and arguing your case and then being proven right is much more likely to predict this behavior in the future.

Questions About Increasing Connectivity

Question: "How Much Time and Effort Are You Prepared to Put into Coaching an Underperformer?"

No one wants to be seen as an insensitive and impatient leader who terminates people quickly after failing to invest sufficient time in helping them correct their behavior or performance. But how much time is the right amount to invest? A consistent response heard from managers who have lived through this situation is the regret that they failed to act soon enough, that they let the situation drag on too long, which wasn't good for the company or the employee. Professional and responsible employees who are failing or struggling in a role aren't having fun, yet their loyalty might be misplaced, and they soldier on for longer than is sensible. A caring manager and a responsible employee are never a good combination when seeking a resolution to poor performance. As an interviewee works through their reasoning, guard against an endless series of "last chances." It is far better to terminate an employee than to coach them to death. The time that should be given to try to turn this bad situation around is three months.

Answer

Listen for the interviewee to put in place clear expectations with a development plan to assist, with the intention of reaching a conclusion after three months. Three months is long enough to show evidence of improvement for pretty much every scenario. In some cases, you should see evidence of improvement much sooner. This is the kind of clarity you should hear from a top candidate.

Question: "How Large Are Your Social and Professional Networks? By What Percentage Has Each of These Networks Grown over the Last Year?"

Few high-performing leaders make a distinction between their social and professional networks, so be wary of interviewees who point to that distinction as though it is significant for them. Organizational network analysis shows that key individuals serve as "communication nodes" with strong connectivity to others and information flowing through them. Those leaders occupying those nodes have phenomenal influence in a company—they are "go-to" people and have connectivity to many major issues in the organization. Social and professional networks aren't static; they are growing, and every year, high-performing leaders seek to expand their connectivity—converting distant connections to closer connections, converting closer connections to advocates and friends. They reach out and drive connections before work requires them to do so, and they exploit their network for advice, direct help, and support during times of need. The two key issues are that their network is large and they are growing it intentionally.

Answer

You should hear a specific number that exceeds one thousand, and you should expect a growth rate of about 10 percent per annum. Vague responses suggest that an interviewee has never really thought about this before, and that should tell you everything you need to know.

Question: "For What Reasons Would You Choose Not to Delegate a Task to a Direct Report?"

When candidates are asked about their delegation capabilities and practice, they know the correct answer—of course they delegate...of course they do it all the time...they are always looking for opportunities to delegate...yes, employees in their care grow enormously because of how good their delegation skills are. Everyone is that good. This question cuts through the obvious question with something that is much more difficult to answer.

Answer

This is a smart question because nearly everyone who struggles with delegation can see an obvious affirmative answer—you would never delegate to a person who wasn't competent, right? This is a smart question to ask because it tends to draw out responses like this one. Think of it this way: high-performing leaders don't have team members with low competence on their teams. They don't tolerate them. When a high-performing leader hears this question, they can't think of a good reason not to delegate to a team member because they've built incredibly strong teams, and any of their team members could take on the most challenging of tasks. Low-performing leaders don't build strong teams because they tend to fear Talented people. They exercise extreme caution delegating some tasks because they doubt their team members can handle the complexity and worry that a poor outcome would reflect badly on their leadership.

Questions About Controlling Traffic

Question: "How Would You Describe Your Process of Planning?"

A common, and incorrect, assumption is that planning is a ubiquitous capability, with individuals differing only in the level of detail they describe in their plans. Everyone knows that the best plan starts with the end in mind—the future state or objective—and works back from there to the starting point in a version of reverse engineering. All the resources of the organization are identified to assist in pursuit of the goal, and the leader's job is to keep things on track and drive toward achievement of the goal. High-performing leaders are different. They don't start with a singular goal; they start with a series of possible objectives, and their process of planning enables flexibility in execution such that, if circumstances rapidly change, they can be flexible and switch their approach midplan and midexecution.

Answer

Multiple possible goals should lie at the heart of a plan that shows executional flexibility. Typically, an interviewee will identify only the different planning stages and highlight the various resource requirements they will manage. But the key to effective planning is how to handle the unexpected and unpredictable elements that will inevitably interject and potentially knock you off course. High-performing leaders place great importance on contingency planning for this very reason.

Question: "How Would You Describe a Time When You Were Surprised at Work?"

Surprises happen, and they affect everyone. High-performing leaders, though, experience fewer surprises. This question provides an opportunity to tease this out. One of the first considerations is how recently the interviewee describes their surprise—was it earlier this week, last week? Maybe yesterday. High-performing leaders might have to go back a little in time because their experience suggests fewer occasions. It is also important to exercise some judgment over the significance of the surprise and whether it could reasonably have been predicted.

Answer
An infrequent, difficult-to-predict surprise.

Question: "How Do You Feel About Getting a Constant Stream of Interruptions at Work?"

The very thought of frequent interruptions is annoying and frustrating to some people. Such people tend to be more focused, more rigid, less open, and more self-contained. Interruptions prevent them from getting their work done. Such people might say, "My door is always open," yet few feel inclined to enter. High-performing leaders welcome interruption because it provides them with an opportunity to discuss, to question, and to engage others. They might also say, "My door is always open," but they also know it has a hinge that swings both ways, and they are as likely to emerge, engage others, and "interrupt" them as they are to enjoy the same behavior in reverse. Whenever a person comes to talk—to interrupt—a high-performing leader is focused on what benefit can come from that, and they welcome and encourage it.

Answer
Interruptions are a welcome sign that others want to engage and discuss important issues—important enough to drive the interruption.

We don't expect companies to entirely retire unstructured, face-to-face interviews. However, we do suggest pairing them with structured interviews with questions like those listed here. With three interviewers, each taking about five of these questions, asking these in addition to what else might be important should cause little disruption to a candidate's experience.

OBJECTIVELY EVALUATE EACH CANDIDATE'S EXPERIENCE

In our work helping clients to redefine their selection criteria, we often ask whether it's possible for a leadership candidate to be highly tenured but relatively inexperienced. We use this thought experiment to make the point that time served—the number of years a candidate has occupied a role—doesn't guarantee that they will have encountered (and successfully navigated) a broad enough range of experiences and developmental opportunities to excel in the role they're now being considered for.

It's common for job descriptions to specify a minimum number of years of experience that all candidates should possess. Instead, we advocate that you identify the specific experiences—and the expected outcomes—that more accurately reflect the work environment and help identify candidates with the greatest chance of success. Before we outline our framework for analyzing candidate experiences for their potential value, we briefly discuss the experiences that shouldn't contribute much to your final decision.

Experiences That (Barely) Matter

Expat Assignment
We have lost count of the number of times leaders, both exceptional and not, have told us that their expat assignment was critical in their leadership journey. Those who have experienced an overseas assignment describe it in very personal terms with respect to its impact on their self-identity as leaders.

We don't deny the value of these assignments, but while these opportunities are treasured by the individuals privileged enough to have them, something more mundane achieves just as much, if not more—leading a business with an international scope and presence.

Rather than operating in a single foreign market, why wouldn't we challenge and develop our most Talented leaders to manage a business across multiple geographies? This kind of experience requires a degree of accountability for performance outcomes in these foreign countries, not just visiting them occasionally. Leaders would need to engage with a range of external stakeholders, work alongside local employees to codevelop strategy and execution, and understand the local market dynamics and competitive landscape. Accomplishing this within multiple, varied sociocultural realities—rather than a single country, as is typical of an expat assignment—requires much greater degrees of attention and effort.

While commercial leadership roles will most often provide development experiences across multiple geographies, nearly every functional part of a business can have similar exposure, whether it be operations, supply chain, HR, finance, or legal. The precise focus and experience might vary, but the opportunities to provide emerging leaders with the experiences that matter exist in all functional areas of a business. Unfortunately, too much thinking in this respect is unidirectional. US businesses see these development opportunities as important for their US leaders and work hard to provide them. It is rare for companies to obsess equally about providing the same experiences for their developing leaders within their non-US divisions. In most cases, "expat" means an American abroad, which makes little sense.

New Business Acquisition

Some companies mistakenly place a high weight on a leader's experience in acquiring new business. We understand why—these can be highly complex and difficult projects. There is no doubt that leading an acquisition presents all kinds of valuable learning opportunities, but many companies become confused when they are asked which of these opportunities is most important to a person's growth. There are three critical aspects that contribute to a successful new business acquisition:

1. Researching and selecting the target to acquire
2. Conducting the due diligence necessary before issuing a letter of interest and developing the initial offer and deal structure
3. Managing the postacquisition integration

Companies often fail to recognize the important differences between each of the three stages in the process. The development value of these stages can be vastly different depending on the specific context of the acquisition. Our point isn't that these add zero value to a leader's experiential capabilities but that there is no reliability to the claim that new business acquisition provides meaningful development experience for leaders that necessarily has causal value in improving their leadership.

There are many other experiences that we see touted as integral to every successful leader's development. Each of the following examples highlights important experiential additions to a leader's résumé, and each can be extremely challenging and difficult. But just because something is difficult doesn't make it more important in experiential terms. In fact, we believe that degree of difficulty is a low bar when setting experiential standards for most leaders.

Here are a few "difficult" issues that should occupy a position on every leader's résumé:

- Downsizing an organization
- Terminating a close team member
- Closing a business
- Divesting a business
- Building a new business unit from scratch
- Restructuring a significant part of a business
- Having public visibility and exposure to external investors and shareholders

There are degrees of difficulty and opportunity in each of these examples that could elevate their importance to that of an overall business, but our view is that examples such as these are the table stakes in an experiential analysis of what leaders offer. When hiring an executive leader from external candidates, each would need to be checked off, but none adds real weight to the final decision—absence might detract, but presence doesn't add. If you work for an organization that does place high value on these issues over others, it may indicate more serious problems in senior leadership that need addressing.

Experiences That Do Matter

We conducted substantial experiential research in many organizations in an attempt to discover the ones that seemed important and were additive to the

Talents we have described here. We found that although some experiences were extremely common—like spending time in a marketing role—they rarely contributed much to a leader's overall success and effectiveness and were little more than "pass-through" experiences that might have added knowledge about the company but little else. The following experiences, however, did seem to add value. Across all the organizations we studied, these were the experiences that helped multiply a person's Talents and capabilities.

We don't have a list of specific experiences that leaders need to have accomplished in order to be the very best. Instead, we have defined a descriptive framework for analyzing experiences for their potential value. Risk is a consistent element in all the best leadership development and growth opportunities, and each of the following experiences should make that clear.

Delivering a High-Risk, Out-of-Expertise Project

"Delivering" means a successful outcome on predefined terms expressed in revenue, margin, or other measurable criteria. "High-risk" can mean a few things. It could be a high opportunity cost, where a multimillion-dollar investment has 1.5–2× potential first-year gains. Alternatively, the outcome could be closely linked to the leader's career development, the implication being that failure likely results in termination.

"Out-of-expertise" means that the leader is operating away from their comfort zone. They are leading the project not because of technical expertise but because they are believed to be the best at coordinating everyone else's technical expertise. Other team members on the project might have more expertise than they do.

An interesting feature of this type of experience is that it typically occurs earlier in a leader's career so that they are thrown far outside their comfort zone. It amounts to being given assignments or promoted to roles beyond their capability (in terms of experience, skills, and knowledge—not Talent), with significant visibility by upper management, a great deal of autonomy, and deep functional focus. These experiences have major financial consequences and expose these individuals to executive-level leaders. Quite often these are classic "sink-or-swim" situations.

Turnaround of a Complete Business

Whom would you pick to lead a business turnaround? We suspect it might depend on the state of the business: how toxic it is, how much stress it is suffering, and whether the turnaround has the aim of stabilizing costs or a complete transformation and conversion to growth. Could it potentially lead to divestment? One thing should be clear: it will not be an easy assignment. This is why it appears on our list of critically important experiences that help shape a future leader's growth and development.

The context is key to business turnaround, but typically it reflects a leader either volunteering or being asked to take charge of a stressed or toxic business division. The toxicity can be either external and market-driven (such as competitor activity) or internal (like a facility that is precariously operating with deleterious engagement). This experience isn't about just optimizing an opportunity; it is about arresting a potentially fatal decline. It must be significant enough that the failure, if it wasn't reversed, could stress the overall company.

Leading a Significant Client-Focused Initiative

The people whom organizations entrust with high-stakes client initiatives are often their most trusted leaders. Many businesses allow their customer relationships to be defined by their lowest-paid, client-facing employees. Investing in programs and initiatives that shape how client relationships are managed over the long term has significant risk but huge potential upside. Assignments like these require leaders to stay especially connected to the essence of their business. It requires a deep understanding of the core operations and interpreting the motivations of clients to develop unique insights.

While leaders experience client-facing roles early in their careers, these projects are significant to the high-performing leaders we study because they tend to occur much later in their career, quite often after they have established themselves as leaders. The projects may have some technical problem-solving requirements but are much more demanding because they involve the following:

- Profound relationship awareness and cultivation
- The need to contextualize decisions within broad scopes

- A mastery of skills—like communication, delegation, planning, and strategy—expressed and used differently in this role than in any previous role
- Full accountability for financial, operational, client, and employee outcomes
- Leading assignments in a significantly new direction with direct, experiential impact on the client

Successful Leadership of a Complex Technical Project

Almost every major project tackled by an executive leader is both complex and technical. However, the experience we describe here is reserved for the most complex and those with the highest technical elements. An example might be leading the integration of a new enterprise resource planning platform, such as Oracle or SAP. Even mentioning projects of this scope and complexity will cause dread and anxiety in those who truly understand their magnitude. They are definitely the most complex, and in each functional area, they are certainly extremely technical.

These experiences require leaders to change their attitudes from "I can do it on my own" to "I need to do it through other people." It is through this transition that leaders show evidence of a systematic, holistic focus. Such roles and assignments require leaders to let go of the pieces (individual products, services, clients) and focus on the whole—how well do we conceive, develop, produce, and market to all clients? This attitudinal transition is achieved through the complexity of the project and the need to play a skillful coordinating role.

Building and Leading a Cross-Functional Team

This might seem like a relatively easy bar, but the critical component is that the leader is required to select the team. In most projects, a leader is typically assigned to lead a project with a team already in place. They might already be part of the team and elevated to lead it. Selecting a team is extremely difficult and often has to be done under extreme time pressure with the project already underway and up against rapidly approaching deadlines and deliverables.

The cross-functional element makes team selection more complex and demanding. A new team leader has to assess future team members and depend on recommendations from business partners, some of whom they might not know well or have any relationship with. The leader needs to help the team navigate through issues like project management and measurement, stage gates, updates, and presentations. They accomplish this while being the face of the project to the organization in terms of accountability. Projects of this kind are successful only if team members feel a high degree of engagement with the issues being resolved, which is nearly always the product of effective management and team leadership.

Interview Questions to Evaluate Experience
For Delivering a High-Risk, Out-of-Expertise Project
- Have you ever led a project where failure could have seriously damaged your career?
- Have you ever been asked to lead a significant initiative that you knew nothing about?
- What level of sponsorship did you have for this project?
- To whom did you report the outcomes?
- How would you describe the people and teams you were expected to pull together?
- How successful was the project? What were the measurable outcomes?

For Complete Turnaround of a Business
- Have you ever been placed in charge or volunteered for an assignment involving a business turnaround that had potentially fatal consequences?
- To what extent were you in complete charge?
- To whom did you report the outcomes?
- How would you describe the people and teams you built?
- How did you quantify your success?

For Leading a Significant Client-Focused Initiative
- Have you ever developed and implemented an idea that had a huge impact on clients or changed the way your company did business with clients?

- Did your idea solve an existing problem or define a new opportunity?
- What structural/behavioral impact did your idea have on the company?
- What was the revenue impact of your idea?

For Successful Leadership of a Complex Technical Project
- When do you first recall facing a project where you realized you couldn't complete it on your own?
- How would you describe how you reached a successful outcome?
- What did you learn from this experience that influenced how you managed similar projects in the future?
- How do you assign responsibilities for complex projects of this kind?
- Have you ever delegated responsibility and had it backfire? Why did it backfire?
- How has this influenced your leadership behavior?

For Building and Leading a Cross-Functional Team
- How would you describe a time when you were asked to lead a cross-functional team of people you hadn't managed before?
- Who picked you and why?
- What was the nature of the project you were leading?
- How did you go about selecting who would be on this team?
- How would you evaluate how well you did?
- What do you think you learned?
- How successful was the project?
- How did the outcome of this project affect how you were perceived as a leader?

These questions and their analysis need not be used only for selection. We recommend that any organization that takes succession planning seriously utilize these to ensure that future leaders are appropriately challenged with these rare and powerful experiences. Many companies lose the opportunity to test their growing leaders through these experiences in favor of their already established leaders. We suggest keeping track of your internal leadership Talent and the key experiences they need or have already been exposed to.

This information should be the product of an interview with each leader or potential future leader. The best preparation for that interview is to send each leader the aforementioned questions so that they can answer and be prepared to discuss them. The result will be a chart that might have some "traffic-light" qualities—some areas will be obviously green, and some elements will be obviously red. The remainder will be yellow, where there is no certainty about what has been achieved. The outcome, however, will be a plan that should inform higher-level discussions of overall succession planning. It is important for organizations to approach this work with diligence and care to get it right.

Two further suggestions will help your organization improve its overall selection process; they concern making the decision and how candidates should be treated.

HOLD OUT FOR THE VERY BEST CANDIDATE

At the end of the selection process, a candidate likely needs to be selected, although if no single candidate meets the predefined criteria, we may recommend starting over rather than investing in a predictably worse option. The aim should be to consider two or three of the strongest candidates against all the evidence sources available. This can be a challenge when hiring managers have developed a strong liking for one candidate based on little more than the relational connection they built with them during one interview.

Some of the best examples we have seen of how multiple credible candidates have been evaluated are those that developed a weighting and scoring system in advance. For example, 60 percent of the decision might be determined by formal assessment, 30 percent based on predefined attributes and characteristics determined during interviews, and 10 percent based on an evaluation of experience. These weightings and scores could vary by job/role, but the idea of having scored criteria is extremely important. Without this, it isn't always clear to us how companies balance the various evidence sources available to them. This process should be effective in trimming down a heavy field or narrowing a small field to one final candidate. Companies should be discouraged from reaching a quick "consensus" decision and hold out for the very best candidate instead.

Companies should also be resistant to the pressure sometimes exerted by candidates who are holding out offers from other companies for other jobs. This is akin to a hostage situation, and companies shouldn't play that game. It is all too easy to convince yourself that you are about to lose your best candidate unless an offer can be made quickly. This nearly always involves the kind of compromise that is rarely justified. We often hear from HR leaders who are keen to fill a vacancy and don't want to incur the wrath of hiring managers at "losing" a candidate whom they were seriously considering. Our advice, every time, is to let them go.

TREAT EVERY CANDIDATE WITH CARE AND DIGNITY

A key component of our assessment process is providing feedback to every leadership candidate, regardless of selection outcome. During these conversations, the criticism most consistently shared by rejected candidates is the abrupt silence after an otherwise positive experience. A candidate goes through a barrage of interviews, then hears nothing at all. This is especially jarring in conjunction with the encouragement they received during the interviews. Multiple attempts to contact HR or a hiring manager led to no response. The failure to appropriately address these candidates happens at nearly every level of an organization and is in direct contradiction to the purported "value of people" that most companies profess.

The lack of effort to provide even a courtesy telephone call to thank a candidate and inform them that they weren't successful will slowly diminish the company's pool of future applicants.

Candidates, especially for executive leadership roles, are already operating in a highly competitive selection environment, and the very best are often weighing multiple job options. Although a candidate might not be an appropriate match for a particular role, they could be exceptionally well suited for a different position in the future. Candidates who have been rejected need to feel positive about their experience if they are to consider joining a company at another time. They are not different from unhappy customers who need careful attention and management. Getting this part wrong invariably results in rejected candidates sharing their negative experience with their peers, which can further hamstring efforts to recruit the very best.

We recommend retaining communication with all candidates regardless of outcome and informing rejected candidates promptly when a decision has been made. This is especially important when an organization utilizes a selection methodology that measures future role performance, as this rejected candidate may be better suited to a different role in the future. Staying in the good graces of rejected candidates can make future selection decisions that much easier.

CHAPTER 11

Four Harsh Truths

OUR RESEARCH HAS GIVEN US IMMENSELY VALUABLE INSIGHT INTO THE hidden realities of modern selection, leadership, and Talent. Some of these discoveries are controversial, but we stand by our data and findings. They are supported by other research conducted in a variety of fields, and we draw analogies between that research and our own. If you find yourself instinctively disagreeing with any of the following topics—and we suspect you might—we ask that you use the same tools to validate or invalidate your opinion.

We are not shy about highlighting and challenging nonsense wherever we find it, and we find a lot. The field of human selection, it seems, provides a target-rich environment. The persistence in France of using handwriting to determine human personality is just one ridiculous example. The pervasiveness of those who believe that the human brain is like a malleable piece of putty that can be molded into any shape is another. And we are almost (but not completely) out of energy from debunking the claims of so-called body-language experts who claim to be able to detect when a person is lying by how they scratch their nose. As scientist Massimo Pigliucci summarized perfectly in the title of his book on the subject, *Nonsense on Stilts: How to Tell Science from Bunk*, there's just so much bunk.[1]

Critical review is a foundational component of the scientific method, and we have provided the citations for the studies we reference so that anyone can read the source material and decide for themselves whether we are accurately representing the information. We always consider the quality of research, the reputation of authors, and the history of the journal that published it. Science is not immune from fraud and controversy. Websites such as Retraction Watch, where scientific journal retractions are tracked, are helpful tools to ensure that a journal or researcher is trustworthy. The articles we use in the following conclusions are not without their critics, but they are well-founded and reliable. They are harsh truths about leadership, and you might not like them.

NOT EVERYONE IS OR CAN BE A LEADER

Utilizing objective measures with predictive value will increase the efficacy of any organization's selection process. In this book, we have focused mostly on leaders and our Executive Leadership Assessment, but this methodology works for any role, although the questions and assessments will be different. We have created similar assessments for sales managers, entry-level professionals, hourly paid workers, frontline managers, managers of managers, and so on. The patterns that we see in the data remain the same—some people are exceptional, and the vast majority are not.

You may have already reached this logical conclusion, but we feel that it needs to be made explicit: not everyone can be exceptional at everything. The majority of people will never measure as good leaders, and even fewer will measure as exceptional. The very best leaders are measured by their astounding performance and explained and predicted by their innate Talents. The same is true for sales managers and all the other roles we just highlighted. Some people simply do not have the requisite Talents for certain role types, which results in mediocre or worse performance when they are expected to perform such a role. For someone to be exceptional, they must stand out among the majority. They are the exception. Organizations should be as focused on finding the very best entry-level employees and frontline managers as they claim to be on finding the very best leaders. Our evidence suggests that this is far from the truth.

Although self-help gurus and pop psychology business books might try to persuade you differently, a person doesn't change all that much over the course of their life. Their innate characteristics and Talents remain consistent. Consider one of your own core predispositions, perhaps your fear or love of public speaking—has it changed over your life? Research indicates that it probably has not. Have you ever been able to use hard work and effort to become an expert at something that you previously struggled with? The same stability that we see in the Talents we measure in our assessments is true for other psychometric measurements and IQ. This kind of consistency is an indication that these psychological features are difficult to change because they are determined by genetics.

Right at the beginning of this book, I mentioned that a career program recommended that I become a funeral director as one possible career option. Although this career never materialized, the underlying assessment of my traits, dispositions, and characteristics that predicted this possibility has held true throughout my life. To this day, I continue to tire at the thought of complex social interactions and prefer my own company to that of others. I might have learned how to deal with this more effectively as my life has progressed, but the obdurate nature of my need for social disengagement has persisted.

Consequently, as you think about how your own career might progress, you have to balance aspiration with a heavy dose of reality. As much as you might want to climb the ladder and become a top-level leader in a company, only the initial rungs might be accessible to you. As your ego convinces you to do more, your capabilities might set you at a lower level. As hard as it might be to settle for that reality, it might be better for you in the long run. Far better to be happy and productive in a lower-level role than unhappy, stressed, and less productive in a role with a more important-sounding title. It will also be better for the people who might end up working for you.

LEADERSHIP CHARACTERISTICS ARE HARD TO DEVELOP

Treat with a grain of salt the proclamations of those who claim that leadership can be taught and learned. This is true only if you possess the necessary Talents, traits, dispositions, and characteristics described in this book. Many of you won't. If you disagree with us when we say that leadership can't be taught to those who don't possess these Talents, consider how effective you have been at changing some of the less desirable characteristics of your partner or significant other over the time you have known each other. Changing people—teaching them, if you will—is extremely difficult, and particularly so for leadership. It can be dispiriting to learn that characteristics that are beyond your reach might forever be so, but that's why this section is entitled "harsh truths." If everyone could learn leadership, we wouldn't see such a dearth of Talent at the top of companies...yet we do. Too many people believe that leadership can be taught, which is similar to the "nature/nurture" debate—and not a lot of personal improvement comes from nurture.

If you ask nearly anyone about which has *more* impact on a person's psychology, nature or nurture, they'll probably tell you that it's a nearly even mix. Both are important and inform our development in different ways, they might say. By claiming that it's a "bit of both," you avoid a difficult and technical argument in which few are qualified to engage. If you ask a neuroscientist, they will likely tell you that the dominant force is *nature*—our genetic makeup.

Our Genes Set the Stage for Who We Become

The composition of our genes has greater influence than nurture in shaping who we are and what we have become. This may be controversial, but it is a necessary truth to accept if we ever hope to see a world where the very best people are matched with the roles for which they are best suited. Training and development gurus, and the brain plasticity movement, hate this reality because it gives them a much smaller world in which to peddle their unscientific claims. No, the brain isn't infinitely malleable. No, personal courage isn't something that can be fixed on a training program. *You can try to teach me to show empathy, but you'll only succeed in helping me say nice things in menacing and threatening ways.*

Why is nature the strongest of the variables influencing who we are? Humans have tendencies and capacities across the species because we all share the same DNA. DNA is the code that builds each human and leads to variable expression of traits and characteristics that are either innate or prewired in the brain. These characteristics emerge through maturation, development, or experience. Kevin Mitchell wrote,

> Somehow, in the molecules of DNA in a fertilized egg from any of
> these species is a code or program of development that will produce an

organism with its species-typical nature. Most importantly, that entails the specification of how the brain develops in such a way that wires in these behavioral tendencies and capacities. Human nature, thus defined, is encoded in our genomes and wired into our brains in just the same way.[2]

A person's nature is a direct product of their brain—it certainly doesn't exist apart from it, contrary to the claims of those who argue for the existence of a human "soul." Some of the variable traits and characteristics that we observe in people, even close relatives, arise from real differences in the physical structure of different brains, such as size, structural organization, strength of connection between different regions of the brain, how microcircuits are wired, the volume and density of different cell types, the neurochemical balance between cells, and so on. These all contribute to the variability and range of behavioral expression that characterize each individual within each species. This is the fundamental reason why people are different from each other, sometimes in extremely subtle ways.

We are far from the time when we might be able to draw a strong connection between specific genes and certain psychological traits, such as *extraversion*. The brain might not even work that way. Our differences are explained by how each of our brains was wired before we were born. But if our genes are a major part of what makes us who we are, those same genes lay out a program for development that shapes exactly who we become. And it is in this development (which is also genetic) that many of our differences emerge.

Developmental Versus Environmental Influences on Development

The fact that variation in many of our traits is only partly genetic doesn't mean the default assumptions regarding the environment (nurture) fill the remaining gap; much of what does fill the gap is developmental (nature). Even if two people had identical genetic coding, they would still turn out differently to some degree, and this difference might be developmental rather than environmental and might even further strengthen the argument that our tendencies and capabilities are more innate, more driven by genetics, more an argument for nature. Keeping these three stages close to hand is extremely important in understanding variability in humans—genes (nature), development (nature—how genes are expressed over time), and environment (nurture—the specific conditions in which we experience life). This has been found in countless studies of identical and nonidentical twins.

Measures of IQ at a young age show some similarities based on family and environment that suggest that these factors do have an early impact on intelligence. However, over time, these similarities revert to differences that accentuate the starting IQs of children. When the same adoptive siblings who initially scored similar IQs at a young age were retested in their teenage years, they were no longer any more like each other than two strangers. The only logical conclusion is that the effect of environment tends to be early and short-lived rather than permanent and cumulative. Indeed, once the familial effect on IQ lessens over time, the genetic basis for intelligence accounts for between 75 and 80 percent of the variability we see, and the variance attributed to the family environment is zero.

Although IQ provides the strongest example of environmental impact, the variability is still modest, and much of it is based on the heritability of intelligence. There is a strong correlation between children with higher IQ and their parents having higher IQ. Smarter kids benefit from living in homes where there are more books because smarter parents read books and place a higher value on education. So even though there are environmental factors that influence growth in intelligence, heritability (genetics) still contributes the lion's share.

Results of twin studies have shown exactly what we would expect if our nature—genetics—is the dominant influence in our development.

Are Leaders Born or Made?

The nature vs. nurture debate should be settled, but this conclusion might matter less in thinking about leadership and the quest to help leaders improve. Whether leaders are born or made is the leadership equivalent of the nature/nurture question. Plenty of research evidence supports the "improvement" argument, but the question remains of how much of our genetic information—our natural Talents, characteristics, traits, and dispositions—provides us with an effective starting point, a "leg up." We know, for example, that we can teach people that certain desirable behaviors in one situation can be problematic in another. Just think of a person who is excellent at asserting a strong argument in a robust debate turning their attention to coaching a sensitive employee.

We know that we can teach leaders to slow down their action drive and more carefully consider the options in front of them. What we don't know is whether these behavioral improvements change the underlying traits and characteristics of the individual or if we just end up teaching them a way to manage them. This is important because changes in behavior are more fragile and more likely to revert to default under pressure or where the acquired behavioral adjustment is challenged. But getting this answer right might not matter.

If we are able to help people behave in ways that are more beneficial to them and others, then who cares? What cannot be denied is that the presence of certain dispositions favorable to effective leadership will advantage those who possess those dispositions and disadvantage those who don't. While we know we can help individuals improve in specific ways, it is unlikely that they can improve to the point that it makes a telling impact. The best we might achieve is to find ways of helping people manage their low spots—to stop these deficiencies from negatively affecting their overall contribution. Self-help gurus may believe that our greatest weaknesses can become towering strengths, but we know they can't.

WE MIGHT NEVER SOLVE THE LACK OF WORKPLACE DIVERSITY

In 2023, Fortune 500 companies hit a new record for Black CEOs with eight executives.[3] Although double the four recorded in 2020, this abysmally small number is an embarrassment and an indictment of how little the very largest companies have done to ensure fairness and representation in overall selection and particularly in leadership roles. How can a group such as Black Americans, who are 13.6 percent of the US population, account for only 1.6 percent of CEOs in the top five hundred companies? Why do so many companies still struggle to create organizations that are representative of the population or even their local communities? In the past two decades of our analysis, we have seen both global conglomerates and regional players fail to create approaches to selection that engender truly diverse, equitable, and inclusive workplaces.

In Chapter 2, we explained the problematic selection methods that most companies use to hire candidates. In that context, we were concerned mainly with the lack of predictive value provided by status quo selection processes. Selection methodologies that rely heavily on face-to-face interviews rarely produce consistently good results in terms of future role performance. However there is another—perhaps greater—danger in relying on selection processes that are not specifically tempered with statistical validity measures such as adverse impact.[4]

There is a growing body of scientific research examining the damaging impact of face-to-face interviews. A 2020 study found that in video interviews, "stigmatized applicants (compared to equally qualified, non-stigmatized applicants) receive lower interview judgements."[5] In this study, "stigmatized" was defined as individuals who were members of an ethnic minority, obese, physically disabled, or facially unattractive. Other research has found that face-to-face interviews suffer from a first-impression problem: "When interviewing stigmatized applicants, the alternative judgment…is likely constructed from biased information (e.g., responses to interview questions attempting to confirm the initial impression). The final judgment will thus not sufficiently deviate from the initial impression."[6]

Awareness of, and scientific insight into, the biases inherent in face-to-face interviews isn't new. In 1929, Rice noted "the possibility that the interviewer, however impartial in intent, may bias not merely the selection or the recording of the information in the minds of the interviewed, but the substance of that information itself, seems always present unless the conditions of the interview are rigidly controlled."[7] This proposed effect has been measured again and again, as in a 1993 study that showed that in college admissions, "attractiveness was significantly related to interviewer judgments of applicants in a face-to-face interview."[8]

Most companies are oblivious to the problems that start long before bias impacts their in-person selection process. Even before a candidate has been seen or interviewed, subliminal bias disadvantages those applicants who don't have English-sounding names. Second names tend to reflect race or ethnic origin, which impacts how candidate résumés are evaluated. A 2023 study sent twelve thousand identical résumés reflecting six ethnic groups to four thousand job openings and discovered that applicants with English-sounding names were twice as likely to receive a positive response from companies than candidates with ethnic-sounding names.[9] This was found to be true for both leadership and nonleadership roles and was particularly pronounced for roles requiring direct contact with customers. This occurs despite the focus and emphasis of companies on hiring people from "diverse slates" of applicants. It includes companies that had appointed DEI officers and that claimed to have invested heavily in DEI initiatives and training. It seems that most diverse applicants aren't even getting noticed. Résumés of equally qualified diverse candidates are liberally sprinkled through the trash can. Of course, every HR leader in every company will deny this. And search firms seem oblivious to these influences and incapable of offering help to address this reality. None are prepared to share data on the ethnicity of the candidates on their books.

The biases that disproportionately affect marginalized individuals are not limited to interviews. Discriminatory systems are rampant in modern business, and every organization must aggressively invest in eradicating them. In the past decade especially, we have been glad to see that many companies are starting to pay attention to this complex problem. Remediating the damage caused by these systems is not simple, and companies have frantically struggled to create fair and just workplaces. This anxiety has been exacerbated by the social climate of the digital age, where injustice is quickly exposed and brands are at the mercy of their next headline appearance. In this environment, organizations have thrown almost everything at the wall, but what has stuck? Which DEI initiatives actually work?

Appointing Chief Diversity Officers

Many companies keen to resolve discrimination issues have opted to appoint chief diversity officers (CDOs). These executive-level positions are tasked with inculcating justice and fairness within the organization through a variety of means, such as encouraging diverse hiring and promotion, organizing diversity training programs, addressing discriminatory systems and events, and advising other leaders about legal requirements and diversity concerns. Companies that have introduced the CDO position should be praised for their effort, but such decisions may not change their organizations as much as they expect.

Research by the National Bureau of Economic Research that studied 462 universities between 2001 and 2016 found that "the proportion of underrepresented tenured faculty hired in universities with a CDO present is 2.8 percentage points less diverse than in universities without a CDO at a 10 percent level of significance."[10] This is surprising, as we would expect and hope that universities with a CDO role would hire and retain diverse faculty at a higher rate than those without. This single study is certainly not evidence that CDO positions are irrelevant or a negative problem; however, it highlights a clear need for greater research on the efficacy of the role.

One potential cause for results like these is that despite the very best of intentions of statutory organizations like the EEOC (US) or the Equal Opportunities Commission (UK) and requirements like the General Data Protection Regulation (GDPR) (EU), the collection of identifying demographic details about job applicants prior to hiring is legally prohibited. This makes it nearly impossible for well-intentioned and concerned CDOs and organizations to determine whether the candidates subsequently appointed are a good statistical representation of the candidates who applied or were considered for the job.

Because CDOs are restricted from measuring their hiring efficacy, as in the case of the studied universities, they end up with relatively unchanged organizational representation. Many of the companies that we work with saw limited changes in demographic distribution after their appointment of a CDO. Additionally, it seems that CDO appointment has little effect on the rate of discriminatory event occurrence. This is supported by research indicating that diversity training programs are not very effective. A meta-analysis of various studies across both academic and business organizations reveals a multitude of reasons why these training programs fail to deliver results:

- A meta-analysis of 426 studies found weak immediate effects on unconscious bias and weaker effects on explicit bias. A side-by-side test of 17 interventions to reduce white bias toward blacks found that eight reduced unconscious bias, but in a follow-up examining eight implicit bias interventions and one sham, all nine worked, suggesting that subjects may have learned how to game the bias test....

- Decades of research on workplace training of all sorts suggests that by itself, training does not do much....

- Field and laboratory studies find that asking people to suppress stereotypes tends to reinforce them—making them more cognitively accessible to people....

- Recent research suggests that training inspires unrealistic confidence in antidiscrimination programs, making employees complacent about their own biases....

- When subjects are told that their employers have prodiversity measures such as training, they presume that the workplace is free of bias and react harshly to claims of discrimination....

- Self-determination research shows that when organizations frame motivation for pursuing a goal as originating internally, commitment rises, but when they frame motivation as originating externally, rebellion increases.[11]

As much as diversity training programs feel important and necessary in the fight against injustice, research does not support their efficacy. This may feel disheartening, and for us, it is. How can organizations become diverse, equitable, and inclusive if an intelligent and intentional exploration of biases and positionality doesn't work?

Why Diversity Might Be Beyond Reach

Why aren't organizations already diverse? Because historically, they hired disproportionately in favor of a privileged group. Why did they disproportionately hire white men? Because selection decisions were made using methodologies rife with bias. To revisit the 1929 article on bias in face-to-face interviews, Rice concluded, "The moral as to the need in any given inquiry of a *controlled* interviewing technique scarcely needs to be mentioned"[12] (emphasis ours). In this context,

Rice is describing a means of interviewing that is standardized, structured, and measurable. He advocates for an interview process that aims to cut through the bias inextricable from human interaction.

Demographic distinctions such as race and gender have no bearing on how well an individual scores on objective measures. Whether Black, Asian, white, or Hispanic or Latino, individuals are equally capable of measuring high or low. Being female or male has no influence on a person's capacity for Talent. Whether individuals are or are not high performers does not correlate to demographic groupings. This means that if selection decisions are based on solely objective measures, the resulting appointments should be nearly exact representations of the population at large. Any organization that struggles with diversity needs only to recognize that this underlying objectivity is the key to reversing decades of racial and gender discrimination.

The selection process is at the core of an organization's representation distribution, yet too many companies rely on the instincts of their hiring managers and interviewers to ensure an equitable workforce. This will never work. CDOs have their hands tied when it comes to measuring the fairness of their hiring process, and so their efficacy is difficult to prove. The biases that cause discriminatory hiring don't change through training programs and may even worsen the problem by providing a false sense of security.

We suggest that companies seeking to inculcate true diversity ensure that the CDO role is occupied by an individual who

- is well-versed in psychometric assessment;
- has experience in statistical measures of validity, reliability, and fairness; and
- is tasked with solving the danger of unchecked bias in selection processes.

The role of CDO is an excellent choice for an organization looking to incorporate objective measures of predictability into the selection process. CDOs are uniquely positioned to understand the biases inherent in all interactions and can become powerful advocates for systems that diminish the effects of these biases on an organization's operation. The right CDO will see the benefit of a data-driven approach.

Diversity Through Data

One of the most rewarding aspects of our work with our clients has been our ability to provide objective advocacy for underrepresented candidates who qualify for leadership positions. We described one such example in the Preface of this book, but that was hardly a unique experience. We are continuously discovering exceptional leaders hidden within the organizations we assess. These are people who have been passed over for various (irrelevant) reasons, the victims of bias-ridden processes. They overwhelmingly come from underrepresented groups and are subject to the systemic historical discrimination intrinsic to generic selection methodologies.

An astounding finding that emerged through the creation and administration of our Executive Leadership Assessment is that individuals from underrepresented groups who are already in leadership roles test measurably higher than their colleagues. Prior to organizations using our assessment in their selection process, women leaders, Black leaders, Asian leaders, and Hispanic or Latino leaders needed to be far stronger in their innate Talents than their white male peers. This didn't surprise us, but it was still shocking to see the story told through objective measurement.

Is this the case in your organization? Do individuals from underrepresented groups need to prove themselves measurably more to be hired or promoted? Unless your selection process incorporates objective measures using methodologies that specifically measure for adverse impact, then the answer is probably yes. We hope this frustrates you. It frustrates us.

The injustice in selection that most companies propagate is unnecessary and overcoming it has become a core mission of our company. We want to live in a world where the most exceptional candidates are appointed to the roles that are best suited to their innate Talents. To this end, we have developed dozens of assessments that predict future performance for a variety of roles, the most popular of which is our Executive Leadership Assessment, but we don't want to require organizations to become our clients to bring about this necessary change. We want to see companies everywhere use objective, fair, validated measurements to make selection decisions that truly produce DEI.

PERSONALITIES AND TALENTS AREN'T THE SAME THING

Measures of personality have been around for almost one hundred years, and assessment tools like the Myers-Briggs Type Indicator (MBTI) have increased their popularity as a means of categorizing people into generic personality types. Despite its popularity, the MBTI is rank pseudoscience competing with astrology rather than meteorology in terms of efficacy. It isn't the purpose of this book to pour even more scorn on discredited assessments, although companies should exercise caution before using them and should never use them as part of a selection process.[13]

Most tests of personality are based on the "Big Five" theory, which lists the myriad descriptors of personality in five broad types—conscientiousness, agreeableness, neuroticism, openness to experience, and extraversion.[14] These broad groups of personality are fundamentally different from Talent. Personality can be measured in all people across all levels and ages across society. Talent tends to express itself in a much narrower subset of society with respect to characteristics, traits, and dispositions that are essential for high performance in a specific role or job. The two should never be confused or conflated.

Consequently, if you are using a personality assessment for job hiring and selection, the results will likely be unimpressive and the effect size barely relevant. Quite simply, when personality-based assessments are used for selection, they lack strong predictive validity, and some have a rather poor record on the previously discussed issue—adverse impact and diversity more broadly. An HBO Max documentary called *Persona: The Dark Truth Behind Personality Tests* did an excellent job of highlighting why personality assessments shouldn't be used for employee selection, as Aimee Harel noted in her article "The Problems with Using Personality Tests for Hiring."[15]

Talent assessments, on the other hand, are typically built to predict success in specific roles and are much more reliable, fair, and valid. If you want to make a start on improving your company's selection practices, then stop using personality assessments for job selection.

SUMMARY

This book has brought you on a journey—part personal and part organizational—that introduces you to The Five Talents That Really Matter in leadership. The findings described in this book are based on credible research—lots of it—and we've provided some tools and resources along the way. Some of these tools will be useful to you in your personal leadership journey, and others will be helpful for you to introduce into your organization. Helping you to improve your leadership while also helping organizations improve their whole approach to leadership selection is intentional on our part. The two improvements need to go hand in hand. Aiding you as a leader while leaving your organization in the nineteenth century won't be a great help. Change and improvement need to be across the board. We hope you are up to the task.

The final section of the book describes how you can take our Executive Leadership Assessment.

CHAPTER 12

Are You an Exceptional Leader?

I T IS OUR HOPE THAT THIS BOOK INSPIRES A NEW GENERATION OF LEADERS who see in themselves the Talents that really matter when it comes to deciding who could be an effective leader. Countless exceptional leaders are hidden in their own organizations. Our Executive Leadership Assessment has the unique ability to discover such individuals. It shines a bright light on Talents, the essence of a leader. Our hope is to continue finding the very best leaders and ensuring that they are put on the path that best suits them.

No leader possesses every Talent, disposition, or trait that captures the extent of high-performance leadership, and you certainly won't be the first. Furthermore, there is no single path that leaders take to achieve their success and no single mold that shapes all great leaders. There is no common starting point, no consistent role or set of experiences. Your differences are what make you unique. But we can certainly learn from individuals leading teams and companies who do achieve world-class results, and their story has been told in these pages. Make no mistake, the performance of leaders is measurable, and it is by learning from the very best that we can begin to understand what really matters in leadership.

In previous chapters, we've illustrated a more effective selection process for leaders in companies that emphasizes the innate characteristics that drive the highest levels of executive performance. We focus on executive selection because the cost of getting these decisions wrong is so high. It's not just the costs of recruitment, relocation, and induction that companies need to consider when appointing candidates to leadership positions. They must also consider how great the opportunity is to grow, and potentially transform, a business while positively impacting the lives of all those who inhabit its sphere of influence.

Companies will always be battling the reality that no leader is perfect. For as many areas that stand out as phenomenal strengths, there will be others where a candidate struggles. Those struggles can be limiting and are nearly always visible. Leadership is about making trade-offs regarding where to spend time and energy. When weighing these trade-offs, it's important that we understand the limits of what can be developed and start to prioritize the unchanging characteristics that are often assumed, poorly measured, or altogether ignored when we're evaluating who is the best leader for the job.

For individuals looking to develop and improve, it can be difficult to make an accurate determination of your own capabilities as a leader. Those lucky enough to have been given fair, direct, and accurate feedback still don't know how those opinions rank against leaders outside their company and industry. The standard of comparison is always subjective and questionable. We have tried, in this book, to focus your self-awareness on the things that really matter in leadership, but we recognize that this will always be a difficult comparison for you to make with yourself. While we have provided a framework to help you consider your development, you have no initial measurement starting point and certainly no potential measurement of improvement over time.

The reality is that you don't know how good you are now, and you don't know how good you might be in the future. You certainly have potential—but for what?

A good psychometric assessment of the kinds of characteristics that we define in this book is the best starting point for evaluating yourself. There are few credible offerings for individuals, as most assessment providers require company-level contracts and have no flexibility to provide benefits for individuals. You might work in an organization that deploys a personality inventory as part of their development offering, but the results, which come in vaguely illustrated archetypes and styles, fail to provide the kind of insight that gives you a language for understanding what makes you unique and how to apply the right focus to your development as a leader. We aim to address that problem.

We're offering you the chance to take our powerful Executive Leadership Assessment. This assessment isn't for everyone—it isn't a measure of sweetness and light; it's a measure of potential leadership effectiveness. Here are some considerations to determine whether this is the right assessment for you:

- Are you currently in a role where you have a legitimate "line of sight" to a top executive leadership position? Remember, this assessment is making a prediction regarding success in executive leadership roles that are no more than three levels away from the company's CEO. If you are below that level, this assessment isn't for you . . . but it might be one day.

- Are you above the age of thirty-two? We see greater variability in the results for the few people below that age who have taken this assessment.

- Do you actively seek feedback about yourself and your performance, and do you receive this feedback positively? If you find it hard to listen to feedback about yourself (and many people do), then you should pause and consider this carefully before going ahead.

- Do you tend to have a more positive view of yourself than other people do when they evaluate your capabilities? Again, consider carefully whether you want to go through this process. This assessment can be humbling and won't calibrate its results to the fragility of your ego.

- Are you actively seeking a new job opportunity and want an objective evaluation of your leadership capabilities? This assessment could be of great help to you.

- Are you currently in a top leadership position and want some insights to inform your future development? This assessment could be of great help to you.

You can access all the information you need to complete the assessment and discover your unique leadership Talents on our website. We hope you enjoy answering our questions, and we're excited to engage with those who desire more direct feedback:

www.conchie.com

ACKNOWLEDGMENTS

W E PAY TRIBUTE TO THE ALMOST SIXTY THOUSAND LEADERS IN OUR assessment database and the clients and organizations that we have worked with over the years. Their anonymized data helped us build and validate our whole assessment approach, and without their involvement, our insights and discoveries would have remained unknown.

We want to issue a broad and general "thank you" to all our clients, friends, and associates who helped through providing observations and comments during the early drafting of the book manuscript. Manuscripts don't just appear intact; they evolve based on the influence of many people, and although there are too many to name individually, we appreciate their contributions.

We would particularly like to thank our wonderful publishing agent, Leah Spiro, who provided invaluable guidance and advice through this process. She introduced us to our proposal writer, Lisa Shannon, and our publishing partner and editor, Dan Ambrosio at Hachette Go. We've enjoyed our long partnership with Barbara Cave Hendricks, going back to her help marketing *Strengths Based Leadership*, and we are fortunate, and grateful, for her help again here.

Front and center in our thanks are two individuals with recognizable second names who played powerful roles early and later in our initial editing process. Amy Conchie has prior editing experience and helped keep us on track when we needed to focus our manuscript and tighten our message. Thomas Conchie was a phenomenal help in carefully crafting the sequence and flow of our content. He brought not only intelligence and subject matter expertise but also his ability to be specific in making arguments and producing a powerful narrative. We are indebted to them both. The apple clearly does not fall far from the tree, and this was a family effort. Along with Barry's wife, Nicola Conchie, they served to keep the writing project on track.

We also want to highlight the contribution of our executive analysts, Keith Conchie and Jasmin Lillesve. Keith has diligently assessed, analyzed, and coded hundreds of leaders and helped ensure the reliability and validity of our data. Jasmin, in addition to her excellent analyst work, curated and designed the graphics for the book. Her creative vision and attention to detail brought these pages to life, ensuring that the visual elements seamlessly complemented and enhanced our message.

I want to highlight three strong female leaders who were not only extremely Talented and capable leaders in their own right, but who also set an exceptional example to female leaders everywhere. Anne Precious was a senior leader at Honley High School in Huddersfield, UK—a truly remarkable leader; Liz Ryan was a board chair and lawyer specializing in representing families of children with special needs, and a professional with an incredible, positive vision for education; and Connie Rath, PhD, was dean of Gallup University, my boss and professional guide when I arrived in Washington, DC. All had a very different but profound influence on my life and professional development. I thank them here. This book would not be possible without their involvement in shaping my professional career.

There are some individuals who have been a constant presence in our professional work and lives, and their influence can be felt in these pages—Ali Bebo was one of the very first clients I met when I arrived in the US, and she has been ever-present in my professional life. The very best non-HR CHRO, her contribution has had a profound influence on my work. I am proud to be associated with her. Other valuable contributions have come from John Clendening, Kevin Christoffersen, Curt Hartman, Shaelie Lambarth, Heather Cohen, Ken Shearer, Stefan Larsson, Ted Hayes, PhD, Pat Beyer, Jim Heath, JP Lebudel, Jennifer Meade, PhD, Tom Rath, PhD, Alex LeJeune, Adam Burke, Don Ronchi, PhD, Mark Lipscomb, Tim Scannell, Erik Anderson, Essex Mitchell, Steve MacMillan, Elie Azar, John Kibarian, John Ferrell, and Maria Brinck. Finally, a special thank you to Pamela Stroko, for her belief in the integrity of our work, and for her advocacy ensuring this book gets the right visibility in the HCM marketplace. There are hundreds of others, too numerous to name, and we thank all those who've made telling contributions to our work and thinking.

NOTES

Preface

1. Brian Kennedy and Meg Hefferon, "What Americans Know About Science," Pew Research Center, March 28, 2019, https://www.pewresearch.org/science/2019/03/28/what-americans-know-about-science/. The scientific method is not well understood outside the natural sciences, so the results of this research should not surprise us. It is not realistic for us to advise everyone to read Karl Popper on "falsification," but this concept does lie at the heart of scientific inquiry.

2. Michael Shermer, *Why Smart People Believe Weird Things: Pseudoscience, Superstition, and Other Confusions of Our Time* (New York: Holt McDougal, 2002).

Chapter 1: What People and Companies Get Wrong About Leadership

1. Jim Collins, *Good to Great: Why Some Companies Make the Leap and Others Don't* (London: Random House Business Books, 2001).

2. Steven D. Levitt, "From Good to Great...to Below Average," *Freakonomics*, July 28, 2008, https://freakonomics.com/2008/07/from-good-to-great-to-below-average/. We think Levitt is too kind in his treatment of this iconic book. The title, in our view, should have been *Good to Great and Back Again*.

3. Robert K. Greenleaf, *Servant Leadership: A Journey into the Nature of Legitimate Power and Greatness*, 25th anniversary ed. (Mahwah, NJ: Paulist Press, 2002).

4. Hermann Hesse, *The Journey to the East* (New York: Picador, 1956).

5. Nathan Eva, Mulyadi Robin, Sen Sendjaya, Dirk Dierendonk, and Robert C. Liden, "Servant Leadership: A Systematic Review and Call for Future Research," *Leadership Quarterly* 30, no. 1 (2019): 111–132, https://doi.org/10.1016/j.leaqua.2018.07.004.

6. Philip Rosenzweig, *The Halo Effect...and the Eight Other Business Delusions That Deceive Managers* (New York: Free Press, 2007).

7. Stephen R. Covey, *The 7 Habits of Highly Effective People* (London: Simon & Schuster UK, 2020). As revered as Covey is for this definitive book, he failed to address whether the "habits" he advocated were even capable of being learned. It is remarkable how many people believe that anything can be learned by everyone with the right application. Not only does this belief fly in the face of everyone's direct experience at school, but it inflicts the accusation of "lazy" on all those who fail to learn a desired skill.

8. Glenn Llopis, "The Most Successful Leaders Do 15 Things Automatically, Every Day," *Forbes*, February 18, 2013, https://www.forbes.com/sites/glennllopis/2013/02/18/the-most-successful-leaders-do-15-things-automatically-every-day/?sh=58107a6869d7.

9. Michael Page, "8 Must-Have Qualities of an Effective Leader," https://www.michaelpage.com/advice/management-advice/development-and-retention/8-must-have-qualities-effective-leader.

10. James Collins and Jerry Porras, *Built to Last: Successful Habits of Visionary Companies* (New York: HarperBusiness Essentials, 1994).

11. Jennifer Reingold and Ryan Underwood, "Was 'Built to Last' Built to Last?" *Fast Company*, November 1, 2004, https://www.fastcompany.com/50992/was-built-last-built-last.

12. Daniel Kahneman, *Thinking, Fast and Slow* (New York: Farrar, Straus and Giroux, 2011).

13. John Geirland, "Go with the Flow," *Wired*, September 1, 1996, https://www.wired.com/1996/09/czik/. This book is equally brilliant and disliked depending on whom you talk to. I had the privilege of speaking on the same stage as Mike Csikszentmihalyi at a psychology conference in Italy in 2005, and his description of "flow states" and how they can be intentionally crafted was inspiring. A must-read book for anyone interested in optimal flourishing.

14. Barbara Fredrickson, "The Broaden-and-Build Theory of Positive Emotions," *Philosophical Transactions of the Royal Society B: Biological Sciences* 359, no. 1449 (September 29, 2004): 1367–1378, doi:10.1098/rstb.2004.1512. Barb has been much maligned by the psychological thought police who derided her work with Lombardi on praise ratios. The idea that there is an effective means of quantifying praise over criticism was too much for the bullies who saw a downside in every human endeavor and derided this idea as "happy talk." However, her excellent work on "broaden and build" remains a cogent argument for expanding human capability.

15. Adam Grant and Barry Schwartz, "Too Much of a Good Thing: The Challenge and Opportunity of the Inverted U," *Perspectives on Psychological Science* 6, no. 1 (February 3, 2011): 61–76, https://doi.org/10.1177/1745691610393523. This paper, more than many others, is guilty of a significant misattribution error—the idea, based on the inverted U, that everything in excess can turn into a weakness. It's complete nonsense. They use linear, quantitative examples, such as the idea that a deficiency of courage is cowardice but an excess of courage is recklessness. A deficiency of pride is humility, but an excess of pride is vanity. They go on in this vein...tediously. But they get it completely wrong. A strength is a strength, and as we think of an attribute such as courage representing a strength, it is a misattribution to describe any aspect of this as a weakness. Think of communication. At what point does being an effective communicator become a problem—an excess?

16. Grant and Schwartz.

17. Robert M. Yerkes and John D. Dodson, "The Relation of Strength of Stimulus to Rapidity of Habit-Formation," *Journal of Comparative Neurology and Psychology* 18, no. 5 (1908): 459–482, https://doi.org/10.1002/cne.920180503.

18. Tomas Chamorro-Premuzic, *The Talent Delusion: Why Data, Not Intuition, Is the Key to Unlocking Human Potential* (London: Little, Brown, 2017).

19. Dan Rockwell, "Your Greatest Strength Is Your Weakness," *Leadership Freak*, March 8, 2010, https://leadershipfreak.blog/2010/03/08/your-greatest-strength-is-your-weakness/.

20. "Survivorship Bias," Wikipedia, https://en.wikipedia.org/wiki/Survivorship_bias #:~:text=Survivorship%20bias%20or%20survival%20bias,conclusions%20because%20of %20incomplete%20data.

Chapter 2: What Companies Get Wrong About Selection

1. Peter Cappelli and J. R. Keller, "Talent Management: Conceptual Approaches and Practical Challenges," *Annual Review of Organizational Psychology & Behavior* 1 (2014): 305–331, https://doi.org/10.1146/annurev-orgpsych-031413-091314.

2. Gallup, "State of the American Workplace," 2013, https://mediaassets.kjrh.com/html /pdfs/unhappyemployees_gallup.pdf. Gallup is the foremost organization in measures of employee engagement, and although the study referenced here is from 2013, annual updates are available at www.gallup.com.

3. Gallup, "Employee Engagement," 2023, https://www.gallup.com/394373/indicator -employee-engagement.aspx.

4. Peter Cappelli and J. R. Keller, "Talent Management: Conceptual Approaches and Practical Challenges," *Annual Review of Organizational Psychology and Organizational Behavior* 1 (March 2014): 305–331, https://doi.org/10.1146/annurev-orgpsych-031413-091314; Gallup.

5. Beatrice I. J. M. van der Heijden and André H. J. Nijhof, "The Value of Subjectivity: Problems and Prospects for 360-Degree Appraisal Systems," *International Journal of Human Resource Management* 15, no. 3 (2004): 493–511, doi:10.1080/0958519042000181223.

6. Jack Zenger and Joseph Folkman, "What Makes a 360-Degree Review Successful?" *Harvard Business Review*, December 2020, https://hbr.org/2020/12/what-makes-a-360 -degree-review-successful. We advise caution regarding Zenger and Folkman and their claims regarding 360 assessments because their entire business model is built around them. It's a little like the conversation I once had with a chiropractor who claimed that every ailment and disease afflicting the human body, from Parkinson's disease to cancer, could be cured by back and spine manipulation.

7. Emma Rachel Andersson, Carolina E. Hagberg, and Sara Hagg, "Gender Bias Impacts Top-Merited Candidates," *Frontiers in Research Metrics and Analytics* 6 (2021), https://www.frontiersin.org/articles/10.3389/frma.2021.594424/full, doi:10.3389/frma.2021 .594424.

8. AESC, "The Role of Executive Assessments in the Search Process," https://www .aesc.org/insights/research/assessments-executive-selection.

9. F. L. Schmidt and J. E. Hunter, "The Validity and Utility of Selection Methods in Personnel Psychology: Practical and Theoretical Implications of 85 Years of Research Findings," *Psychological Bulletin* 124, no. 2 (1998): 262–274, https://doi.org/10.1037/0033-2909.124.2.262.

Chapter 3: Researching the Very Best Leaders

1. Emma Hinchliffe, "Women CEOs Run 10.4% of Fortune 500 Companies. A Quarter of the 52 Leaders Became CEO in the Last Year," *Fortune*, June 5, 2023, https://fortune.com/2023/06/05/fortune-500-companies-2023-women-10-percent/.

2. Anthony J. Kunnan, "Test Fairness," in *European Language Testing in a Global Context*, ed. Michael Milanovic and Cyril J. Weir (Cambridge, UK: Cambridge University Press), 27–48, https://www.cambridgeenglish.org/Images/329229-studies-in-language-testing-volume-18.pdf#page=48. One equally interesting example showing how culture and language intersect is the question "Why are manholes round?" It's an excellent critical thinking question, and relatively few respondents are able to state that a round shape is the only one that can't fall through itself, which makes it safe for workers below to push the manhole cover up without it falling back on them and through the hole. Unfortunately, quite a few European countries have no concept of "manhole cover," and the question doesn't effectively translate.

3. The literature on test-retest reliability in the nursing and health professions is presented at "Test Retest Reliability," *ScienceDirect*, https://www.sciencedirect.com/topics/nursing-and-health-professions/test-retest-reliability.

4. The literature on Cronbach's alpha coefficient in the nursing and health professions is presented at "Cronbach Alpha Coefficient," *ScienceDirect*, https://www.sciencedirect.com/topics/nursing-and-health-professions/cronbach-alpha-coefficient#:~:text=Cronbach's%20alpha%20is%20a%20way,items%20relative%20to%20the%20varianc.

Chapter 4: What Have We Learned?

1. Marshall Goldsmith and Mark Reiter, *What Got You Here Won't Get You There* (New York: Hyperion, 2007). This isn't a very good book, but it's an excellent title.

2. "Action Bias," Wikipedia, https://en.wikipedia.org/wiki/Action_bias. The bias to action is the most common bias affecting executive teams.

3. Michael P. Wilmot and Deniz S. Ones, "Agreeableness and Its Consequences: A Quantitative Review of Meta-analytic Findings," *Personality and Social Psychology Review* 26, no. 3 (2022), https://doi.org/10.1177/10888683211073007.

4. Gwendolyn Seidman, "Why Do We Like People Who Are Similar to Us?" *Psychology Today*, December 18, 2018, https://www.psychologytoday.com/us/blog/close-encounters/201812/why-do-we-people-who-are-similar-us#:~:text=Consensual%20validation%3A%20Meeting%20people%20who,and%20maybe%20even%20a%20virtue. See also Kendra Cherry, "What Is the Halo Effect?" *Verywell Mind*, October 24, 2022, https://www.verywellmind.com/what-is-the-halo-effect-2795906.

Chapter 5: Setting Direction

1. Adrienne Fox, "Raising Engagement," *HR Magazine*, Society for Human Resource Management (SHRM), May 1, 2010, https://www.shrm.org/hr-today/news/hr-magazine/pages/0510fox.aspx.

2. "Marx's Theory of Alienation," Wikipedia, https://en.wikipedia.org/wiki/Marx%27s_theory_of_alienation.

3. Amanda Shantz, Kerstin Alfes, and Catherine Truss, "Alienation from Work: Marxist Ideologies and Twenty-First-Century Practice," *International Journal of Human Resource Management* 25, no. 18 (2014): 2529–2550, doi:10.1080/09585192.2012.667431.

4. Bryant P. H. Hui, Jacky C. K. Ng, Erica Berzaghi, Lauren A. Cunningham-Amos, and Aleksandr Kogan, "Rewards of Kindness? A Meta-analysis of the Link Between Prosociality and Well-Being," *Psychological Bulletin* 146, no. 12 (2020): 1084–1116, doi:10.1037/bul0000298.

5. Adam M. Kuczynski, Max A. Halvorson, Lily R. Slater, and Jonathan W. Kanter, "The Effect of Social Interaction Quantity and Quality on Depressed Mood and Loneliness: A Daily Diary Study," *Journal of Social and Personal Relationships* 39, no. 3 (2022): 734–756, https://doi.org/10.1177/02654075211045717. Much has been written in recent years about the significance of generational differences in the workplace. Members of Gen Z, for example, are thought to need a sense of mission, purpose, and value in their work more than previous generations. There is no credible research to support this rather tired, lazy hypothesis. Rather than talking about the overlapping bell curve as an explanation of this nonsense, let's just say that variation on this issue is far greater within a so-called generation and always exceeds the variation between so-called generations. People are first and foremost individuals and need to be treated as such.

6. Sasmit Patra and Vijay Pratap Singh, "The Challenge of Retaining Employees: Employee Engagement, Reducing Cynicism and Determinants of Employee Retention," *Global Journal of Arts & Management* 2, no. 1 (2012): 53–60, http://www.rrjp.in/admin/papers/P-12%20Vijay%20Pratap%20Singh.pdf.

7. Marshall Goldsmith and Mark Reiter. *What Got You Here Won't Get You There: How Successful People Become Even More Successful* (New York: Hyperion, 2007).

8. Karolina Hübner, "Spinoza's Epistemology and Philosophy of Mind," *The Stanford Encyclopedia of Philosophy*, ed. Edward N. Zalta, Spring 2022, https://plato.stanford.edu/archives/spr2022/entries/spinoza-epistemology-mind/.

9. Javier DeFelipe, "The Evolution of the Brain, the Human Nature of Cortical Circuits, and Intellectual Creativity," *Frontiers in Neuroanatomy* 5 (May 16, 2011), https://www.frontiersin.org/articles/10.3389/fnana.2011.00029/full, https://doi.org/10.3389/fnana.2011.00029.

10. Mark P. Mattson, "Superior Pattern Processing Is the Essence of the Evolved Human Brain," *Frontiers in Neuroscience* 8 (2014), doi:10.3389/fnins.2014.00265.

11. Hiroshi Ito and Aki Sakurai, "Familiar and Unfamiliar Face Recognition in a Crowd," *Psychology* 5, no. 9 (2014): 1011–1018, doi:10.4236/psych.2014.59113. A fascinating experiment in artificial intelligence (AI) generated faces (https://this-person-does-not-exist.com/en) that fooled most people into thinking they were real. Researchers found that

AI-generated white faces were judged to be human more than actual human faces. See Elizabeth J. Miller, Ben A. Steward, Zak Witkower, Clare A. M. Sutherland, Eva G. Krumhuber, and Amy Dawel, "AI Hyperrealism: Why AI Faces Are Perceived as More Real Than Human Ones," *Psychological Science* 34, no. 12 (November 13, 2023), https://journals.sagepub.com, doi:10.1177/09567976231207095.

12. Anne Treisman, "How the Deployment of Attention Determines What We See," *Visual Cognition* 14, nos. 4–8 (2006): 411–443, doi:10.1080/13506280500195250.

13. Genevieve Mortimer, "Business Planning for Unintended Consequences," *International Journal of Sustainable Strategic Management* 5, no. 2 (2016): 87–102, https://doi.org/10.1504/IJSSM.2016.080467.

14. Carey K. Morewedge and Daniel Kahneman, "Associative Processes in Intuitive Judgment," *Trends in Cognitive Sciences* 14, no. 10 (2010): 435–440, https://doi.org/10.1016/j.tics.2010.07.004.

15. Amos Tversky and Daniel Kahneman, "Availability: A Heuristic for Judging Frequency and Probability," *Cognitive Psychology* 5, no. 2 (1973): 207–232, https://doi.org/10.1016/0010-0285(73)90033-9.

16. Nassim Nicholas Taleb, *The Black Swan: The Impact of the Highly Improbable* (New York: Random House, 2007).

17. "Cognitive Bias," Wikipedia, https://en.wikipedia.org/wiki/Cognitive_bias.

18. Glenn S. Sanders and Robert S. Baron, "The Motivating Effects of Distraction on Task Performance," *Journal of Personality and Social Psychology* 32, no. 6 (1975): 956–963, https://doi.org/10.1037/0022-3514.32.6.956.

19. Todd Vogel, Zachary Savelson, A. Ross Otto, and Mathieu Roy, "Forced Choices Reveal a Trade-off Between Cognitive Effort and Physical Pain," *eLife* 9 (November 17, 2020), doi:10.7554/eLife.59410.

20. Karen E. Jacowitz and Daniel Kahneman, "Measures of Anchoring in Estimation Tasks," *Personality and Social Psychology Bulletin* 21, no. 11 (1995): 1161–1166, https://doi.org/10.1177/01461672952111004.

21. Lisa K. Fazio, David G. Rand, and Gordon Pennycook, "Repetition Increases Perceived Truth Equally for Plausible and Implausible Statements," *Psychonomic Bulletin & Review* 26 (2019): 1705–1710, https://doi.org/10.3758/s13423-019-01651-4.

22. Thomas Koch and Thomas Zerback, "Helpful or Harmful? How Frequent Repetition Affects Perceived Statement Credibility," *Journal of Communication* 63, no. 6 (2013): 993–1010, https://doi.org/10.1111/jcom.12063.

23. Daniel Kahneman, "A Psychological Point of View: Violations of Rational Rules as a Diagnostic of Mental Processes," *Behavioral and Brain Sciences* 23, no. 5 (2000): 681–683, doi:10.1017/S0140525X00403432.

24. Solomon E. Asch, "Forming Impressions of Personality," *Journal of Abnormal and Social Psychology* 411, no. 3 (1946): 258–290, https://doi.org/10.1037/h0055756, https://www.romolocapuano.com/wp-content/uploads/2013/08/Asch-Forming-Impressions-Of-Personality.pdf.

25. Asch, 270.

26. Solomon E. Asch, "Studies of Independence and Conformity: I. A Minority of One Against a Unanimous Majority," *Psychological Monographs: General and Applied* 70, no 9 (1956): 1–70, https://doi.org/10.1037/h0093718.

27. Daniel Kahneman, *Thinking, Fast and Slow* (New York: Farrar, Straus and Giroux, 2011), 82.

28. "Dunning-Kruger Effect," *Psychology Today*, https://www.psychologytoday.com/us /basics/dunning-kruger-effect.

29. Emily Pronin and Kathleen Schmidt, "Claims and Denials of Bias and Their Implications for Policy," in *The Behavioral Foundations of Public Policy*, ed. E. Shafir (Princeton, NJ: Princeton University Press, 2013), 195–216, https://psycnet.apa.org/record/2013-00609 -011.

30. Kahneman, *Thinking, Fast and Slow*.

31. Kahneman.

32. Hugh M. Culbertson, "Breadth of Perspective: An Important Concept for Public Relations," *Public Relations Research Annual* 1, nos. 1–4 (1989): 3–25, doi:10.1207/ s1532754xjprr0101-4_1.

33. Vanderbilt University, "The Brain Doesn't Like Visual Gaps and Fills Them In," *ScienceDaily*, August 21, 2007, www.sciencedaily.com/releases/2007/08/070820135833.htm. This article provides lots of examples, some counterintuitive, that explain how research into the visual cortex leads humans to see the frame of images and then fill in gaps that are missing.

34. Caleb Crain, "Why We Don't Read, Revisited," *New Yorker*, June 14, 2018, https:// www.newyorker.com/culture/cultural-comment/why-we-dont-read-revisited.

35. Paul Leinwand, Cesare Mainardi, and Art Kleiner, "Only 8% of Leaders Are Good at Both Strategy and Execution," *Harvard Business Review*, December 30, 2015, https://hbr .org/2015/12/only-8-of-leaders-are-good-at-both-strategy-and-execution.

36. Michael D. Watkins, "Demystifying Strategy: The What, Who, How, and Why." *Harvard Business Review*, September 10, 2007, https://hbr.org/2007/09/demystifying-strategy -the-what.

37. John M. Bryson and André L. Delbecq, "A Contingent Approach to Strategy and Tactics in Project Planning," *Journal of the American Planning Association* 45, no. 2 (1979): 167–179, doi:10.1080/01944367908976955.

38. Carol S. Dweck, *Mindset: The New Psychology of Success* (New York: Ballantine Books, 2008).

39. Yue Li and Timothy C. Bates, "Does Growth Mindset Improve Children's IQ, Educational Attainment or Response to Setbacks? Active-Control Interventions and Data on Children's Own Mindsets," *SocArXiv*, https://doi.org/10.31235/osf.io/tsdwy. See also "Growth Mindset Fails to Increase Grades or Non-cognitive Skills. What Now?" *Psychbrief*, July 23, 2019, https://psychbrief.wordpress.com/2019/07/23/growth-mindset-fails/; and Zhen Huang, Xiangdong Wei, Runhao Lu, and Jiannong Shi, "Whether and How Can a Growth Mindset Intervention Help Students in a Non-Western Culture? Evidence from a Field Experiment in China," *Educational Psychology* 42, no. 7 (2022): 913–929, https://doi .org/10.1080/01443410.2022.2085669.

40. A. Tversky and D. Kahneman. "Advances in Prospect Theory: Cumulative Representation of Uncertainty." *Journal of Risk and Uncertainty* 5 (1992): 297–323.

41. Daniel J. Sweeney, "What Drives Growth: Analyzing Quantitative Factors and Their Variation Across Sectors," *UF Journal of Undergraduate Research* 23 (2021), https://doi.org/10.32473/ufjur.v23i.128438.

42. Geremy Cepin, "Talent Acquisition: What It Is, Why You Need It, What Is Involved, and Where to Start," *CPA Practice Management Forum* 13 (December 2013), https://heinonline.org/HOL/LandingPage?handle=hein.journals/cpamanf9&div=148&id=&page=.

43. Kirsten Weir, "Why We Believe Alternative Facts," *Monitor on Psychology* 48, no. 5 (2017), https://www.apa.org/monitor/2017/05/alternative-facts.

44. George Sher, "But I Could Be Wrong," *Social Philosophy and Policy* 18, no. 2 (2001): 64–78, doi:10.1017/S0265052500002909.

45. Jonathan Masur and Eric A. Posner, "Against Feasibility Studies," 77 *University of Chicago Law Review* 657 (2010), https://chicagounbound.uchicago.edu/cgi/viewcontent.cgi?article=2785&context=journal_articles.

46. Eva M. Krockow, "Are You Too Smart to Think Wisely?" *Psychology Today*, March 2019, https://www.psychologytoday.com/us/blog/stretching-theory/201903/are-you-too-smart-think-wisely.

47. Michael G. H. Coles, Marten K. Scheffers, and Lisa Fournier, "Where Did You Go Wrong? Errors, Partial Errors, and the Nature of Human Information Processing," *Acta Psychologica* 90, nos. 1–3 (1995): 129–144, https://doi.org/10.1016/0001-6918(95)00020-U.

48. Michael Roberto, "Strong Leaders Encourage Dissent and Gain Commitment," *Wharton School Publishing*, November 2005, https://knowledge.wharton.upenn.edu/article/strong-leaders-encourage-dissent-and-gain-commitment/.

49. David Eagleman, *Livewired: The Inside Story of the Ever-Changing Brain* (New York: Pantheon Books, 2020).

50. J. Benitez, X. Delgado-Galvan, J. A. Gutierrez, and J. Izquierdo, "Balancing Consistency and Expert Judgement in AHP," *Mathematical and Computer Modelling* 54, nos. 7–8 (2011): 1785–1790, https://doi.org/10.1016/j.mcm.2010.12.023.

51. Ian Steadman, "Deepak Chopra Doesn't Understand Quantum Physics, So Brian Cox Wants $1,000,000 from Him," *New Statesman, Science & Tech*, July 7, 2014, https://www.newstatesman.com/science-tech/2014/07/deepak-chopra-doesnt-understand-quantum-physics-so-brian-cox-wants-1000000-him. For more entertainment on the ridiculous pronouncements of Deepak Chopra, many examples abound on the Internet, but this is probably one of the best: "Deepak Chopra Faces a Real Theoretical Physicist," YouTube, https://www.youtube.com/watch?v=0qFGs-SIWB4.

52. Christine K. Volkmann, Kim Oliver Tokarski, and Kati Ernst, *Social Entrepreneurship and Social Business: An Introduction and Discussion with Case Studies* (Wiesbaden, Germany: Gabler Verlag, 2012), https://doi.org/10.1007/978-3-8349-7093-0.

53. Vivian Hunt, Dennis Layton, and Sara Prince, "Why Diversity Matters," McKinsey & Company, January 2015, https://www.mckinsey.com/capabilities/people-and-organizational-performance/our-insights/why-diversity-matters. See also Vivian Hunt, Lareina Yee, Sara

Hunt, and Sundiatu Dixon-Fyle, "Delivering Through Diversity." McKinsey & Company, January 2018, https://www.mckinsey.com/capabilities/people-and-organizational-performance /our-insights/delivering-through-diversity; and Vivian Hunt, Sundiatu Dixon-Fyle, Sara Prince, and Kevin Dolan, "Diversity Wins: How Inclusion Matters," McKinsey & Company, May 2020, https://www.mckinsey.com/~/media/mckinsey/featured%20insights/diversity %20and%20inclusion/diversity%20wins%20how%20inclusion%20matters/diversity-wins -how-inclusion-matters-vf.pdf. For far better and more meaningful research on the place of women in leadership, Caroline Criado Perez's excellent book *Invisible Women: Exposing Data Bias in a World Designed for Men* (New York: Vintage, 2020) is highly recommended.

54. Juliet Bourke, "The Diversity and Inclusion Revolution: Eight Powerful Truths," *Deloitte Review* 22 (January 22, 2018), https://www2.deloitte.com/us/en/insights/deloitte -review/issue-22/diversity-and-inclusion-at-work-eight-powerful-truths.html?zd_source =hrt&zd_campaign=5328&zd_term=chiradeepbasumallick; Katherine W. Phillips, "How Diversity Makes Us Smarter" (citing the research of Anthony Antonio), *Scientific American*, October 1, 2014, https://www.scientificamerican.com/article/how-diversity-makes-us -smarter/; Robert D. Austin and Gary P. Pisano, "Neurodiversity as a Competitive Advantage: Why You Should Embrace It in Your Workforce," *Harvard Business Review*, May–June 2017, 96–103, https://hbr.org/2017/05/neurodiversity-as-a-competitive-advantage.

55. Barry Richmond, "Operational Thinking," *The Systems Thinker* 9, https://thesystems thinker.com/operational-thinking/.

56. Reagan Panelli, "An Introduction to Agile Thinking and Agile Principles," *Leanscape*, June 18, 2021, https://leanscape.io/introduction-to-agile-thinking/.

57. "Convergent Thinking," Wikipedia, https://en.wikipedia.org/wiki/Convergent _thinking.

58. "Divergent Thinking," Wikipedia, https://en.wikipedia.org/wiki/Divergent_thinking.

59. "Critical Thinking," Wikipedia, https://en.wikipedia.org/wiki/Critical_thinking.

60. Dara Ramalingam, Prue Anderson, Daniel Duckworth, Claire Scoular, and Jonathan Heard, "Creative Thinking: Definition and Structure," Australian Council for Educational Research, February 25, 2020, https://research.acer.edu.au/ar_misc/43/.

61. "The Discovery of DNA's Structure," PBS Evolution Library, https://www.pbs .org/wgbh/evolution/library/06/3/l_063_01.html#:~:text=Taken%20in%201952%2C%20 this%20image,shape%20of%20the%20DNA%20molecule.

62. Barbara Steinmann, Hannah Klug, and Gunter Maier, "The Path Is the Goal: How Transformational Leaders Enhance Followers' Job Attitudes and Proactive Behavior," *Frontiers in Psychology* 9 (2018), doi:10.3389/fpsyg.2018.02338.

Chapter 6: Harnessing Energy

1. V. H. Medvec, S. F. Madey, and T. Gilovich, "When Less Is More: Counterfactual Thinking and Satisfaction Among Olympic Medalists," *Journal of Personality and Social Psychology* 69, no. 4 (1995): 603–610, https://doi.org/10.1037/0022-3514.69.4.603.

2. Dani Peled, "Competitors vs. Achievers," Wix.com, https://www.liniyari.com/single -post/2017/11/10/Competitors-Vs-Achievers.

3. Jennifer A. Epstein and Judith M. Harackiewicz, "Winning Is Not Enough: The Effects of Competition and Achievement Orientation on Intrinsic Interest," *Personality and Social Psychology Bulletin* 18, no. 2 (1992), https://doi.org/10.1177/01461672921820.

4. William W. George, *True North: Discover Your Authentic Leadership* (San Francisco: Jossey-Bass, 2007).

5. Barbara L. Fredrickson, "The Broaden-and-Build Theory of Positive Emotions," *Philosophical Transactions of the Royal Society London B* 359 (2004): 1367–1377, http://doi.org/10.1098/rstb.2004.1512.

6. Robert E. Kaplan and Robert B. Kaiser, "Stop Overdoing Your Strengths," *Harvard Business Review*, February 2009. Available at: https://hbr.org/2009/02/stop-overdoing-your-strengths; Robert E. Kaplan and Rob B. Kaiser, *Fear Your Strengths: What You Are Best at Could Be Your Biggest Problem* (Oakland, CA: Berrett-Koehler Publishers, 2013).

7. Jerry L. Harbour, *The Basics of Performance Management* (Boca Raton, FL: CRC Press, 2017).

8. Paul R. Sackett, Charlene Zhang, Christopher M. Berry, and Filip Lievens, "Revisiting Meta-analytic Estimates of Validity in Personnel Selection: Addressing Systematic Overcorrection for Restriction of Range," *Journal of Applied Psychology* 107, no. 11 (2022): 2040–2068, doi:10.1037/apl0000994.

9. J. R. Spence and L. M. Keeping, "The Impact of Non-performance Information on Ratings of Job Performance: A Policy-Capturing Approach," *Journal of Organizational Behavior* 31, no. 4 (2010): 587–608, https://doi.org/10.1002/job.648.

10. Steve Scullen, Michael K. Mount, and Maynard Goff, "Understanding the Latent Structure of Job Performance Ratings," *Journal of Applied Psychology* 85, no. 6 (2001): 956–970, doi:10.1037//0021-9010.85.6.956.

11. Chockalingam Viswesvaran, Deniz S. Ones, and Leatta M. Hough, "Do Impression Management Scales in Personality Inventories Predict Managerial Job Performance Ratings?" *International Journal of Selection and Assessment* 9, no. 4 (2002): 277–289, https://doi.org/10.1111/1468-2389.00180.

12. Viswesvaran, Ones, and Hough.

13. Nancy Befort and Keith Hattrup, "Valuing Task and Contextual Performance: Experience, Job Roles, and Ratings of the Importance of Job Behaviors," *Applied Human Resource Management Research* 8, no. 1 (2003): 17–32, https://psycnet.apa.org/record/2004-11250-002.

14. Jasmijn C. Bol, "The Determinants and Performance Effects of Managers' Performance Evaluation Biases," *Accounting Review* 86, no. 5 (2011): 1549–1575, https://doi.org/10.2308/accr-10099.

15. Allen Smith, "More Employers Ditch Performance Appraisals," *Society for Human Resource Management*, May 18, 2018, https://www.shrm.org/resourcesandtools/legal-and-compliance/employment-law/pages/more-employers-ditch-performance-appraisals.aspx.

16. Jack Welch, "The Biggest Thief in Your Organization: Employee Performance," Jack Welch Management Institute, May 7, 2017, https://jackwelch.strayer.edu/winning/weak-employee-performance-steals/.

17. Robert Half International, "Survey: Managers Spend Nearly One Day a Week Managing Poor Performers," November 8, 2012, https://press.roberthalf.com/2012-11-08-Survey-Managers-Spend-Nearly-One-Day-a-Week-Managing-Poor-Performers.

Chapter 7: Exerting Pressure

1. Pew Research Center, "Attitudes and Beliefs on Science and Technology Topics," January 29, 2015, https://www.pewresearch.org/science/2015/01/29/chapter-3-attitudes-and-beliefs-on-science-and-technology-topics/. See also Pew Research Center, "The Evolution of Pew Research Center's Survey Questions About the Origins and Development of Life on Earth," February 6, 2019, https://www.pewresearch.org/religion/2019/02/06/the-evolution-of-pew-research-centers-survey-questions-about-the-origins-and-development-of-life-on-earth/.

2. Kristy Sproles, Sullivan Central High School, "Scopes Trial," Lesson Plans for Primary Sources at the Tennessee State Library & Archives, 2015, https://sharetngov.tnsosfiles.com/tsla/educationoutreach/Lesson%20Plans/Scopes%20Trial.pdf.

3. James C. Foster, "Scopes Monkey Trial," Free Speech Center at Middle Tennessee State University, September 19, 2023, https://www.mtsu.edu/first-amendment/article/1100/scopes-monkey-trial.

4. Independence Hall Association, "The Monkey Trial," U.S. History, https://www.ushistory.org/us/47b.asp.

5. American Civil Liberties Union, "State of Tennessee vs. Scopes," July 1925, https://www.aclu.org/documents/state-tennessee-v-scopes.

6. Marjorie Bloy, "William Cobbett (1763–1835)," *A Web of English History*, January 2016, https://www.historyhome.co.uk/people/cobbett.htm.

7. Alice Shepherd and Steve Toms, "Entrepreneurship, Business Strategy and Philanthropy: Competition and Regulation in Nineteenth Century British Cotton Textiles," Leeds University Business School Working Paper No. 18-04, June 28, 2017, http://dx.doi.org/10.2139/ssrn.2993304.

8. John P. Kotter, *John P. Kotter on What Leaders Really Do* (Boston: Harvard Business School Press, 1999).

9. Noel M. Tichy and Ram Charan, "The CEO as Coach: An Interview with Allied-Signal's Lawrence A. Bossidy," *Harvard Business Review*, March–April 1995, https://hbr.org/1995/03/the-ceo-as-coach-an-interview-with-alliedsignals-lawrence-a-bossidy.

10. Barry Z. Posner and James M. Kouzes, "Relating Leadership and Credibility," *Psychological Reports* 63, no. 2 (1988): 527–530, https://doi.org/10.2466/pr0.1988.63.2.527.

11. Kim Scott, *Radical Candor: Be a Kick-Ass Boss Without Losing Your Humanity* (New York: St. Martin's Press, 2019).

12. Marcus Buckingham and Ashley Goodall, "The Feedback Fallacy," *Harvard Business Review*, March–April 2019, https://hbr.org/2019/03/the-feedback-fallacy. This excellent article should be essential reading for all those claiming that "feedback is a gift." The authors show that feedback is anything but a gift and that most attempts at giving feedback completely miss the mark.

13. Jeffry A. Simpson, Allison K. Farrell, Minda M. Orina, and Alexander J. Rothman, "Power and Social Influence in Relationships," in *APA Handbook of Personality and Social*

Psychology, vol. 3: *Interpersonal Relations*, ed. M. Mikulincer, P. R. Shaver, J. A. Simpson, and J. F. Dovidio (Washington, DC: American Psychological Association, 2015), 393–420, https://doi.org/10.1037/14344-015.

14. M. A. Drescher, M. A. Korsgaard, I. M. Welpe, A. Picot, and R. T. Wigand, "The Dynamics of Shared Leadership: Building Trust and Enhancing Performance," *Journal of Applied Psychology* 99, no. 5 (2014): 771–783, https://doi.org/10.1037/a0036474.

15. James N. Druckman, "Evaluating Framing Effects," *Journal of Economic Psychology* 22, no. 1 (2001): 99–101, https://doi.org/10.1016/S0167-4870(00)00032-5.

16. Bruce Bower, "Think Like a Scientist," *Science News* 175, no. 13 (2009): 20, https://www.cmu.edu/dietrich/psychology/pdf/klahr/Think%20Like%20A%20Scientist%20_%20Science%20News.pdf.

17. Tommi Auvinen, Liris Aaltio, and Kirsimarja Blomqvist, "Constructing Leadership by Storytelling—the Meaning of Trust and Narratives," *Leadership & Organization Development Journal* 34, no. 6 (2013): 496–514, https://doi.org/10.1108/LODJ-10-2011-0102.

18. Jay A. Conger, "The Necessary Art of Persuasion," *Harvard Business Review*, May–June 2018, https://hbr.org/1998/05/the-necessary-art-of-persuasion.

19. Conger.

20. Nico H. Frijda, Antony S. R. Manstead, and Sacha Bem, *Emotions and Beliefs: How Feelings Influence Thoughts* (Cambridge, UK: Cambridge University Press: 2000).

21. C. K. Prahalad and Venkat Ramaswamy, "Co-creating Unique Value with Customers," *Strategy & Leadership* 32, no. 3 (2004): 4–9, https://doi.org/10.1108/10878570410699249.

22. Herbert D. Saltzstein and Louis Sandberg, "The Relative Effectiveness of Direct and Indirect Persuasion," *Journal of Psychology* 91, no. 1 (1975): 39–48, https://doi.org/10.1080/00223980.1975.9915795.

23. Daniel Ames, Alice Lee, and Abbie Wazlawek, "Interpersonal Assertiveness: Inside the Balancing Act," *Social & Personality Psychology Compass* 11, no. 6 (2017), https://doi.org/10.1111/spc3.12317. The article abstract explains that "interpersonal assertiveness [reflects] the degree to which someone stands up and speaks out for their own positions when they are faced with someone else who does not want the same outcomes. In this article, we review long-standing and recent scholarship to characterize the curvilinear consequences of assertiveness (both 'too little' and 'too much' can be problematic). We consider the sources of accommodating and assertive behavior, such as motivations, expectancies, and failures of self-regulation. We also examine ways in which people can assert themselves effectively, ranging from making precise offers in negotiations to employing rationales as part of their proposals."

24. Richard Banks, *The Keys to Being Brilliantly Confident and More Assertive: A Vital Guide to Enhancing Your Communication Skills, Getting Rid of Anxiety, and Building Assertiveness* (independently published, 2020).

25. "Straw Man," Wikipedia, https://en.wikipedia.org/wiki/Straw_man.

26. Ryan O. Murphy, Kurt Alexander Ackermann, and Michel Handgraaf, "Measuring Social Value Orientation," *Judgment and Decision Making* 6, no. 8 (2011): 771–781, http://dx.doi.org/10.2139/ssrn.1804189.

27. Jeremy Sutton, "Assertiveness in Leadership: 19 Techniques for Managers," Positivepsychology.com, February 24, 2021, https://positivepsychology.com/assertiveness-in-leadership/.

28. Mary E. Maloney and Patricia Moore, "From Aggressive to Assertive," *International Journal of Women's Dermatology* 6, no. 1 (2019): 46-49, https://www.sciencedirect.com/science/article/pii/S2352647519301054?via%3Dihub.

29. Christopher Clarey, "Are Women Penalized More Than Men in Tennis? Data on Fines Says No," *New York Times*, September 14, 2018, https://www.nytimes.com/2018/09/14/sports/tennis-fines-men-women.html.

30. Tamela Rags and Cindy Boren, "Serena Williams Fined $17,000 for U.S. Open Outburst; Billie Jean King Calls Out 'Double Standard,'" *Washington Post*, September 8, 2018, https://www.washingtonpost.com/news/early-lead/wp/2018/09/08/serena-williamss-game-penalty-at-u-s-open-final-sparks-torrent-of-reactions/.

31. Dan Cancian, "John McEnroe Defends Serena Williams' U.S. Open Outburst: 'Women and Men Are Treated Differently,'" *Newsweek*, March 29, 2019, https://www.newsweek.com/serena-williams-john-mcenroe-sexism-row-us-open-ladies-final-1379501.f.

32. Wei Zheng, Ronit Kark, and Alyson Meister, "How Women Manage the Gendered Norms of Leadership," *Harvard Business Review*, November 2018, https://hbr.org/2018/11/how-women-manage-the-gendered-norms-of-leadership.

33. Zheng, Kark, and Meister.

34. Victoria L. Brescoll, "Who Takes the Floor and Why: Gender, Power, and Volubility," *Administrative Science Quarterly* 56, no. 4 (2011): 622–641, https://doi.org/10.1177/0001839212439994.

35. Mark Spranca, Elisa Minsk, and Jonathan Baron, "Omission and Commission in Judgment and Choice," *Journal of Experimental Social Psychology* 27, no. 1 (1991): 76–105, https://doi.org/10.1016/0022-1031(91)90011-T.

36. Michael E. Palanski, Kristin L. Cullen, William A. Gentry, and Chelsea M. Nichols, "Virtuous Leadership: Exploring the Effects of Leader Courage and Behavioral Integrity on Leader Performance and Image," *Journal of Business Ethics* 132 (2015): 297–310, https://doi.org/10.1007/s10551-014-2317-2.

Chapter 8: Increasing Connectivity

1. Nicholas A. Christakis and James H. Fowler, *Connected: The Surprising Power of Our Social Networks and How They Shape Our Lives* (New York: Little, Brown, 2009).

2. David G. Rand, Samuel Arbesman, and Nicholas A. Christakis, "Dynamic Social Networks Promote Cooperation in Experiments with Humans," *Proceedings of the National Academy of Sciences* 108, no. 48 (2011): 19193–19198, https://doi.org/10.1073/pnas.1108243108.

3. Nichola Raihani, *The Social Instinct: How Cooperation Shaped the World* (New York: St. Martin's Press, 2023).

4. Philippe Rochat, "Five Levels of Self Awareness as They Unfold Early in Life," *Consciousness and Cognition* 12, no. 4 (2003): 717–731, https://doi.org/10.1016/S1053-8100(03)00081-3.

5. Albert Bandura, "Self-Efficacy: Toward a Unifying Theory of Behavioral Change," *Psychology Review* 84, no. 2 (1977): 191–215, doi:10.1037//0033-295X.84.2.191.

6. "Self-Awareness," Wikipedia, https://en.wikipedia.org/wiki/Self-awareness.

7. David Brooks, *How to Know a Person: The Art of Seeing Others Deeply and Being Deeply Seen* (New York: Random House, October 2023).

8. Annamarie Mann, "Why We Need Best Friends at Work," Gallup, January 15, 2018, https://www.gallup.com/workplace/236213/why-need-best-friends-work.aspx. See also Alok Patel and Stephanie Plowman, "The Increasing Importance of a Best Friend at Work," Gallup, August 17, 2022, https://www.gallup.com/workplace/397058/increasing-importance-best-friend-work.aspx.

9. Patel and Plowman.

10. John P. Kotter, "What Effective General Managers Really Do," in *Managerial Work*, ed. Rosemary Stuart (New York: Routledge, 1998).

11. Marc Hauser, *Moral Minds: How Nature Designed Our Universal Sense of Right and Wrong* (New York: Ecco Press, 2006).

12. George Lakoff, *Moral Politics: How Liberals and Conservatives Think* (Chicago: University of Chicago Press, 1996).

13. J. Russell, C. Jarrold, and D. Potel, "What Makes Strategic Deception Difficult for Children—the Deception or the Strategy?" *British Journal of Developmental Psychology* 12, no. 3 (1994): 301–314, https://doi.org/10.1111/j.2044-835X.1994.tb00636.x.

14. Michael Tomasello, Malinda Carpenter, Josep Call, Tanya Behne, and Henrike Moll, "Understanding and Sharing Intentions: The Origins of Cultural Cognition," *Behavioral and Brain Sciences* 28, no. 5 (2005): 675–691, https://doi.org/10.1017/S0140525X0500 0129.

15. "Wells Fargo Cross-Selling Scandal," Wikipedia, https://en.wikipedia.org/wiki/Wells_Fargo_account_fraud_scandal.

16. Jeffrey Moriarty, "Business Ethics," *The Stanford Encyclopedia of Philosophy*, ed. Edward N. Zalta, Fall 2021, https://plato.stanford.edu/archives/fall2021/entries/ethics-business/.

17. Wex Definitions Team, "Legal Ethics," Legal Information Institute of Cornell Law School, last updated March 2023, https://www.law.cornell.edu/wex/legal_ethics.

18. US Office of Government Ethics, https://www.oge.gov/.

19. Finance Code of Ethics, https://www.sec.gov/Archives/edgar/data/1396279/00011 9312507083128/dex141.htm.

Chapter 9: Controlling Traffic

1. Federal Aviation Administration, *The United States of America Aeronautical Information Publication*, 27th ed., Department of Transportation, October 2023, https://www.faa.gov/air_traffic/publications/atpubs/aip_html/part2_enr_section_1.1.html.

2. Roger Martin, "The Execution Trap," *Harvard Business Review* (July–August 2010), https://hbr.org/2010/07/the-execution-trap.

3. Donald Sull and Charles Spinosa, "Promise-Based Management: The Essence of Execution," *Harvard Business Review*, April 2007, https://hbr.org/2007/04/promise-based -management-the-essence-of-execution.

4. Donald Sull, Rebecca Homkes, and Charles Sull, "Why Strategy Execution Unravels—and What to Do About It," *Harvard Business Review*, March 2015, https://hbr .org/2015/03/why-strategy-execution-unravelsand-what-to-do-about-it.

5. D. Kahneman and A. Tversky, "Prospect Theory: An Analysis of Decisions Under Risk," *Econometrica* 47, no. 2 (1979): 263–292.

6. John N. Warfield and Scott M. Staley, "Structural Thinking: Organizing Complexity Through Disciplined Activity," *Systems Research* 13, no. 1 (1996): 47–67, https://doi .org/10.1002/(SICI)1099-1735(199603)13:1%3C47:AID-SRES27%3E3.0.CO;2-A.

7. Jens Roehrich, "Complexity," in *Wiley Encyclopedia of Management*, vol. 10, *Operations Management*, ed. C. L. Cooper, S. Roden, M. Lewis, and N. Slack, https://onlinelibrary.wiley .com/doi/10.1002/9781118785317.weom100003https://doi.org/10.1002/9781118785317 .weom100003.

8. Barry Conchie, "The Demands of Executive Leadership," Gallup, May 13, 2004, https://news.gallup.com/businessjournal/11614/seven-demands-leadership.aspx.

9. Derek Cabrera, Laura Cabrera, and Hise Gibson, "Leapfrog Leaders: Accelerating Systems Leadership Skills," in *Routledge Handbook of Systems Thinking*, ed. D. Cabrera, L. Cabrera, and G. Midgley (London: Routledge, 2021), https://www.researchgate.net /publication/349850342_Leapfrog_Leaders.

10. Linda Booth Sweeney, "Systems Thinking: A Means to Understanding Our Complex World," adapted from *When a Butterfly Sneezes: A Guide for Helping Kids Explore Interconnections in Our World Through Favorite Stories* (Waltham, MA: Pegasus Communications, 2001), https://scpsystem.weebly.com/uploads/2/1/3/3/21333498/linda_booth_sweeney_-_systems _thinking_a_means_to_understanding_our_complex_world.pdf.

11. Lori Fry, "Don't Gamble with Your Company's Culture," Edwards Deming Institute, June 8, 2017, https://deming.org/2589-2/.

12. "Root Cause Analysis," Patient Safety Network, Agency for Healthcare Research and Quality (AHRQ), https://psnet.ahrq.gov/primer/root-cause-analysis.

13. "Root Cause Analysis Explained: Definition, Examples, and Methods," Tableau, https://www.tableau.com/learn/articles/root-cause-analysis#:~:text=Root%20cause%20 analysis%20(RCA)%20is,symptoms%20and%20putting%20out%20fires.

14. Gale Thompson, "The 5 Principles of Gestalt," Sciencing.com, April 24, 2017, https://sciencing.com/5-principles-gestalt-8430201.html.

15. Ignacio Esponda and Emanuel Vespa, "Contingent Preferences and the Sure-Thing Principle: Revisiting Classic Anomalies in the Laboratory," *Review of Economic Studies* (2016), https://doi.org/10.1093/restud/rdad102.

16. Alejandro Martínez-Marquina, Muriel Niederle, and Emanuel Vespa, "Failures in Contingent Reasoning: The Role of Uncertainty," *American Economic Review* 109, no. 10 (2019): 3437–3474, https://web.stanford.edu/~niederle/mnv_paper.pdf, doi:10.1257/aer.20171764.

17. W. F. Samuelson and M. H. Bazerman, "The Winner's Curse in Bilateral Negotiations," in *Research in Experimental Economics*, ed. V. Smith (Boston: Boston University and Massachusetts Institute of Technology, 1985), https://dspace.mit.edu/bitstream/handle/1721.1/49408/winnerscurseinbi00samu.pdf.

18. Gary Charness and Dan Levin, "The Origin of the Winner's Curse: A Laboratory Study," *American Economic Journal: Microeconomics* 1, no. 1 (2009): 207–236, http://www.jstor.org/stable/25760353.

19. Harver Team, "Learning Agility: What It Is and How to Access It," Harver.com, August 2023, https://harver.com/blog/learning-agility/.

20. Marjorie Bloy, "Disraeli's Speech on the Third Reading of the Bill for the Repeal of the Corn Laws: 15 May 1846," *A Web of English History*, March 4, 2016, https://www.historyhome.co.uk/polspeech/dizcorn.htm.

21. Gary Burnison, "The Tuna Fish Sandwich Test," Kornferry.com, https://www.kornferry.com/insights/this-week-in-leadership/burnison-learning-agility-test.

22. Leading Effectively Staff, "Tips for Improving Learning Agility," Center for Creative Leadership, December 2020, https://www.ccl.org/articles/leading-effectively-articles/tips-for-improving-your-learning-agility/.

23. Gary M. Grobman, "Complexity Theory: A New Way to Look at Organizational Change," *Public Administration Quarterly* 29, no. 3 (2005): 350, http://www.complexityforum.com/members/Grobman%202005%20Complexity%20theory.pdf.

24. Paul Plsek, Curt Lindberg, and Brenda Zimmerman, "Some Emerging Principles for Managing Complex, Adaptive Systems," working paper, Plexus Institute, November 25, 1997, http://www.plexusinstitute.com/edgeware/archive/think/main_filing1.html.

25. Grobman, "Complexity Theory," 376–377.

26. Mary Uhl-Bien and Russ Marion, "Complexity Leadership in Bureaucratic Forms of Organizing: A Meso Model," *Leadership Quarterly* 20, no. 4 (2009): 631–650; doi:10.1016/j.leaqua.2009.04.007.

Chapter 11: Four Harsh Truths

1. Massimo Pigliucci, *Nonsense on Stilts: How to Tell Science from Bunk* (Chicago: University of Chicago Press, 2018).

2. Kevin J. Mitchell, *Innate: How the Wiring of Our Brain Shapes Who We Are* (Princeton, NJ: Princeton University Press, 2018).

3. Paige McGlauflin, "Black CEOs on the Fortune 500 Reach New Record High in 2023—Meet the 8 Executives," *Fortune*, June 5, 2023, https://fortune.com/2023/06/05/black-ceos-fortune-500-record-high-2023/.

4. Martha Gill, "If Chatbots Can Ace Job Interviews for Us, Maybe It's Time to Scrap this Ordeal," *Guardian*, November 4, 2023, https://www.theguardian.com/commentisfree/2023/nov/04/if-chatbots-can-ace-job-interviews-for-us-maybe-its-time-to-scrap-this-ordeal?CMP=Share_iOSApp_Other.

5. Alexander Buijsrogge, Wouter Duyck, and Eva Derous, "Initial Impression Formation During the Job Interview: Anchors That Drive Biased Decision-Making Against

Stigmatized Applicants," *European Journal of Work and Organizational Psychology* 30, no. 2 (2020), 305–318, doi:10.1080/1359432x.2020.1833980.

6. Eva Derous, Alexander Buijsrogge, Nicolas Roulin, and Wouter Duyck, "Why Your Stigma Isn't Hired: A Dual-Process Framework of Interview Bias," *Human Resource Management Review* 26, no. 2 (2016): 90–111, doi:10.1016/j.hrmr.2015.09.006.

7. Stuart A. Rice, "Contagious Bias in the Interview: A Methodological Note," *American Journal of Sociology* 35, no. 3 (1929): 420–423, doi:10.1086/215055.

8. Comila Shahani, Robert L. Dipboye, and Thomas M. Gehrlein, "Attractiveness Bias in the Interview: Exploring the Boundaries of an Effect," *Basic and Applied Social Psychology* 14, no. 3 (1993): 317–328, doi:10.1207/s15324834basp1403_5.

9. Mladen Adamovic and Andreas Leibbrandt, "Is There a Glass Ceiling for Ethnic Minorities to Enter Leadership Positions? Evidence from a Field Experiment with over 12,000 Job Applications," *Leadership Quarterly* 34, no. 2 (April 2023), https://doi.org/10.1016/j.leaqua.2022.101655.

10. Steven W. Bradley, James R. Garven, Wilson W. Law, and James E. West, "The Impact of Chief Diversity Officers on Diverse Faculty Hiring," *Southern Economic Association* 89, no. 1 (2018): 3–36, doi:10.3386/w24969.

11. Frank Dobbin and Alexandra Kalev, "Why Doesn't Diversity Training Work? The Challenge for Industry and Academia," *Anthropology Now* 10, no. 2 (2018): 48–55, doi:10.1080/19428200.2018.1493182.

12. Rice, "Contagious Bias in the Interview."

13. Dean Burnett, "Nothing Personal: The Questionable Myers-Briggs Test," *Guardian*, March 19, 2013, https://www.theguardian.com/science/brain-flapping/2013/mar/19/myers-briggs-test-unscientific.

14. "Big Five Personality Traits," Wikipedia, https://en.wikipedia.org/wiki/Big_Five_personality_traits.

15. Aimee Harel, "The Problems with Using Personality Tests for Hiring," Vervoe.com, updated January 29, 2024, https://vervoe.com/personality-tests-hiring/.

INDEX

Index

Index